A Fan's Guide To
dc Talk

The Music, the Tours, and the Story behind Christian Music's Groundbreaking Trio.

By K. Andrew Komosinski

This book was written *by* dc Talk fans, *for* dc Talk fans. It is not endorsed, affiliated, or in any way officially connected with dc Talk, their management, their label, or any other business or governmental entity referenced within. The views expressed in this book are those of the author alone.

This book is an independent publication. Any references to copyrighted or trademarked intellectual property of dc Talk or any other rights-holders are made strictly for editorial purposes. No commercial claim upon that property is made by the author or any contributors. The book itself is copyright the author, but the recordings and audiovisual material mentioned in this book are copyright their respective owners.

Although every precaution has been taken to verify the accuracy of the information contained herein, no responsibility is assumed for any errors or omissions, and no liability is assumed for damages that may result from the use of this information.

All rights reserved. No part of this book my be reproduced in any written or electronic medium without written permission of the author, except in the case of brief quotations or excerpts embodied in critical articles or reviews provided to the public free of charge and for non-commercial purposes.

Special thanks to Bert Gangl for his immeasurable contributions to the information regarding dc Talk concerts and tours.

For more information, visit www.dctalkfreaks.com

Copyright © 2019 K. Andrew Komosinski

ISBN: 978-1-7342119-0-0

Table of Contents

Word 2 the Readers!	1
Liberty University	6
Christian Rhymes to a Rhythm	10
At the ForeFront	16
DC Talk (1989)	19
Early DC Talk Shows	37
Nu Thang (1990)	40
Yo Ho Ho! (1990)	74
Go West Young Man Tour	80
Addicted to Jesus	83
Nu Skool Jam Tour	85
Rap, Rock, and Soul	89
Free at Last (1992)	91
Free at Last EP	137
Change Your World Tour	139
The Free at Last Tour (1994)	141
Free at Last: The Movie	145
The Jesus Freak Era	149
Jesus Freak (the single)	157
Jesus Freak (the album)	166
1995 Jesus Freak Tour	214
Freak Show Tour (1996)	216
Welcome to the Freak Show	220
My Will (1998)	222
Supernatural (1998)	227
The Supernatural Experience Tour	270
Supernatural Experience VHS/DVD	274
Spirit in the Sky (2000)	276
Intermission (2000)	277
Solo EP (2001)	286
Solo Tours (2001-2002)	290
Let's Roll (2002)	294

The Hardway (Revisited)	296
Atmosphere (2004)	298
The Cross (2007)	300
Love Feels Like (2015)	301
2017 Jesus Freak Cruise	303
2019 Jesus Freak Cruise	306
TobyMac's Solo Career	308
Tait and the Newsboys	319
Kevin Max's Solo Career	329
My Friend, So Long!	338
Bibliography	340

Word 2 the Readers!

Welcome to the Freak Show! For the uninitiated, dc Talk is a groundbreaking musical trio whose output in the 1990s helped define an entire generation of music – particularly in the contemporary Christian market. Originally a hip-hop group made up of college roommates, dc Talk's unlikely journey from a dormitory praise act to an arena-shaking, record-breaking phenomenon is certainly a story worth telling.

Made up of members Toby McKeehan, Michael Tait, and Kevin Max, dc Talk recorded five major studio albums (three of which went Platinum), won four Grammy Awards as a trio, and nabbed countless Dove Awards throughout their careers together. The group is widely known for its seminal album, *Jesus Freak*.

While you probably know most of that, what you might *not* know is the story of how dc Talk was formed, how they found their footing and came into their own, how they changed with the times to create landmark albums, and how they eventually went their separate ways to climb new mountains. We'll be discussing all of that—and much more—in this book.

Truly, if you have even the slightest interest in the band or the Christian music world at large, you've come to the right place. This is your companion piece to the legacy of some of the most influential artists of our time. It's an encyclopedia to every aspect of dc Talk's history—on the stage and in the studio—with an in-

Word 2 the Readers!

depth look at the songs that helped redefine an industry. From dc Talk's self-titled 1989 release to their 2019 Jesus Freak Cruise reunion shows, this is thirty year's worth of fandom distilled into a single volume.

A brief note about the layout: the chapters are organized as a chronological look at the dc Talk story with pit-stops at every major entry in their discography. Some entries are purely narrative while others serve to introduce the creation of a specific album or project. For example, the next chapter discusses the group's college years at Liberty University, then subsequent sections pause to analyze the demo tape that they released in those years, and then the book picks up with the next phase of their lives. In short, after each album or project is introduced, there's a section that examines each and every song from it. The stories behind the songs, the meaning of the lyrics, the musical structures, various trivia, and several other aspects of the tracks are discussed. If the songs were released as singles, chart positions are noted. Alternate, rare, or collectible versions (if they exist) are accounted for. So are live performances. If there was ever a music video or live clip available, those things are in there, too. Once the album has been thoroughly covered, the main narrative resumes.

While the information in this book encapsulates the recordings, tours, and major events in the band's life, there's been far more to the careers of these three men than the time they spent as dc Talk. Though their last full album together was released in 1998, they've continued to develop their artistry apart from each other and have each succeeded in making a positive mark on a world that desperately needs it. A section at the end gives a bird's-eye view of their solo careers.

Before we get too far into any of that, though, let's give a broad introduction to the three members of dc Talk:

A Fan's Guide to dc Talk

Toby McKeehan (a.k.a. "TobyMac")

Kevin Michael McKeehan (known as "Toby McKeehan" or "TobyMac") was born on October 22nd, 1964. In an ironic twist, his birth name contained the first names of both future bandmates. While growing up in northern Virginia, Toby famously took the bus to Washington D.C. to pick up early hip-hop records. He quickly developed a fascination with the genre and began creating his own music. In college, he began pursuing it with a passion. Settling on the name "DC Talk" (the "DC" originally stood for "Washington D.C."), he put together a demo tape with some friends in 1987 and the rest, as you'll soon read, is history.

Toby married his college sweetheart Amanda Levy in 1994. That same year, as he began work on dc Talk's fourth album, he helped create Gotee Records. While Gotee was originally just a production house, it soon grew to be one of the hottest labels in Christian music. Toby currently serves as the president of Gotee Records. Under his watch, the label has signed numerous talented and popular artists.

Over the course of his career with dc Talk, Toby went from a rapper to an alternative rocker to a pop vocalist. After the group went on indefinite hiatus in the early 2000s, he embarked on a solo career under the name "TobyMac." As TobyMac, he's explored every genre under the sun with his backup band, Diverse City. By most metrics, Toby's solo work over the past fifteen years has even eclipsed his tenure with dc Talk.

Michael Tait

Michael DeWayne Tait, the second member of dc Talk, was born on May 18th, 1966. He grew up as the youngest in a large family in the Washington D.C. area. His father, a major influence in Michael's life, was a cab driver known for evangelizing to his passengers. As a young adult, Michael's vocal talent was so highly

Word 2 the Readers!

regarded that he received national attention even before his career with dc Talk.

Tait met Toby McKeehan while attending Liberty University. After the two became fast friends and roommates, Toby wasted no time in enlisting Tait as the first member of his new musical outfit, "DC Talk and the One Way Crew." In 2000, after over a dozen years of Platinum records and sold-out arenas as a member of dc Talk, Michael formed a rock band named "Tait." "Tait" was named after his father, who had recently passed. The group released two albums. In 2009, Michael was tapped to become the new lead singer of the Newsboys, a mega-popular band who had gone on tour with dc Talk in their early days. With Michael Tait at the helm, the Newsboys have continued to achieve commercial success through album releases and international concert tours.

Kevin Max

Kevin Max Smith (known to fans as "Kevin Max") was born on August 17th, 1967 in Grand Rapids, Michigan. He met Toby and Michael while attending Liberty University. Kevin gained recognition on campus for being an incredible vocalist in a band called "The Connection," but it was ultimately a chapel performance that caught Toby and Michael's attention. Once Kevin's distinctive voice was added to the mix, the dc Talk sound was complete.

Throughout the 1990s, Kevin Max stood out in the group with his incredible vibrato, an improvisational performance style, and a spoken-word poetry project titled *At the Foot of Heaven*. After the dc Talk years were over, Max built a devoted following through a prolific recording career, additional books of poetry, and even a novel. He married Amanda MacDonald, his second wife, in 2005.

So that's a quick look at the three heads of our musical hydra. If those introductions seemed a little brief, don't worry – we'll be spending the next three hundred pages filling in the blanks. As each bio mentioned, the dc Talk story started while the trio was in college together. The next chapter takes us back to that time and place.

Liberty University

Founded in the early 1970s by the famous evangelist Jerry Falwell and the prolific author and academic Elmer L. Towns, Liberty University has grown to become one of the most well-known Christian institutions in the United States. Nestled in the foothills of the Blue Ridge Mountains in the city of Lynchburg, Virginia, "LU" is known for its comprehensive curriculums, Bible-based value systems, robust online education programs, and famous alumni. Few alumni are as famous, though, as the three members of dc Talk.

While growing up in Fairfax, Virginia, Toby McKeehan took a keen interest in hip-hop music. In high school, he even began recording a few rap verses and scratching turntables under the name "Sir CaucaTalk." While music was a passion of his, it probably wasn't his focus in those years.

When Toby went to Liberty to help kick off their brand new golf program in the mid-1980s, his music finally started landing on the green when he met a vocal powerhouse named Michael Tait. Inspired by the possibilities of harnessing Tait's velvety baritone to drive his own rhythms, "Sir CaucaTalk" reimagined himself as "DC Talk" and dove head-first into music. Influenced by the evangelical atmosphere of his college environment, Toby's lyrics adopted an overtly spiritual tone. Friends Mike Valliere and Vic Mignogna teamed up with him for beats and instrumental tracks. As Toby's rhythms and rhymes were fleshed out, Michael Tait stepped in to sing choruses. The nucleus of dc Talk's early sound was formed.

Even though Toby's rap verses and Michael's singing gelled to create compelling music, it probably didn't seem obvious that the two would be together long-term. Hip-hop was an extra-curricular activity for Tait, who was known on campus for his gospel performances. As his hymn repertoire and flawless solo spots were gaining notice even outside of Virginia, the path he traveled was far more conventional than the one Toby was carving for himself. Still, as McKeehan continued to formulate rap tracks as "DC Talk," Michael happily donated his time as the inaugural member of what they were calling the "One Way Crew."

Liberty University was rife with opportunities for DC Talk and the One Way Crew to perform. While chapel services at Liberty were fairly traditional, Toby was able to push the envelope a bit and sometimes shoehorn in a dc Talk performance at the end of a Michael Tait solo. The community at Liberty was supportive of these worship-oriented hip-hop songs. In fact, the first official dc Talk concert was held in Jerry Fallwell's own backyard.

One of the first serious steps for any musical group is to record a demo tape. Toby and the One Way Crew cobbled together an earnest, two-track hip-hop cassette called *Christian Rhymes to a Rhythm*. Side A featured a song called "Heavenbound." It was an amateur production, to be sure, but the synthesized beats and keyboard trumpets took a back seat to Toby's competent, breezy delivery and Michael Tait's soaring vocals.

The demo was popular on campus. But even with the tape flying off the merch table, Michael Tait probably still had no intentions of a future with dc Talk. To help get his own career off the ground, Michael recorded a demo album of his own called *Burden Lifter*. His cassette, comprised of traditional gospel tracks and hymns, began making its way to industry contacts.

Meanwhile, chapel services at Liberty had done more for Toby and Michael than give them a platform to perform. At one of the services, they were drawn in by a crisp, dynamic rendition of a hymn called "Lord of the Harvest." The singer was a waterfall of a vocalist named Kevin Max Smith.

Kevin, a transplant from Grand Rapids, Michigan, had a rocky start at LU. When he bent the rules too many times, Liberty expelled him. After he spent some time soul-searching at his old home in The Wolverine State, Liberty gave him a second chance. Getting together with Toby and Michael at LU not only helped Kevin become more entrenched in his studies once he came back, but it gave the One Way Crew a new member with plenty of vocal horsepower. With the dc Talk sound now complete, the group moved into an apartment together.

dc Talk set their sights on a record deal. As Toby's graduation date drew nearer, though, more than one of his professors took him aside and gently tried to point him away from rapping and back to his studies. To everyone's relief, he did both: Toby ended up graduating from Liberty in 1988 with a Political Science degree while still pursuing his dreams of being a recording artist.

As time went on and the possibility of a record contract started to become a reality, Michael Tait also felt himself being pulled in a different direction. Bill Gaither, the legendary leader of the famous Gaither Vocal Trio / Gaither Vocal Band, began looking for a new baritone after singer Gary McSpadden left to cut a solo album called *Hymns From The Heart*. Michael Tait, who excelled at the type of southern gospel music that the Gaither Vocal Band performed, was a serious candidate. On the 2019 Jesus Freak Cruise, Toby recalled how he and Kevin had met for chicken sandwiches to discuss what to do about DC Talk and the One

Way Crew if Michael, their core singer in the early days, were to leave the group. They never had to decide; Gaither went with a singer/comedian named Mark Lowry instead. Tait and Lowry *both* consider the move a good one: Tait went on to an illustrious career on his own terms and Lowry thrived in the Gaither group for a total of twenty years.

Liberty University represented a time of growth, learning, creativity, and possibility for the young men of dc Talk. It was where they first met and first gained a following. The education, friendships, and opportunities at LU were certainly instrumental to their success, but one of the essential benefits of these years was also the spiritual background and fortitude that they began to develop. As their success grew over the next decade, the road was paved with trials, temptations, stressors, and difficulties. This bedrock of Biblical knowledge that they were given formed more than the basis of their early lyrics – it gave them something to rely on when they were faced with these challenges.

Of course, another important benefit of their time at Liberty University was that it served as a rich testing ground for the type of material that they were producing at the time. Our cataloging of dc Talk's discography starts with their very first project: the aforementioned demo cassette called *Christian Rhymes to a Rhythm*.

Christian Rhymes to a Rhythm

The *Christian Rhymes to a Rhythm* tape was where it all began. dc Talk's first two songs were released a full two years before the band was even signed.

The cassette, produced in stereo, had a very limited printing of only 3,000 units. Toby and Michael actually sold these tapes themselves, offering them at gigs and even selling them door-to-door. It was a popular item. In a January 24th, 1994 article by Steve Dougherty in *People Magazine,* Michael Tait recalled that all 3,000 of the tapes sold briskly.

In modern times, *Christian Rhymes to a Rhythm* is the holy grail of dc Talk collectibles. Because of its importance to the band's career, the project's age, and its limited production number, very few are found in the wild. On the rare occasion that one materializes, it's usually at an online auction or a collector's show. The price *begins* at $500 and can easily go past $1000. To give an idea of its rarity, only two were offered for sale over the past twenty-four months.

The cassette features a stylized line drawing of the US Capitol building on the front with the words "DC TALK" directly below it. The back features a mailing address (a Washington D.C. Post Office Box) and the line "Ministries of Tait and McKeehan." The copyright date is 1987.

A Fan's Guide to dc Talk

Kevin Max hadn't joined the group yet, so his voice isn't featured on the tape.

The first side is a little song called "Heavenbound," and the second is a song called "Always Leaning." The next sections dive deeper into both tracks.

Christian Rhymes to a Rhythm Side A:
Heavenbound

"Heavenbound" was the track that first put the band on the map. With a synthetic trumpet opening to the tune of "Rule, Britannia!" and a breathtakingly earnest effort of the group's rapper to "cut it up," listeners could surely sense that they were embarking on a somewhat experimental musical journey. And what a journey it's been.

Despite the track being an early demo, this signature song of dc Talk's early days was offered in a fairly complete and polished form. The song was spruced up and released again on the group's debut record two years later, but the lyrics, beat, and instruments on the later version were virtually identical to *this* take's. The main difference between the demo version and the final version was a replacement vocal track by McKeehan and extra backing vocals from Tait, especially during the bridge. The snare drum sounded a little different in the demo version, as did some of the percussion, but the general structure of the song (and its signature brass) remained the same.

Here, Toby's vocals are delivered in a higher register. He's quite a bit more subdued than he is in the 1989 version. Some collectors feel that McKeehan's less aggressive approach to the song sounds better than the 1989 vocals. Michael Tait's voice is given more room to shine on *Christian Rhymes to a Rhythm*: his tracks lack the extra processing and background vocals of the final album version. One blemish on this production is the overuse of reverb (an echo effect) toward the end of the song on McKeehan's part, though that's a classic mistake with budding recording artists. Obviously, this version of "Heavenbound" sounds quite a bit more raw than the 1989 version, but in many ways, that's a good thing. dc Talk always sounds better when a little bit of the polish is left off.

As dc Talk's career progressed, "Heavenbound" appeared in various incarnations throughout the years. The rest of its history will be explored in the "DC Talk (1989)" chapter.

Christian Rhymes to a Rhythm Side B:
Always Leaning

The B-side (second side) of the *Christian Rhymes to a Rhythm* cassette is the rarest song in the history of dc Talk: a song called "Always Leaning."

This was the *only release* of "Always Leaning," making it a true unheard gem for most fans since the cassette tape was pressed in such a limited quantity. The song was never re-recorded or released on any future project, so this offers an interesting glimpse at the original style of one of the biggest Christian bands in history.

The song follows "Heavenbound's" formula in the sense that it has keyboard-based instrumentation, verses rapped by Toby McKeehan, and a chorus sung by Michael Tait. The instrumentation during the verses is quite a bit busier than "Heavenbound," with a synthy bassline playing in octaves and some really dated brass synths punctuating the verses. The chorus, too, has a busy arrangement, with harmonizing vocal tracks by Michael Tait and guitar samples from keyboards throughout. One of the highlights of the arrangement is a saxophone solo after the bridge. The solo has plenty of growl and a sound so good that it might as well be live.

The songs that went on to be featured on the group's debut album typically had much simpler arrangements. It seems that one of the things they learned from "Always Leaning" is that for early dc Talk records, less would be more.

The lyrics are notable for including references to guns and crack cocaine. The message, of course, was that the group should be "Always Leaning" on Jesus. *Always*, not just when they found themselves with dangerous people. The theme would be brought back in a more subdued form on dc Talk's sophomore album in the song "He Works" where the protagonist of the song is offered drugs at school but is able to lean on his faith to decline.

Toby's performance on this track isn't as engaging as it was on the "Heavenbound" track, probably owing more to "Heavenbound" being a better song rather than any lack of effort on Toby's part. Michael Tait's performance is nothing short of fantastic, though he delivers his lines in such a strong baritone in that modern Tait fans would probably have a hard time recognizing him. While he focused on keeping a pure and enthusiastic tone in "Heavenbound," here he follows the saxophone's lead and puts some growl into his voice.

This wasn't the strongest song of dc Talk's early career, but the 1989 debut album only had eight tracks and this one was clearly in a fairly ready state, so it's a little puzzling that it was left off. The most common theory is that the lyrics were considered a little too edgy for the overall spirit of the debut album, which focused more on praise music and "safer," more mainstream evangelical messages. Thirty years later, very little of the music produced during the 1980s seems very "edgy," so the song can be appreciated for what is: a fascinating, rarely heard time capsule of dc Talk's early years.

At the ForeFront

As more songs were completed, dc Talk began sending demo tapes out to different record executives. Time was growing short. Toby had graduated in 1988, but he was able to buy a few more months by taking graduate courses in business. The group continued to hone its sound with live performances, new material, and even by singing Christmas carols door-to-door. If a record deal didn't materialize soon, though, the three of them would undoubtedly be forced to go their separate ways.

While dc Talk's enthusiastic rap-chorus-rap style had been well-received at Liberty, the music industry as a whole felt quite differently. According to record executives of the era, the labels weren't terribly impressed, some going as far as passing the demo around as a "joke." Apparently, a college-aged Christian hip-hop outfit wasn't what the industry was looking for. dc Talk was passed over time and time again. There was *one* label, however, that had been on the lookout for a group that rapped its verses and sang its choruses. It was ForeFront Records, a record company that had entered the Christian music scene in 1987.

As mentioned in the July 13th, 1996 article in *Billboard Magazine* by Deborah Evans Price, the founders of ForeFront Records were Dan R. Brock, Eddie DeGarmo, Ron W. Griffin, and Dana Key. Founders DeGarmo and Key were a famous Christian rock group that had been going strong since the 1970s. By the time they were inducted into the Gospel Music Association's Hall of Fame in 2011, they'd been nominated for seven Grammy Awards and nearly twenty Dove Awards.

This small, trendy, upstart label was still in the process of signing and developing artists when dc Talk's demo came across their desk. At that point, the only albums ForeFront had put out were Eddie DeGarmo's *Feels Good to be Forgiven*, Jeoffrey Benward's *The Redeemer*, and a live DeGarmo and Key record.

It was Ron Griffin who first heard the dc Talk demo tape. He, Dan Brock, and the other executives at ForeFront Records were already seeing more potential in Christian hip-hop than their contemporaries were. They felt that by taking it a step further and infusing rap with more melody and vocals, they could create a product that would interest a wide base of consumers for the long-term. When dc Talk's demo fell into their hands, they realized that this energetic trio might be just what they were looking for.

The lines of communication were opened up between dc Talk and ForeFront, and it soon became apparent that the label might be a good home for the fledgling group. While the members of dc Talk had each had different musical interests and different ideas of what their careers would look like, it seemed that fate had thrust them together as a hip-hop group. When ForeFront offered them a serious deal, they decided that it was worth a shot to sign it. If they didn't work out as a hip-hop trio, well… the label would drop them and they'd be free to take their musical careers in any direction they chose. There really wasn't much downside.

In January 1989, Forefront Records sat down in the group's apartment near Liberty University. Toby McKeehan, Michael Tait, and Kevin Max Smith—along with Vic Mignogna and Mike Valliere—signed their names on the dotted line. Before the ink was even dry, they began packing up for a move to Nashville, Tennessee.

At a panel on the first Jesus Freak Cruise, Dan R. Brock mentioned that throughout the 1990s, other record executives would often ask him how he was able to woo dc Talk over to ForeFront. Even now, he seems amused by the question. Brock has to remind his peers that ForeFront was the only company who would give dc Talk a chance!

And indeed, the foresight and the risk that ForeFront took on this unproven hip-hop group eventually paid off in spades. But first, dc Talk needed to find their way. Throughout the early weeks and months of 1989, the group readied their debut album and began performing on an international stage for the first time.

DC Talk (1989)

After making a beeline for Nashville, ForeFront worked with dc Talk to assemble a product for the marketplace. The group had recorded several original songs already, so the process of putting together a debut album moved quickly. Vic Mignogna had done musical arrangements for several tracks (particularly "Final Days"), but with the label involved, his role was reduced. Mike Valliere (the "Valet Beat" referred to on some of the songs) recorded several beatboxing tracks. Overdubs, edits, mixes, and various vocal takes were done at studios in Tennessee and New Jersey.

The biggest addition to the team was producer/arranger Richard Hartline. In addition to various engineering tasks, Hartline wrote and arranged large portions of the tracks "Voices Praise Him" and "He Loves Me." This was the only album that Richard Hartline worked on for dc Talk, but he continued to be active in the industry until 1996.

The album ended up sounding fairly clean and polished, but since so much of it relied on what the band had produced before they were picked up by ForeFront, the sound wasn't exactly top of the line... even for 1989. Live instruments were virtually absent from the album, with keyboard sounds from only a couple synths being used for almost everything (even the guitar parts).

At the ForeFront

The project was recorded as quickly as possible, which also meant that there were some tough decisions to make. Additional songs were in the works, but there was no time to finish them and they had to be cut. At the end of the recording period, there were only seven songs and an extended interlude ready to be released.

The marketing machine was fired up while these were finalized. Promotional shots were taken (including a few shots of the group re-enacting the signing of their contract: the main trio was seated while Mignogna and Valliere high-fived each other behind them). dc Talk was sent out to perform with DeGarmo and Key for spring concert dates. The idea of a music video was floated around. Plans were made for the group to appear at several summer festivals.

The self-titled debut album, *DC Talk*, was pressed and ready in an impressive amount of time. While one of the dc Talk newsletters lists its release as February 1989, most catalogues and release information peg the date as June 13th, 1989. This was barely five months after the group was signed.

Containing eight tracks and running about thirty minutes, the record didn't seem to gain very much traction initially. Sales fell below expectations, though the official Spring '91 newsletter announced that it had broken the 100,000 mark by the end of 1990.

While subsequent dc Talk records fared much better, the debut never seemed to keep pace. As it stands, it's the only dc Talk album to never sell over 500,000 units and achieve gold status with the RIAA.

DC Talk Album, Track 01:
Heavenbound

"Heavenbound," the group's first signature song, wedged its way into the hearts of early fans quite easily. With its onslaught of synths and beats, its catchy chorus, and an unabashedly enthusiastic performance from rapper Toby McKeehan, "Heavenbound" was the first song to pass as a "hit" from the group. Even today, despite elements that could easily be described as "amateurish," something about the song really *works*. Toby's natural talent and charisma is highlighted more here than on almost any other *DC Talk* track due to the sparse musical accompaniment during the verses. More background vocals from Michael Tait were added to the bridge to give the song a more polished feel than the version from *Christian Rhymes to a Rhythm*, but even so, it seems that Kevin Max was still nowhere to be found on the track.

This was the only radio single from the album, though a couple of other songs ("Gah Ta Be" and "Spinnin' Round") also received a bit of airplay. Stations didn't quite know what to *do* with dc Talk's debut material, so it was clear early on that if the band was to find a pathway to success, the airwaves wouldn't be the easiest way to go.

Alternate Versions:
There aren't a lot of alternate versions of dc Talk's early material,

DC Talk (self-titled album)

but "Heavenbound" has a few cousins out there. The version from the 1987 *Christian Rhymes to a Rhythm* cassette has already been discussed, of course. In 1989, two different companies released an accompaniment track of "Heavenbound" without the main rap and chorus vocals. The one not directly affiliated with ForeFront has fewer background vocals than the ForeFront one, getting as close to a true instrumental track as can be. It's amazing how bare the verses sound without Toby's rap vocals.

In 1998, the ForeFront Records band "Bleach" recorded a cover of "Heavenbound" for *Forefront X: The Birthday Album*. Aside from the lyrics, the cover doesn't really resemble dc Talk's original very much. Bleach's version is alternative rock with a bridge that takes a mellow turn and introduces some original lyrics. This was the only dc Talk cover that Bleach ever recorded. After releasing three albums with ForeFront Records between 1996 and 1999, Bleach left ForeFront for another label and eventually disbanded after playing together for more than ten years. In 2010, they reunited to record a new EP and embark on a new tour.

Live Versions:
"Heavenbound" was the backbone of dc Talk's early performances. From the years before they were even signed to their first huge headlining tour in 1994, "Heavenbound" was a stalwart mainstay in an ever-changing dc Talk setlist. In fact, it's the only dc Talk song to appear in one form or another on almost every major tour. The big exceptions were the 1995 and 1996 tours in support of the *Jesus Freak* album and the Solo tours in the early 2000s. During 1999's Supernatural Experience Tour, the first verse of "Heavenbound" was performed during an "old school" rap breakdown that took place after an extended disco set that included band introductions. On that same tour, portions

of the 1989 recording of the song were played back by the on-stage DJ (Ric "DJ Form" Robbins) during the show's intermission. That practice was repeated by DJ Maj on the 2017 and 2019 Jesus Freak Cruises.

The best live version of "Heavenbound" was undoubtedly the arrangement played during 1994's Free at Last Tour. Performed completely with live musicians, this crowd favorite followed a string of older dc Talk songs (including "Nu Thang" and "Walls" from their second album) and was typically the last song of the show before the encore. Will Denton's drums added a much more organic feel to the song, Jason Halbert's soaring synths (especially the solo) kept the performance rooted to its 80s origins but added new, almost jazzy musical textures, Otto Price's bass gave the song a deeper bottom, and Brent Barcus' electric guitar gave the song a new edge (similar to how his guitars brought "Word 2 the Father" (a *Free at Last* era song from 1992) out from a laid-back jam to a scathing live piece). Toby McKeehan's delivery of the rap verses had become completely fluid by this time, Michael Tait had raised his baritone to a smoother, more modern register, and Kevin Max played adeptly with new background vocal arrangements. A clip of the group performing this version of the song can be found on *Free at Last: The Movie*.

Videos:
"Heavenbound" was dc Talk's first official music video, though they'd performed "Time Ta Jam" for television a few months after being signed. The "Heavenbound" video was produced and directed by Deaton Flanigen Productions, an outfit founded by the talented team of Robert Deaton and George J. Flanigen IV. In modern times, Deaton and Flanigan have continued to be active in the music video scene. They've produced projects for Kid Rock,

DC Talk (self-titled album)

Carrie Underwood, Rascal Flatts, and many others (mostly in the country music genre).

The "Heavenbound" video features the 1989 recording of the song played over concert footage, scenes with dc Talk on a bridge, shots of them literally dancing in the street, and short clips of the group performing unsafe vehicular maneuvers. Toward the end, they also "break it down" in a shopping mall by a jewelry store and help a baby in a stroller learn some dance moves. Lots of interesting hats, matching outfits, and even a mullet or two also make an appearance. In other words, the video is pure, high-octane 80s fun.

According to an article in the June/July 1990 issue of *Inside Music*, the BET network added the "Heavenbound" video to its "Video Vibrations" and "Rap City" shows. The television rotations gave the group its first taste of mainstream exposure.

Toby McKeehan, in a recent interview shown on the 2017 Jesus Freak Cruise television loop, explained what a surreal feeling it was to see himself in a music video for the first time. It's probably become a little more routine by now: as a part of dc Talk and as a solo artist, he's gone on to make nearly two dozen music videos in his career.

DC Talk Album, Track 02:
Gah Ta Be

With a gospel flair and a shot of hip-hop at its core, "Gah Ta Be" is an up-tempo number that mostly features Toby McKeehan and Michael Tait.

Rather than simply crafting something that only Christians can enjoy, this song is an early example of Toby writing lyrics that were meant for the world at large. The song attempts to dissuade its listeners from being caught up in material trappings by giving them a spiritual alternative.

Portions of the track resemble a jam session among talented musicians. That's was quite an accomplishment considering that the group was relying on keyboard synths for the majority of their work. 1980s technology was used to its full advantage here, and the resulting synthesized guitar work in particular is actually quite funky. And while "Heavenbound" was the only song officially released as a single, this song garnered some acclaim, as well.

Live Versions:
"Gah Ta Be" was performed off and on all the way until the summer of 1992, making it one of the more popular songs from the first album. It was often used as an encore piece. Kevin was featured more heavily in the live versions.

DC Talk Album, Track 03:
Final Days

Foreboding, fiery synths march the listener through the scorched earth of the apocalypse. The warnings in Toby's rapped verses erupt into a sublime, textured chorus that's heavy with the Kevin Max sound. At a particularly effective breakdown, the group's talented beat-boxer, "Valet Beat" (a.k.a. Mike Valliere) urges us to "get busy" – a 1980s phrase, to be sure. The tempo is a bit slower on this one, which only serves to help the track communicate the feeling of impending doom. The synth chosen for the main riff is addictive, sounding almost like a vocalization.

One of the highlights of the track comes at the very end when the music drops out and the Kevin Max chorus plays by itself. It's disappointing that this vocal section wasn't picked up and used in more remixes and DJ sets by other artists. dc Talk wouldn't put out another song with such a haunting and catchy Kevin Max passage until the *Nu Thang's* similarly-themed "Things of This World."

DC Talk Album, Track 04:
The King (Allelujah)

This was Kevin's big feature on the album ("He Loves Me" being Michael's). dc Talk considered itself a trio of three complementary but very different parts: "Rap, Rock, and Soul." Kevin Max Smith was the "Rock" of the group, and the feel of this song was a bit more in line with the style of music he excelled in at the time.

If "Final Days" wasn't enough of an introduction to Kevin's unique voice and talent, then this song surely did the trick. After a good introduction to Michael through the first two tracks and to Kevin through "Final Days" and "The King (Allelujah)," there was no doubt in any listener's mind that dc Talk had uniquely accomplished singers in its ranks.

Perhaps in an effort to match the distorted guitar sound on the track, Toby's delivery during the raps is more aggressive here than on the rest of the album. While Kevin's chorus is usually the song's most noticeable feature, this is one of Toby's best performances in the entire canon of early dc Talk material.

The song was featured on a 1990 ForeFront Christmas compilation called *Yo Ho Ho!* dc Talk contributed two *new* original songs to that project, as well.

DC Talk (self-titled album)

Live Versions:

"The King (Allelujah)" was a pretty regular inclusion in the live show until the summer festival season of 1992 when it was finally dropped to make way for new material. Even for audiences unfamiliar with dc Talk's work, the chorus' lyrics were so easy to learn that several members of the crowd found themselves singing along halfway through their first listen.

In the early days, "The King (Allelujah)" was sometimes performed as part of dc Talk's encore.

DC Talk Album, Track 05:
Spinnin' Round

With its great bass riff, generous servings of "Valet Beat," and a drum track programmed with gravitas, "Spinnin' Round" is almost as much of an accomplishment as "Heavenbound." Unlike most of the songs on the debut album, "Spinnin' Round" allows plenty of room for all three dc Talk elements to be highlighted in their own unique ways.

Toby has some great moments, primarily in the third verse, where he demonstrates an almost supernatural ability to become one with the rhythm. The spoken word portion sounds like it was tailor-made made for their live show, and most listeners can envision scenarios where it might be extended during a performance to give Toby an opportunity to speak to the crowd. This song was used as a finale in a few shows, which would make that segment an ideal place for a spoken testimony.

The chorus is primarily Kevin Max, but it also contains some great moments from Michael Tait. The arrangement manages to highlight the talents of *both* singers, serving as one of the first examples of the vocal interplay that would later become the bread and butter of dc Talk albums.

Alternate Versions:
An instrumental/accompaniment track was released under

DC Talk (self-titled album)

ForeFront's "Street Trax" karaoke banner. Like the other "karaoke-style" releases of the era, the tape contained the original mix of the song with the main vocals taken out. This particular mix was a little odd in that all of Toby and Michael's segments are cut out, but most of Kevin's remain. Some of the "shouting" tracks in the verses can still be heard, too.

A huge highlight of the accompaniment version is that the listener is treated to the raw "Valet Beat" portions of the track. Those segments sound *incredible* without anything else playing over them.

Live Versions:
When Kevin Max discusses dc Talk's early years, he almost always mentions this song. Perhaps it sticks out in his memory because he was the primary singer for the choruses during the live show, or perhaps because it was used as a lively encore piece for a period of time. It was also one of the only songs from the debut album to rival the material from their *next* album, Nu Thang, which meant that it was a mainstay at live shows until their third album was almost complete.

The song made its final live appearance on the 1992 summer festival circuit. It was often performed as the first third of a high-energy three-part main-set closer that also included "Nu Thang" and "Heavenbound."

DC Talk Album, Track 06:
Voices Praise Him

This is one of the most musically advanced songs on the album, possibly because of producer Richard Hartline's involvement. The soaring synths evoke the same feeling of "praise" that "Heavenbound" does, and the pumping bassline during the verse gives way to a great muted bass riff that was way ahead of its time.

It was one of the tracks that came together after the group was signed, thus giving fans a little sneak preview of how the group might evolve in the future. A highlight of the song is the bridge, where instead of a breakdown or another rapping verse, Michael Tait and Kevin Max trade vocal licks. Their voices also blend seamlessly during the chorus, giving the listeners an early taste of what would later become a signature dc Talk vocal sound.

There's a great call and response section before the bridge that seems like it would've worked well live. The spoken word section toward the end seems like filler, but the surprisingly effective modulation to a higher key makes up for it. The fade-out comes too quickly after the transition, a decision that may have been forced because of the cassette's timing considerations.

DC Talk Album, Track 07:
Time ta Jam

This is the most unique song on the album. That's not just because it lacks Michael and Kevin, but because it lacks any traditional instrumentation *at all*. Those things don't hold it back, though. Toby's rap is the main feature, and his accompaniment—Mike Valliere's multi-tracked "Valet Beat"—is on-point. Particularly impressive is Valliere's emulation of toms. The "zipper" sound is also a perennial favorite.

Too bad there weren't more tracks like this in the early dc Talk years. It's an evocative slice of what it would've been like in the *very* early days of dc Talk: young, hungry college kids with nothing but dreams and a couple of microphones.

The intentional voice squeaking by Toby isn't the best vocal affectation on the record, but it adds some interest to the track in the same way that other singers of the era like Michael Jackson used vocal ticks to add rhythm and dynamic range to otherwise bare performances.

One bonus of the track's lyrics is that we learn everyone's nicknames: apparently Kevin was known as "K Max" (a name that stuck) and Michael Tait was known as "Tater Tot" (a name that didn't).

A Fan's Guide to dc Talk

Live Versions:
Owing to the fact that the song required minimal setup, it was a live staple in the early years and had many impromptu performances. Between Toby's passionate vocal delivery and Mike Valliere's prodigious beat-boxing, it was a crowd-pleaser that could feel more organic than other parts of dc Talk's live show.

Once the ball got rolling, though, it didn't seem to be a particularly integral part of their set. It *did*, however, make a surprising return during 1994's Free at Last Tour. Lines from the song were worked in as part of a band introduction segment called "Back 2 the Basics" (a medley that took its name from a *Free at Last* interlude of the same name).

Video:
Shot at the Cornerstone Television studios in Wall, Pennsylvania for a show called *Lightmusic*, dc Talk performed this song live-to-tape in March 1989. This performance may be the earliest publicly-released footage of the group as a trio. It can be found on the 1992 video release *Rap, Rock, and Soul*.

And who can forget the classic line: "Yo homes, can you hook us up with a cup of coffee?"

Tom Green, the host of *Lightmusic* and the man who helped facilitate dc Talk's appearance, was an innovative musician in his own right. While hosting *Lightmusic*, he was widely known to push for more quality, contemporary content in religious programming. He sometimes even brought in a secular artist or played a mainstream music video with a positive message, something that was rarely done on religious television in those days. Sadly, he passed away in 2003 at the young age of 55.

DC Talk Album, Track 08:
He Loves Me

The only ballad on the album is the well-deserved Michael Tait spotlight "He Loves Me." Though modern fans will hardly recognize Tait's tone and phrasing in this track, this was the general style of music that he was singing when Toby McKeehan first met him. A star performer at chapel during the Liberty University days, it always seemed that Michael Tait was headed for gospel music, not hip-hop. Life certainly had other plans. Fans of this incarnation of Michael Tait should do their best to track down his 1988 demo cassette called *Burden Lifter*, a project that features Tait performing several classic hymns.

To bring this updated take on "Jesus Loves Me" into the dc Talk sound, Toby crafted and delivered some subdued verses for the moments between Michael Tait's incredible renditions of the main chorus. The spoken word/rap portions were a surprisingly perfect fit for the song.

The track benefitted greatly from Richard Hartline's involvement. The background vocals might be a little loud in the mix, but they fit the song well. There's a pristine woodwind sound playing some advanced harmony lines during the final chorus; the passage helps the song (and the whole album) end on a very gentle note.

Alternate Versions:
The instrumental/accompaniment version of this track sounds a little uneven for some reason. But whether it was a bad transfer or whether these were decisions made to enhance the karaoke version of the song, it's difficult to tell.

Live Versions:
This was a huge part of early dc Talk shows, played whenever there was enough time in the set for a slower song. It continued to appear in slightly different formats (and without the rap parts) even into the *Free at Last* years. Later performances feature much sparser instrumentation with just Michael and a keyboard player playing to the audience. As explained in *Free at Last: The Movie*, the keyboard player was terrified of making a mistake: whenever he did, Tait would turn around and shoot him a desperate look.

The song was performed for the last time in 1994.

Video:
The 1991 video *Rap, Rock, and Soul* has footage of dc Talk performing "He Loves Me" at the 1990 Flevo Festival in the Netherlands. Produced by Paul Groeneveld, this clip is one of the earliest dc Talk performances that have been released to the public.

There's also a live video circulating of Michael Tait performing this song during a concert in 1993. The clip is available on a commercially released VHS tape that features the band in a series of interviews and performances.

Free at Last: The Movie contains footage of Michael singing the song at a friend's wedding. Through clever editing, the clip merges into a performance of the song from one of the Spring

DC Talk (self-titled album)

1994 concerts. During that concert series, the song was included as part of the encore. Earlier in the movie, there's footage of dc Talk regrouping backstage before going out to perform their final songs. Michael expresses apprehension about singing the encore because his voice is tired and he's afraid that it'll go out during the more difficult passages. As Toby changes wardrobe for "Socially Acceptable," another number that was also part of the encore, the group urges Tait to go on.

Early DC Talk Shows

"The first festival they were at, they didn't even have an album. They were on the truck with DeGarmo and Key, and they wormed their way onto the stage for five or ten minutes." This was how Denny Keitzman, dc Talk's road manager from 1991 until the end of the band's career, described his first memories of dc Talk's stage career. (The quote appeared in Rona Pryor's "Denny Keitzman: King of the Road" article in the May/June 2001 issue of *Christian Musician*.) It's a perfect summation of the first tours that dc Talk went on.

The thirty minutes that made up the debut album might not have been enough to convince the world that dc Talk members were emerging superstars, but at least it was enough to convince their label that they had promise. ForeFront Records founders (and main act) Eddie DeGarmo and Dana Key threw their weight behind dc Talk and brought them out on tour with them as soon as the ink was dry on their contracts. In a story that band members have repeated several times throughout the years, there was only one string attached: in exchange for a few minutes on stage, the members of dc Talk had to essentially work as roadies by setting up DeGarmo and Key's equipment, keyboards, packing things up, and working the merchandise tables.

DC Talk (self-titled album)

They were more than happy to do it, though. Even thirty years later, Toby, Michael, and Kevin still express gratitude to DeGarmo and Key for giving them their first major opportunity in the music business. The arrangement seemed to work out for everyone, as the up-tempo evangelical style of dc Talk's early music and their energetic live performances started to slowly win them fans and even enhance DeGarmo and Key's concert experience.

Being out on the road with the label's head honchos was probably also a test of sorts to see how well the group fit within the developing culture of the fledgling label. They must have passed, since throughout 1989 and 1990, dc Talk was never far from DeGarmo and Key's side. dc Talk opened for them nearly thirty times in 1989 and nearly twenty times in 1990.

dc Talk was also able to book a couple of appearances at the big summer festivals in 1989. They made appearances at the Encounter Festival, the Fishnet Festival, and Jesus '89. In August, the group secured a spot to perform at the Alleluia '89 festival, an event spread out over Kingston and Montego Bay in Jamaica (where Toby's college sweetheart and future wife, Amanda Levy, was from). The rest of the year was spent in the US and Canada on a busy tour schedule as DeGarmo and Key's opening act. The first half of 1990 was spent the same way.

These early dc Talk shows looked *nothing* like their concerts in the mid-to-late 1990s. Rife with sweeping dance moves, matching outfits, and lots of energy, the three men of dc Talk were fueled by the hunger and drive of a band eager to prove itself and gain its footing.

Early shows weren't without their mishaps, of course. At one show, Toby entered the stage on a skateboard and couldn't quite navigate well enough to avoid a painful crash. Toby was no stranger to danger though: he spent many evenings of his adolescence in the hospital getting sewn up for adventures gone awry. There was also an episode (described by Bruce A. Brown in his article "DC Talk: Def, Not Dumb" for *CCM Magazine's* December 1990 issue) where Kevin Max broke his arm while wrestling on the bus and had to be sent back to his hometown to recuperate. It wouldn't be Kevin's only injury, either. During a show on a later tour, he got behind a backup dancer just as they were diving forward and kicking their legs up and outward. Kevin's lips were busted up when the dancer's feet connected with his microphone and thrust it into his face.

Their adventurous spirit, hard work, and raw talent may have scraped them up a bit, but it was paying off. As the group toured the world and Toby began writing new songs, the label was enthusiastic enough about them to set up production for a second dc Talk album.

Nu Thang (1990)

Throughout their career, every album that dc Talk released was a quantum leap above the previous one in some form or fashion. Even though it was stylistically cut from the same cloth as their debut album, dc Talk's sophomore effort, *Nu Thang*, was no exception to this rule.

It should be noted that the album wasn't *always* a stylistic successor to the debut album, though. For almost a year, *Nu Thang* went in a very different direction. Toby McKeehan most recently discussed the origins of *Nu Thang* in a January 28th, 2019 interview with writer Justin Sarachik for the website *rapzilla.com*. As mentioned in Sarachik's article, the original studio sessions for *Nu Thang* were held in Memphis, Tennessee. Live musicians and drummers were tasked with laying down organic, beat-driven soul tracks with professional backup singers. In between long stretches of dc Talk appearances at DeGarmo and Key concerts, Toby lived out of Memphis hotel rooms and did his best to steer the songs toward his vision. But as time went on, the disconnect between the record in his head and the record being put to tape became too much for him.

Toby and the label had a reckoning over the material. The tracks were good, but they had drifted *very* far from the original *DC Talk* record and weren't on the path that Toby was traveling as an artist. Fortunately, the label understood this. ForeFront had begun taking on more hip-hop artists and producing more rap tracks under their new "Yo! ForeFront" brand. As they made more headway in this space, they gained a much better understanding of the genre. The company needed to rethink the *Nu Thang* album. Production was moved back to the Nashville area for dc Talk to regroup.

Enter Mark Heimermann, the producer who was hired to rework *Nu Thang* and whose eight years of work with the dc Talk would practically make him the "fourth member" of the group. Heimermann was no stranger to the business, having begun his professional career in the mid-1980s as the original keyboard player of budding star Michael W. Smith's backing band. As part of Smith's crew, Heimermann had played alongside future dc Talk session musicians Chris Harris, Chris Rodriguez, David Huff, and future star producer and Grammy winner Wayne Kirkpatrick. During this time, Heimermann had also begun lending his voice as a studio background singer for artists like Amy Grant and Rich Mullins.

Mark Heimermann's first major turn in the producer's chair had come earlier as one of the driving forces behind a unique project from Reunion Records. The Reunion label had already released two of Michael W. Smith's live records that Heimermann had been a part of and had put out a compilation album with a Mullins track that Heimermann had lent his voice to. Their new project, called *Prism*, was a four-volume album series consisting of high-quality contemporary Christian song covers, hymns, and originals aimed at the children's market. Heimermann was in charge of producing the project along with Chris Harris, a friend he had worked with in Michael W. Smith's band. On the *Prism* records, Heimermann and Harris did the majority of the arranging, production, writing, composing, and even the vocals. They brought in *another* Michael W. Smith alumni, guitarist and vocalist Chris Rodriguez, to assist. Each sang a couple of tracks on all four of the albums, and the other tracks featured guest

Nu Thang

vocalists from around the Christian music industry. Some of the other talents who lent their voice to the *Prism* project included Gary Chapman (a popular Christian Music artist and Amy Grant's husband at the time) and First Call (a Christian vocal group that was on the cusp of winning their first Dove Award).

The four *Prism* albums, titled *Blue*, *Red*, *Green*, and *Yellow*, gave Heimermann and Harris ample room to showcase their production talents. After the Prism albums had hit the market, Heimermann found additional work as a session player and background singer for major artists like Kenny Rogers, Stephen Curtis Chapman, and Carman. More production jobs came his way after that: the year that he produced *Nu Thang* for dc Talk, he and Chris Harris also produced Morgan Cryar's *Kingdom Upside Down* album for Reunion Records and the legendary Alabama-based soft rock Christian quartet 4Him's debut record for Benson Records (the same label that DeGarmo and Key were releasing records on when they weren't publishing under ForeFront).

People who worked with Toby McKeehan during the dc Talk days recall that he wasn't usually the most relaxed presence in the studio, but when Mark Heimermann was brought in to rework *Nu Thang's* Memphis sessions, there was a huge feeling of relief. Heimermann understood what Toby wanted and found ways to deliver it. *Nu Thang* was brought to life at places like Nashville's Quad Recording Studios (where Jimmy Buffet's "Margaritaville" was recorded in 1977), OmniSound Studios (a popular choice for Christian artists of the era), the somewhat short-lived Duckworth Studio (where a Petra album had just been mixed), and other well-equipped facilities. Chris Harris came in to do some of the higher-level work while Heimermann was busy in the trenches. The foundations for the tracks were programmed by Heimermann, McKeehan, and future Gotee Brother Todd Collins. Additional contributions from jazz artist Mose Allison's Memphis-based drummer Tom Lonardo were used in the project, too. As the project took shape, an accomplished team of live session players was brought in to flesh out the tracks. Some of the musicians whose work ended up on *Nu Thang* included Steven Curtis Chapman's studio bassist Jackie Street. Guitarist Chris Rodriguez, whom Heimermann and Harris had worked with the Michael W. Smith years and on the *Prism* project, also lent his considerable talents to the record.

Unfortunately, dc Talk's live show and new recording process left nothing for Vic Mignogna, their original musician, or Mike "Valet Beat" Valliere. Professionally, they parted ways with dc Talk. In later years, Vic Mignogna became a prolific musician, a producer for a variety of television and radio commercials, a worship leader for a major church in Houston, TX, and he eventually found worldwide success as an Anime voiceover artist. Mike "Moose" Valliere, who had been studying psychology at Liberty University, picked up his studies again at George Mason University near his hometown. Valliere went on to have a very successful career in real estate. Interestingly, this was the same line of work Toby had planned to go into if dc Talk had failed. On February 26th, 2011, a touching moment for classic dc Talk fans occurred between Toby and Valliere at a TobyMac concert in Fairfax, Virginia when Toby handed the microphone over to Valliere for one more dose of "Valet Beat."

For a Christian hip-hop album recorded at the turn of the decade, the songs put together for *Nu Thang* were solid. More advanced and more diverse than offerings from the debut album, the new material had benefitted greatly from dc Talk's experience on the road, the album's long incubation period, a bigger budget, and the talents of Heimermann's production team.

Not *everyone* was as thrilled with the new tracks as McKeehan, however. Michael Tait half-jokingly makes a horrified facial expression when asked to recall the song "I Luv Rap Music," a reimagining of a 1979 song called "I Love Beach Music," and its accompanying video. Kevin Max, when reminiscing about the first two albums, has mentioned that he was less than enthusiastic about some of the material. At the core of it could have been that Tait and Max were probably still a little hesitant to commit to a career as backup singers for a hip-hop group. Before dc Talk's record deal, they'd entertained very different career paths for themselves. Both singers knew that they had the talent to front their own projects, but *Nu Thang* planted both of their flags firmly in hip-hop territory and seemingly represented a bigger commitment to a future as backup singers.

At the end of the day, though, all three of them obviously felt that there were far more positives than negatives to the project. While there may have been disagreements about a variety of things, the members of dc Talk seemed to believe in the core of what they were doing. *Nu Thang* moved forward.

Kevin Max once shared what many believe to be a secret of the group's success: he said that regardless of how anyone may have felt about particular songs or particular sessions (especially in the early years), at the end of the day, they all strived to be professionals and focused on giving every song the best performance that they could. When listening to the album, it's clear that everyone involved in *Nu Thang* gave a hundred percent of themselves to the work. Some of the less-than-flattering opinions that *all three* members have diplomatically shared about the project in recent years are probably colored more by their *current* thoughts on it rather than how they were feeling at the time. Of course, it's a given that the project hasn't aged as well as their later material. At the very least, it must be acknowledged that *Nu Thang* was a necessary step in dc Talk's evolution. Toby found his voice as a producer, Mark Heimermann was brought into the fold, Michael Tait got his first co-writing writing credit for working on the music to "Walls," and—most important of all—a production team was formed that would later carry the group into more artistic territory.

In September 1990, over a year after dc Talk's debut album was released, *Nu Thang* hit the shelves. The group's small band of followers immediately appreciated it for what it was: a project that took everything that worked well from the group's earlier efforts and built on it exponentially. While the album kept its feet firmly planted in hip-hop and rap, the group was already broadening their horizons by experimenting with guitar tracks and other genres of music.

There was one core difference between the first two albums: while the *DC Talk* record was mostly a praise project directed squarely at the Christian market, *Nu Thang* took a much wider aim. Tackling a variety of social issues (some of them quite heavy, like abortion and racism), the group still offered a positive message and faith-based alternatives. This time, the Gospel was offered while exploring some of the most pervasive problems of society and human nature. Spending a year and a half on tour had exposed the group to many more issues than those that existed inside the walls of Liberty University. The group was no longer content with tailoring dc Talk's message to a built-in, receptive audience when so much good could be done by bringing the ideas of hope and faith to a larger group of people.

Critics who had ignored the *DC Talk* album gave *Nu Thang* a warm reception. The market did too, as it sold 100,000 copies in four months. Concert-goers noticed that the live show was improving dramatically, especially when the group went on tour with Michael W. Smith as his opening band in 1991. Smith, who was burning up the charts with his smash hit song "Place in This World," helped introduce dc Talk's sophomore album to a whole new audience (the tours with Michael W. Smith will be covered

Nu Thang

later in the book).

Nu Thang won a Dove Award in 1991 for Rap/Hip-Hop Album of the Year and eventually sold over half a million copies. It was certified "Gold" by the RIAA on June 6th, 1994.

Nu Thang Album, Track 01:
When DC Talks

A dramatic synth pad opens the *Nu Thang* album before quickly breaking away to the unabashedly 80s bass riff that drives "When DC Talks," making for one of the best moments in the classic dc Talk canon. Written as a mission statement to define the band's work, "When DC Talks" was the perfect way to begin the next chapter of their careers.

The "cutting" of Toby's voice is reminiscent of how "Heavenbound" started. The effect helps tie the two projects together. Tying them together even further is the quick sound sample from the debut album's "Time Ta Jam."

It's immediately apparent that the quality of the sound and production had greatly improved from the 1989 project. The alien-sounding vocoder effect is perfect, not only adding an aura of mystery and suspense to the opening bars but functioning as more weight behind the chorus, too. An observant listener will enjoy the layers of complex vocoder harmonies in the sections toward end of the chorus sections as they transition into verses.

Like the debut album, "When DC Talks" is mostly keyboards and synths. The programming improved quite a bit from the original album, and there's even a very modern sub-kick sound in the verse that repeats every two bars. A few live guitar parts chime in during select parts of the chorus.

Nu Thang

Sampling other songs was a huge trend in hip-hop at the time. dc Talk embraced this practice fully. As detailed on the website *whosampled.com*, the first musical breakdown of "When DC Talks" samples the song "Real Love" as performed by Jody Watley. The "this is serious business" clip comes from "Mind Blowin'" by The D.O.C. "Hit it" was a very popular sample at the time, best known as one of the sounds from Rob Base and DJ E-Z Rock's "It Takes Two." The sample used right after it sounds like the same James Brown clip used later in the song "I Luv Rap Music." The "Aw yeah," sample comes from a live version of Run-DMC's "Here We Go."

For newer fans, "When DC Talks" offers an explanation for the group's name. Folks familiar with their early work knew that they had originally been called "DC Talk" because Toby and Michael were both from the Washington D.C. area. "When DC Talks" retcons the band's name into meaning "Decent Christian Talk" (though the change had already been introduced briefly in "Time Ta Jam"). In the verses for "When DC Talks," Toby promises no obscenities (hence, the "Decent"), affirms that the lyrics come from his stance as a believer (the "Christian"), and explains that his genre of choice is "r-a-p" (the "Talk" portion of the name).

Nu Thang Album, Track 02:
He Works

The song begins with the theme from the Andy Griffith Show, but DJ is promptly told to "drop it." When he does, the album erupts into a spectacular explosion of clav, synth, and drum machines.

"He Works" is one of the funkiest, most upbeat tracks in the dc Talk catalog. One of the highlights here is that Michael Tait debuts his new singing voice: a frosty, smooth, pitch-perfect tone delivered in a higher register than he'd used previously. Current fans will finally recognize him. Toby's rap skills are leaps and bounds above the first album, and he was *already* pretty good there. Kevin is already nailing his parts like a seasoned pro.

The beat and background tracks are quite a bit better than the debut album, too. Much more time was spent arranging the music and adding the different elements that make it interesting. On this track, experienced ears will be able to hear how Heimermann and company used various effects to give the drums a wider stereo separation. A chorus effect (a way of doubling the sound), in particular, makes the beat much thicker.

Hardcore fans will recognize that the second verse takes its lyrical cue from dc Talk's abandoned "Always Leaning" track. Thankfully, it handles the subject of drug use in a much more palatable way. The "God is always workin'" portion of the song is reused on the group's next album during the final main track, "Word 2 the Father," which was created as sort of a career retrospective of dc Talk's work up to that point.

Listeners in 1990 probably didn't recognize the high-pitched sample that appears right before Michael Tait sings "And God is in my life." It comes from a 1972 Lyn Collins song called "Think (About it)." The breakbeat used in this same area was one of the most popular "enhancers" used by DJs at the time. It came from a James Brown track called "Funky Drummer." These connections and more are documented on the website *whosampled.com*.

In recent years, "He Works" has become a favorite track of Christian dance groups who enjoy choreographing routines to "old school" hits.

Alternate Versions:
An instrumental/accompaniment version of this song was offered for sale on cassette in the early 1990s as part of ForeFront's "Street Trax" series. The clavichord track is mixed hotter on the accompaniment track: a wise decision makes the whole production even funkier.

Live Versions:
"He Works" was an underrated part of several *Nu Thang*-era dc Talk shows. It continued to be included in setlists until the end of the summer 1992 festival season. At Cornerstone 1992, it was performed immediately after their brand new song "Luv is a Verb."

Nu Thang Album, Track 03:
I Luv Rap Music

"I Luv Rap Music" was the first single released from *Nu Thang*. A bouncy song with plenty of humor and personality injected into it, the track seemed perfect for radio. Stations seemed to disagree, though... like most of dc Talk's early singles, it failed to earn widespread airplay.

The song differentiated itself from most of the group's other material by not being overtly evangelical. Additionally, most dc Talk fans had no idea that it was a cover of sorts. The track takes most of its cues from a 1979 song called "I Love Beach Music" by Jackie Gore. Gore was known for his work as part of a North Carolina group called the Embers from 1958 until the mid-1990s. During his nearly forty-year tenure with the group, his signature sound was associated with beachy weekends and holidays in the sun. Because of his success in that genre, Jackie Gore is fondly known as "The Father of Beach Music."

"I Luv Rap Music" may not have been successful on the radio, but it did prove its worth by winning a 1992 Dove Award for Rap/Hip-Hop Recorded Song of the Year.

Alternate Versions:
An instrumental/accompaniment cassette was released under the "Street Trax" banner. Some of the transfers for these releases weren't as good as others, but "I Luv Rap Music" is crystal-clear.

Nu Thang

Live Versions:
The song was a mainstay in dc Talk shows for the entire *Nu Thang* period and even through the early *Free at Last* concerts from 1992 to 1993. It was part of the show until the 1994 Free at Last Tour.

Video:
Bright colors, baggy pajamas, loud costumes, oversized props, polka dots, and color-changing dresses don't even begin to describe the joyous mayhem of 1991's "I Luv Rap Music" video. If the early 1990s could dream, this is what it would dream. Some participants may have been worried about something so campy ending up on a blackmail tape in the future, but if they were, they hid their worries well. The band, dancers, and extras were clearly having a good time, perhaps a function of doing something so silly that they felt giddy. dc Talk's backup dancers, notably long-time associates Teron Carter and Juan Otero, were shown in prominent roles wearing costumes and participating in some the oddball vocal sections. Teron Carter received a credit for masterminding the choreography. To add to the fun, the winner of a *Lightmusic* contest got to appear in the video as one of the female "Be-Bop" singers.

The video project was produced by Deaton Flanigen Productions, the same team behind the "Heavenbound" video.

Nu Thang Album, Track 04:
No More

"No More," dc Talk's major rock number on the album, is a pretty intense piece. Kevin Max Smith takes center stage, of course, but Michael Tait gets more microphone time than he did during last album's "The King (Alleluja)." Both singers sound fantastic on this track, and Toby raises his intensity to deliver a stand-out performance, too.

With huge drums and a guitar riff that really shreds, the song has a stadium-sized feel. The crowd echoes add nicely to the effect. In the instrumental of the song (if you can find it), you can hear that the crowd isn't exactly saying "No More," but the sample does its job.

Similar to dc Talk's later track "My Friend (So Long)," there's a speaking part during the bridge that's barely audible. It's only there for effect, but it was once actually transcribed. The words weren't very interesting.

The last section of the song (with more prominent spoken words) is very reminiscent of passages from the debut album that seemed custom-made for concert testimony.

The song ends on a neat (and very 1980s) note as Toby says the word "gone!" and the guitar drones out. The effect is better than a fadeout, but to modern listeners, not by much!

Nu Thang

"No More" was released as a single later in the *Nu Thang* promotional cycle. It was one of the only early dc Talk songs that gained much traction, reaching all the way to number ten on the Christian Rock chart (reportedly dc Talk's highest position on that particular chart until their smash hit song "Jesus Freak").

Alternate Versions:
An instrumental/accompaniment track was available on cassette via the "Street Trax" line, just like several other songs from this album.

Nu Thang Album, Track 05:
Nu Thang (song)

Musically and stylistically, the title track to the *Nu Thang* album is one of the most advanced dc Talk songs of the era. It's aged better than most of their other classic tracks, some of which sounded a bit outdated even within a year of their release.

It's clear that a lot of care went into this song. Some of it was undoubtedly the work of Joel Dobbins, the song's co-writer. Dobbins also got a general credit for programming on the album ("programming" means the assembly of a song with drum machines, samples, and the sequencing of keyboard and other sonic elements), so his involvement ran deep.

The chorus/doubling effect on Toby's voice during the rap adds some thickness to some of the more musically sparse segments. Toby is still employing the "squeak" effect (most noticeably during the phrase "a brand *new* thing to your raggedly walk"), but this is one of its last appearances.

The background singers do a great job, especially during the bridge. The chorus is vocally complex, with Kevin dominating the first phrase, Michael dominating the second, and the background singers cleaning up on the third. Kevin and Michael have some great solo moments toward the end of the song.

The guitar work brings back the mix of rap and rock that dominated "No More." Guitars continued to trend during the rest of the album, especially during the next two tracks: "Things of This World" and "Walls." This early mix of rock and rap had already begun to set the stage for *Jesus Freak*.

Fans of early hip-hop will recognize many of the audio samples in "Nu Thang." The website *whosampled.com* attempts to document them all: the breakdown ("get funky") samples come from James Brown's song "Funky President (People it's Bad)." The "hit me" is from Public Enemy's "911 is a Joke," a clip which they reuse again on "Walls." The extended "yeeeeah" comes from The D.O.C's "It's Funky Enough."

"Nu Thang" was eventually released as a single. It soared to the number three position on one of the Christian charts, giving dc Talk its highest ranking yet as their popularity began to surge.

In the years immediately after the track's release, the "a cappella" (vocal-only) chorus at the beginning of the song was a favorite sample of remixers who worked on Christian tracks. Even Stephen Curtis Chapman, one of the biggest contemporary Christian music stars of the 1990s, included it on a song called "Got 2 B Tru." Chapman's track also featured Toby as a rapper and co-writer. dc Talk even sampled their own song during a breakdown for *Free at Last's* "Socially Acceptable," though it's hard to notice (it's the "Yo who's doin it? Everybody's doin' it" portion).

During the internet era, the song took on a life of its own when an online video of a young boy performing "Nu Thang" on an old television broadcast garnered more than two million views. By several metrics, the "Nu Thang Kid" has actually outperformed dc Talk's original version!

Alternate Versions:
A "Street Trax" edition was released in the early 1990s. A music video was produced for the song, with the version of the song in

the video featuring minor differences from the original track (like the repeated phrase "Peace in your heart, a new start").

Live Versions:
"Nu Thang" was an integral part of the live set from 1990 through most of 1994. One of the most notable performances of it was when the band was invited to sing it at the 1992 Dove Awards. Live footage from this era of dc Talk is rare, so being able to see Toby and Michael execute their choreography (using kids as backup dancers) and hearing Kevin's ad-libs makes for a real time capsule.

On the Free at Last Tour in 1994, "Nu Thang" was sung after "Lean on Me." It was followed by a medley of "Walls" and "Time Is" before the group closed out the main set with "Heavenbound." Despite a *lot* of concert footage being released from this era, there are no videos at all of "Nu Thang" circulating in the public. In fact, it's the only portion of the show that hasn't made its way out yet.

After a considerable absence from dc Talk's live show, "Nu Thang" was resurrected as the second round of Toby's "old school" rap segment in 1999's Supernatural Experience Tour. Along with bassist Otto "Sugarbear" Price, Toby delivered the entire first verse and handed the chorus off to Sugarbear and the crowd. On the various DJ sets that the group employed over the years, including on the Jesus Freak Cruises, the chorus vocals were set to contemporary beats.

Video:
Deaton Flanigen Productions was employed once again to bring dc Talk to the screen. The music video they ended up with for "Nu Thang" had a similar feel to the "Heavenbound" video. There were impromptu concert/dance/keyboard scenes and clips of the group out in the street. This time, they added synchronized dance moves choreographed by a professional dancer named

Nu Thang

Sheron Neverson-Diggs. Baseball jerseys, matching shirts, and identical necklaces rounded out the fun. The shooting of the video must've been a little more arduous than some of the others, as the weather is so cold that you can see the group's breath.

Nu Thang Album, Track 06:
Things of This World

"Things of This World" is *Nu Thang's* answer to "Spinnin' Round," though this time the message of materialism is much more severe. This dark, moody piece has a great keyboard motif that gets explored through different styles of synths and with heavily-phased percussion elements. Some of the percussion is even played on a guitar fretboard. A solid beat and a driving groove steer the track forward and keep it from becoming *too* somber, though the dark message of materialism's effect on the soul is hard to shake.

The mysterious quality of Kevin Max's voice makes him perfect for the lead. When he lets loose toward the end, it's downright chilling. Michael Tait has some great moments toward the end of the song, though for some reason the timbre of his voice sounds more like it did on the debut album.

Clocking in at over five minutes, this is one of the longer songs on *Nu Thang*.

In the acknowledgment section, Toby thanks "Dan and Brigette Laskowski" for the concept behind this song.

Alternate Versions:
Like many *Nu Thang* tracks, an instrumental/accompaniment track was made available on cassette.

Nu Thang

Live Versions:
"Things of This World" wasn't performed very often at all during the *Nu Thang* tours, probably because it was so moody and didn't fit with everything else they had going on. When dc Talk was being invited for longer sets on the 1992 summer festival season, they included it as a medley with another *Nu Thang* track, "Children Can Live (Without It)." This medley was brought over to the first leg of the 1994 Free at Last Tour for a time as the opening song of their encore (it would be followed by "Socially Acceptable" from *Free at Last*). It was dropped after a short run and has never been performed again.

Video:
A video of a live performance from 1994 can be found on *Free at Last: The Movie* (released to DVD in 2002). What's interesting is that in the commentary, Toby and Michael both express disbelief at what they're seeing because neither of them remembered *ever* performing the song. The memories seem to have disappeared forever, just like the *real* things of this world.

The video of the performance is actually worth the price of the DVD itself. Witnessing how dc Talk's talented musicians and vocalists were able to update the *Nu Thang* tracks for a later tour always drives home what a special group they really were. The 1994 live version is a haunting, complex rendition that would hold up even to today's audiences. The synth sounds are thicker, the vocals by Michael and Kevin are delivered with greater power, and the guitars expand greatly on the original's themes. The best part of the whole production is that Toby delivers the rap with much more polished cadence in a deeper register. He'd come a long way since the *DC Talk* and *Nu Thang* days. The better vocals, along with the live instrumentation, makes for pure gold.

Nu Thang Album, Track 07:
Walls

One of the first social issues that dc Talk tackled was racism. They were proud to set an example of "living integration": from its core members to its dancers to its backing band (in the studio and later on the road), dc Talk was proof that different races could live together, work together, create together, and love together. "Walls," a fan favorite from *Nu Thang*, was Toby's first time to not only tell the world what he stood for religiously, but to craft an anthem that explained where he stood when it came to social justice.

The spoken word sample in the introduction emphasizes one of Martin Luther King, Jr.'s most powerful messages from his April 16th, 1963 "Letter From Birmingham Jail": that segregation is not only a sociological wrong, but that it's a *moral* wrong. The quote serves as the perfect start... though we could probably stand to lose the "Yeah, boy!" line. In "Walls," Toby's lyrics work as not only a call to action but as a reminder that nothing about racism or segregation has any roots in a Bible-based faith. In a song filled with spectacular lines, some of the best ones include "Gotta live by example, show brotherly love / We're together on earth, we'll be together above" and "All means all, with no discrimination."

Musically, this is the track from *Nu Thang* that's aged the best. It was clearly the best song at the time, too, and should've been the band's first breakout single. When it was released to radio in

Nu Thang

1992, it did receive *some* airplay, but not nearly enough. It peaked at number 18 on the Contemporary Christian Music Rock chart, which was a decent number for the fledgling band. Its reception was enhanced by the debut of a music video to go along with the single's release.

The guitar work on the track is stellar. dc Talk was already blending rap and rock effortlessly at this stage in their career. The vocals, too, are some of the best on the record. Michael Tait, who earned a co-writing credit for the music on this track, puts his voice to the test in unique ways. Toby's delivery is so unabashedly passionate that it almost feels like a continuation of a song like "Final Days" from the debut album.

Alternate Versions:
You guessed it... an instrumental/accompaniment track was available on cassette. Unlike some of the "Street Trax" releases that have virtually no background vocals, a lot of the vocal tracks remain (even some of the shouting that can be heard during the verses).

Live Versions:
"Walls" was brought into the live show almost immediately. It was so strong that it became a mainstay in dc Talk sets all the way through 1996 – the only track from *Nu Thang* to last through the *Jesus Freak* era.

The Spring/Summer 1992 issue of the *Christian Activities Calendar* magazine detailed a memorable early performance of the song. In an article called "DC Talk: Tearin' Down the Walls," writers Robert Michael and Colleen Hoagland describe the scene: "At a high school in Jackson, Mississippi, the DC Talk'ers noticed that the audience was split down the middle – blacks on one side and whites on the other. At the conclusion of their performance of 'Walls,' a black football player crossed the [aisle] and hugged a white football player, at which point the rest of the students followed the dramatic example."

In 1993, dc Talk began performing "Walls" as a medley with their *Free at Last* rocker "Time Is." When they headlined their 1994 tour, the medley was expanded to include a guest appearance from their opening band's guitarist, Audio Adrenaline's Barry Blair.

The most impressive live version of the song was performed during the 1995 shows and the 1996 Freak Show Tour in support of *Jesus Freak*. Again, it was featured in a medley that included "Time Is." The song began with the opening riff to Jimi Hendrix's "Purple Haze," and the rock flavor only got more intense from there. It was one of the hardest-hitting parts of the show; no easy feat considering that much of the *Jesus Freak* era was pure rock and roll. The medley was technically the last song in the main set, as "Alas My Love," "The Hardway," and "Jesus Freak" followed as an encore.

When *Supernatural* came along, the song disappeared. It made a only a brief comeback during DJ Maj's solo on the 2017 Jesus Freak Cruise when he played the vocals from the chorus over "Intergalactic" by the Beastie Boys.

dc Talk has ventured pretty far from their hip-hop roots, but if they continue to perform reunion shows, it would be great to see the "Walls"/"Time Is" medley make a return.

Video:
Deaton Flanigen Productions and choreographer Sheron Neverson-Diggs brought their talents to the third music video from *Nu Thang*. In "Walls," historic footage from the Civil Rights era and strong imagery are interspersed with clips of dc Talk (at one point in matching red shorts) delivering the song on a dark

street and against projection screens. Throughout the video, a team of muscle men use hammers to destroy a wall, finally succeeding in time for the end of the video. Folks in the background pump their right fist into the air when the word "Walls" is said, a motion that was repeated at concerts from 1990 to 1993. Live musicians and dancers punctuate other portions of the video. It was very well done for the era, making the most of powerful visuals and an even more powerful message.

The video was technically first available on 1991's *Rap, Rock and Soul*, but it made its mainstream debut on Martin Luther King Jr. Day in 1992 on BET's *Rap City* program. As described by the same *Christian Activities Calendar* article quoted earlier, it made national headlines when a premiere was held in Pulaski, Tennessee: a city with a dark history involving the KKK. Pulaski's mayor, Dan Speer, gave the members of dc Talk an award for using their music to help close racial divides. The video also won an award at the International Film Festival in New York.

Nu Thang Album, Track 08:
Talk It Out

As any child of the 1990s will tell you, something about some of the vocal sections on this song sound a little too much like a popular group at the time called "New Kids on the Block." dc Talk had already been compared to them in reviews and conversation, so this fueled the comparison even more. Being held up against one of the best-selling contemporary groups at the time was positive on several levels, though, but dc Talk seemed a little uncomfortable with it.

While most of the songs on *Nu Thang* contained mature themes and were clearly aimed at adults, the intro sample from the 1940's "Howdy Doody Show" was a cue to parents that this one was for the kids. Teens going through their most turbulent years made up the majority of dc Talk's fanbase, so it was nice to have a message tailored specifically to them. The message of "Talk it Out" is that kids don't have to face their problems alone... they can find the help that they need by opening up lines of communication with parents and teachers as opposed to shutting down and dealing with problems themselves.

It wasn't apparent to dc Talk just how well the song actually worked until many years later. On the first Jesus Freak Cruise, several people stepped forward during one of the discussion panels and revealed how that particular song had actually changed their lives. Fan feedback to websites and internet forums has been saying the same thing for years. "Talk it Out" probably wasn't the song that dc Talk or their label had the most faith in when they released it, but its lyrics ended up being quite influential.

Beyond the message, there's a lot to appreciate in the music. The bass riff during the verse is one of the strongest on the album, becoming even *more* effective when the guitar is added during the second verse. Several songs toward the end of the record (this one, "Take It to the Lord," and "Can I Get a Witness") sound like jam sessions, which is rare for a rap record. Some of the great use of guitar was probably the influence of Mark Heimermann, whom some of the dc Talk members used to refer to as a "rock and roll guy." The great guitarists that the band had access to, like Chris Rodriguez, also played a huge part in creating that loose, jam session atmosphere that elevated these tracks.

There's not much of Kevin or Michael in the chorus, but they have a good spotlight during the bridge. Some of their ad-libs toward the end of the song are almost as good as their later work on *Free at Last*.

"Talk it Out" was released as a single in 1991.

Alternate Versions:
A very clean, well-mixed instrumental/accompaniment version of the song was released through the "Street Trax" line.

Live Versions:
In looking at old dc Talk setlists, it's difficult to determine how often this one was played. Several lists have "Talk" as an entry. Did that mean that the group would share something with the audience, or was that short-hand for "Talk it Out"? Entries like "Pray" seem to support that "Talk" may have just been audience banter. To a lesser extent, the same problem crops up when an entry just reads "Witness." Was this a time to share testimony, or

was it a performance of "Can I Get a Witness?" Thirty years later, memories are hazy and while we can "Talk it Out" all we want to, we just may never know.

Nu Thang Album, Track 09:
Take It to the Lord

This is the "DC Go-Go jam," according to the intro. The announcement will probably only excite die-hard hip-hop/funk fans, or at least people who grew up in the Washington D.C. area. "Go-go" is a regional genre of music with distinctive beat patterns that pioneered some of the hip-hop of the era. For folks who'd like to explore the genre's roots, they need look no further than 1970s-1990s albums by the legendary Chuck Brown.

"Take It to the Lord" is a reminder that the listener can shoulder their problems with God at any time. Toby plays it pretty straightforward with the lyrics, joined by *really* strong vocals from Michael and Kevin. Michael, in particular, brought a lot to the song (particularly with the touches he adds during verses). He thoroughly demonstrates why he's the "Soul" of "Rap, Rock, and Soul." There's a sense that he and Kevin were feeding off of each other during the recording session, as each vocal lick traded between the two seems to get more intense as they go. There's an energy that outshines most of their other early efforts in dc Talk.

The bass riff is sparse and actually has an origin in jazz. Some of the orchestral hits and record scratches ensure that the song has a hip-hop feel, but the guitar and keyboard tracks give it plenty of that "Go-go" funk. All in all, "Take it to the Lord" is a great—though often overlooked—song from dc Talk's classic era.

Live Versions:
This was one of the first songs from the record added to the live show, possibly because of the energy that Michael and Kevin brought to their performances. Lacking the more artistic lyrical style demonstrated in some of dc Talk's other work, though, it was dropped during the *Free at Last* era.

Nu Thang Album, Track 10:
Children Can Live (Without It)

dc Talk was overtly religious, but they were rarely political. "Children Can Live (Without It)," a song that examines abortion issues, was one of the few times where they went all-in when it came to that tricky touch-point where religion and politics meet.

Toby McKeehan had actually graduated Liberty University with a degree in politics, so he was certainly adept at understanding the various issues of the day. As a religious institution, the intersection of Christianity and politics had undoubtedly featured into his coursework. Abortion was a heated issue at the time (and still is), so it was certainly a topic that the group had encountered in the news and in society.

The lyrics to the song are predictably heavy. Like the rest of McKeehan's work on *Nu Thang*, he's able to explain the song's position clearly. The lyrics were generally able to avoid some of the pitfalls inherent in the topic, but obviously, as a sensitive issue written about in 1990 and now looked at through a modern lens, it may not have aged well for all listeners. In a concept that was credited to Kevin Max, the bridge offers a moment where the narrative perspective shifts for a bit.

Jeff Silvey, who co-wrote the music/background track of the song, is a well-known Christian songwriter who helped create over four hundred songs in his career. He's written for several different genres but when left to his own devices, his songs take on a more western and country flair.

Musically, the last bars are the best. A new guitar part dominates the right channel and the song takes on a complex chord structure. A great remix for this song could be made by using this guitar part throughout the rest of the song and introducing the complex chord progression earlier.

Casual listeners may not recognize him, but that's Michael Tait during the chorus. He's using what sounds like a stronger, more experienced version of the voice he'd used on the debut album.

Live Versions:
dc Talk didn't always have room for slower, heavier production pieces during their live shows, so this song wasn't always in the mix. In 1992, when they began playing longer sets for summer festivals, they sang "Children Can Live (Without It)" as the second half of a medley with "Things of This World." The medley was brought back for 1994's Free at Last Tour, but it was dropped after a time.

Nu Thang Album, Track 11:
Can I Get a Witness

After the heavy message of "Children Can Live (Without It)," the album takes on a much lighter tone with "Can I Get a Witness." Clocking in at over four minutes, the song has enough rapping, singing, and musical interludes to satisfy any listener. The beat is breezy and loose, and the gospel choir chorus adds a fun swing. A nice, round, intricate bass track and a funky guitar lay the groundwork, and the organ solo cuts through so well that it'll make you wonder whatever happened to organ solos... they sound good!

The fun didn't stop with the live musicians. The programmers had a good time, as well, treating us to the "aw yeah" sample from Run-DMC's "Here We Go (Live at the Funhouse)" again near the 3:00 mark, bringing back the "hit it" from Rob Base & DJ E-Z Rock's "It Takes Two," and throwing in the James Brown sample from "Hot Pants." These clips are documented on the *whosampled.com* website.

Great vocals, a great performance by Toby, top-tier musicianship, and plenty of studio wizardry make this the perfect track to close out *Nu Thang* and set the listener up for *Free at Last*.

"Can I Get a Witness" was the second single released from the *Nu Thang* album, but like most early dc Talk songs, it received little airplay. The song got accolades a few years later, though, when it won a 1993 Dove Award for Rap/Hip-Hop Recorded Song of the Year.

Live Versions:
"Can I Get a Witness" was a mainstay in *Nu Thang*-era live shows. It didn't survive very long into the *Free at Last* era, even though the band's new setup with live musicians (as opposed to backing tracks) was perfect for the song. By the time the 1994 Free at Last Tour was underway, "Can I Get a Witness" was gone. If dc Talk wants to dig deep into their catalog for a reunion show, this song would certainly be an interesting addition.

Yo Ho Ho! (1990)

There was no rest for dc Talk after the release of *Nu Thang*. At the end of the summer festival season, they went straight back to the road with DeGarmo and Key. dc Talk opened several of their shows throughout September and October in 1990.

Around that time, dc Talk contributed two brand new original tracks to a ForeFront holiday compilation called *Yo Ho Ho!*, one of which was the title track. Toby had already been working on some new ideas, so the project was a natural fit. In addition to the two new entries they recorded for the *Yo Ho Ho!* project, an instrumental of the title track was included on the release and "The King (Alleluja)" from the debut album was thrown in, too.

Appearing with dc Talk on the compilation was fellow rap group and labelmates E.T.W. (End Time Warriors). Christian rap pioneer Stephen Wiley was also included, as was a Benson Records group called Transformation Crusade. M.C. Ge Gee (considered the first female Christian rapper to make it big onto the music scene) and her brother, D-Boy Rodriguez also made appearances. Danny "D-Boy" Rodriguez's inclusion was bittersweet... the record was released after he'd been violently murdered on October 6th, 1990 near his East Dallas apartment. During interviews around the release of *Yo Ho Ho!*, Toby expressed grief over the young rapper's tragic death. In an article titled "DC Talk: Def, Not Dumb" by Bruce A. Brown in the December 1990 issue of *CCM Magazine*, Toby had this to say: "D-Boy was very influential on dc

Talk. He had exactly the kind of attitude that we'd like to try and emulate. He encouraged us, telling us he loved us. He wasn't trying to play any kind of games; he was just so humble. Obviously, his ministry was having an impact. Man, we're really gonna miss him."

Yo Ho Ho!, with its two new dc Talk tracks, hit store shelves in time for the 1990 Christmas season.

Yo Ho Ho! Album:
Yo Ho Ho! (song)

"It ain't jingle bells, baby!"

Original Christmas songs are difficult to write. Toby not only churned out *one* of them, but he pulled off *two*. Both songs have a solid Christmas flair to them while still retaining the classic dc Talk sound, which was quite an accomplishment in and of itself.

"Yo Ho Ho!," the title track to the compilation, is the Christmas story translated for a younger, hipper audience. It follows the standard formula of rap verses, a tight-sounding group of background singers during the chorus, a smooth bridge with Michael and Kevin spotlights, a third verse, and then an outro where Michael and Kevin get to ad-lib over the chorus. The formula had worked so well on *Nu Thang*, so why change it?

Mark Heimermann wasn't involved in the *Yo Ho Ho!* project, having moved on to a busy schedule of background vocal appearances and seeking production gigs. Stepping up to the plate for this first track was Joe Hogue, a songwriter and budding producer who had done programming and some arranging on *Nu Thang*. Hogue graduated to co-writer for this song, helping Toby flesh out and assemble the music tracks. The collaboration went well, and Hogue assisted Toby again when he teamed up with Christian superstar Carman for 1991's "Addicted to Jesus" song. The year after *that*, Hogue moved up even further in the food chain and got to occupy one of the producer's chairs during the creation of several *Free at Last* tracks. Hogue was an accomplished background singer too, lending his voice to the covers of "Jesus is Just Alright" and "Lean on Me" on *Free at Last*. On those two songs, he's the only other background singer besides dc Talk, making for a distinctive sound to the chorus. Hogue contributed bass and keyboards to that album, as well.

"Yo Ho Ho!" has plenty of personality, with lines like "Mary was a virgin but laden with child / Yo Doc, ponder that for a while!" and the classic "Where's the little drummer boy? ... Here I am!" moment. The group had fun with it. Somehow, amidst all the festivities, Toby's third verse on the song managed to be one of the tightest rap performances he ever recorded on any of the early dc Talk records.

Alternate Versions:
The instrumental track was available on the *Yo Ho Ho!* cd/cassette itself. A "Street Trax" version of the instrumental was also released.

Live Versions:
If "Yo Ho Ho!" made it into the show's lineup at the end of 1990, no one seems to remember it. Their touring schedule was a little lighter in November and December, but they played a huge show at Knotts Berry Farm in California on New Year's Eve called the "New Year's Jubilation." M.C. Ge Gee (D-Boy Rodriguez's sister and *Yo Ho Ho!* contributor) also performed at that event.

The first bars to "Yo Ho Ho!" were used as the opening number during dc Talk's "Nu Skool Jam Tour" in the fall months of 1991. The tour ran from October 17th to November 20th.

Yo Ho Ho! Album:
Reason for the Season

Jim Ebert, who co-produced this track with Toby, is a major music producer with a discography a mile long. With Jim Ebert at the console, it's no wonder that "Reason for the Season" turned out to be such a tight, well-produced song (especially for a compilation album track). Christmas music wasn't generally known for having great guitar performances or solid rap performances, but "Reason for the Season" had both.

The chord progressions and general rhythms of this song actually sound close to something that Toby McKeehan would've done as a solo artist once dc Talk went on hiatus in the early 2000s. Some of the syncopated rhythms, reggae-like hits, and blocked chords are the same type of instrumentation patterns that make up the foundations of several early TobyMac songs.

Toby's voice and delivery is a little more mature than it was on most of the *Nu Thang* songs, providing a small hint at the major leap in style he'd take while recording *Free at Last*. Not *everything* about the track was more mature, though. "Haha, put that one in your face!" is one of the strangest ad-libs to ever appear on tape. dc Talk also calls God the "Big G" somewhere in this one, a nickname not used by many churches at the time. As one of the better dc Talk tracks from "back in the day," though, it's a shame that it didn't get a wider release.

The general message of "Reason for the Season" is

straightforward: Christmas has become commercialized, and that's not really what the holiday is about.

Alternate Versions:
A "Street Trax" instrumental/accompaniment cassette was put out by ForeFront in 1991.

Go West Young Man Tour

The two years spent touring with DeGarmo and Key were huge for dc Talk. They gained valuable experience, got a tremendous amount of exposure, and established a good working relationship with their label. The year *Nu Thang* was released, Eddie DeGarmo and Dana Key both produced solo albums *and* new material for their 1991 *Go to the Top* record. As their mentors were busy with these projects, dc Talk was given a new touring opportunity.

Nu Thang producer Mark Heimermann's former boss, Christian music artist Michael W. Smith, released an album called *Go West Young Man* a month after dc Talk's *Nu Thang* hit the shelves. Smith's new album took the world by storm. One of the singles, a song called "Place in this World," rose higher and higher in the mainstream Billboard charts and eventually peaked at an incredible number six... a position unheard of for an artist from any Christian genre.

This now-legendary artist (Smith eventually won three Grammy Awards and nearly four dozen Dove Awards) was known for his high-energy, arena-shaking live show. With a new tour coming up and the wind at his sails, Michael W. Smith began looking for a new opening act to captivate his audiences.

He zeroed in on a little Christian rap/rock trio called dc Talk, and they were more than happy to accept his offer. While dc Talk had been touring for nearly two years, most of their appearances had been relegated to school auditoriums, churches, or a festival's B-stage. DeGarmo and Key had certainly been supportive and generous, but dc Talk was aching to see their names in lights. Their opening spot on Michael W. Smith's Go West Young Man Tour would give them the opportunity.

With a brand new album to share, dc Talk was hungry and ready to prove themselves. A new audience for their live show was just what they needed, especially since the traditional path to stardom hadn't worked out as well as they'd hoped up to that point. Many radio stations wouldn't play their singles. Stores wouldn't stock their ads. The only way they ever saw the needle move was by putting on a great show anytime someone would let them take the stage. To that end, dc Talk was very excited about Smith's offer.

The Go West Young Man Tour kicked off on February 21st at the Hersheypark Arena in Pennsylvania. Traveling through New England, then the Midwest, then the South, up to Canada, the Northwestern United States, and finally ending in a scattershot across the US, dc Talk excelled in their role as Smith's energetic warm-up act during the four months that they were on the road with him. As the *Go West Young Man* album and its smash hit "Place in This World" continued its hold on the charts, dc Talk's own sales picked up, too. They began to get more of the recognition they had worked so hard to achieve, and their outing with Smith was instrumental to *Nu Thang's* win at the 1991 Dove Awards for Rap / Hip-Hop Album of the Year.

Looking back so many years later, dc Talk members still speak warmly and enthusiastically about the role that DeGarmo and Key and Michael W. Smith played in their careers. "He is *hugely* instrumental in me sitting here right now," Toby told WAY Nation in a May 20th, 2019 video featuring both him and Michael W.

Go West Young Man Tour

Smith playing a "Guess the 90's Christian Music" game. On the 2019 Jesus Freak Cruise, the band also thanked DeGarmo and Key for including them on their tours. "We are so grateful for that," Toby said. "We have *not* forgotten that." Eddie DeGarmo was on the ship to hear the warm words in-person.

The 1991 outing was obviously a success, so when Michael W. Smith went back to the studio to make a new album in 1992, not only did he bring in Mark Heimermann (who had played keyboard for him in his live band during the 1980s) to produce it, but he brought in dc Talk to co-write a track and sing backup. To return the favor, dc Talk invited Smith to lay down keyboard tracks on their *Free at Last* cover of "Lean on Me." When Michael W. Smith went out again on tour in 1993 to support a new album, he once again brought dc Talk out as his opening act. dc Talk and Smith retain a great personal and professional relationship to this day.

Nearly thirty years later, the Go West Young Man Tour still rightfully occupies a special place in the hearts of all three members of dc Talk. A very poignant moment took place in 2019 when Michael W. Smith went out on tour with Michael Tait's Newsboys band. While singing "Place in This World," Smith brought Tait out to perform the song with him. It was an amazing moment: two friends joining together to sing the song that had defined the tour that they were on so many years before. The historical meaning of the duet may have been lost on most of the crowd, those who knew the backstory knew that it was from the tour that brought "Place in this World" to the public and Smith into dc Talk's lives. It was one of the sweetest moments to ever grace the stage. "Place in this World" had been the background to defining moments in both of their careers, and to see these two artists share the song with each other again was to see Michael Tait's success come full circle.

Nu Thang Era:
Addicted to Jesus

Are you A2J?

Carmelo Licciardello, best known by his stage name "Carman," is a mega-popular Christian artist whose career has spanned forty years. An performer not really known for rap songs, Carman was nevertheless full of surprises in his heyday. With a heart for finding ways to relate to different populations, Carman has always experimented widely with different genres and presentation styles. While observing youth culture in the early 1990s, he decided to try his hand at a few hip-hop songs. For his 1991 album, he penned two tracks that went on to become fairly successful. The first one, "Holy Ghost Hop," was the most well-known of the two. The other one, "Addicted to Jesus," became the title of the record. While putting "Addicted to Jesus" together, he decided to collaborate and wisely enlisted the talents of a new rap group on the rise: dc Talk.

Toby, Michael, and Kevin each get plenty of chances to add spice to Carman's "Addicted to Jesus" track. Carman himself is to be commended for doing most of the rapping himself... and actually doing a pretty decent job of it. His approach was more of a spoken-word kind of delivery, something he excelled at on other projects. One of the most interesting parts of the song is the intro, where we hear multiple tracks of Toby talking to himself to simulate a crowd of friends hanging out.

Addicted to Jesus

The beat was contemporary at the time, and for an artist who wasn't used to making this kind of music, it turned out pretty well. Input from dc Talk and one of their producers probably helped it along. Like most music of the era, though, it doesn't quite hold up to modern sensibilities. However, since it was one of the first times that dc Talk was able to collaborate in the studio with a titan of the music industry, it's certainly an important part of their history.

The *Addicted to Jesus* album was released on October 29th, 1991. It quickly sold over half a million copies and earned "Gold" status. It was also nominated for a Grammy Award. To keep the momentum going, the album was re-released on CD in 1993.

Carman experimented with hip-hop again on his next major album, *The Standard*, with his most popular rap track yet: "Who's in the House?"

Alternate Versions:
An accompaniment version was released by Benson Records.

Video:
The music video for the song is energetic, colorful, and has plenty of dc Talk in it. The props, the humor, the staging of the scenes, and the energy of the production made for a solid romp through the early 1990s. Most impressive of all, Carman really holds his own during the dance numbers.

The fashions and sensibilities are somewhat humorous so many years later (the tagline, "Are you A2J?" didn't age well, either), but it was a contemporary release at the time that did two important things: it showed Carman's range/versatility, and introduced a new set of music fans to a talented group called dc Talk. The video was released on September 9th, 1992 and went "Gold" two months later after selling over 50,000 copies.

Nu Skool Jam Tour

Special thanks to Bert Gangl for assisting with the research for this section and with other concert-related entries.

Two weeks after the Michael W. Smith tour ended, dc Talk kicked off the summer festival season with a June 1st, 1991 appearance at Joyfest (which took place at Six Flags Great America). Capitalizing on their momentum from the Go West Young Man Tour, they booked some of their biggest shows ever, including more prominent appearances at Creationfest and Sonshine Festival. On July 20th, they reunited with DeGarmo and Key to appear at an outdoor festival in their hometown called DC '91 at the Sylvan Theatre.

In September, dc Talk went international. They embarked on a European tour that took them to Germany, Switzerland, and Poland. Seven concerts were played in Germany alone, including one at the Metropolis in Munich. Accompanying them on the tour was the Christian rock band White Heart – a group originally configured from members of Bill Gaither's choir.

dc Talk and White Heart actually have a few more connections beyond the European Tour. Musicians (and brothers) Dann and David Huff had been original members of White Heart from its inception in 1982 until about 1985. After leaving White Heart, both brothers became sought-after studio players. In 1990, they had worked on Michael W. Smith's *Go West Young Man* record,

Nu Skool Jam Tour

with Dann lending several guitar tracks to the project. During the dc Talk's *Jesus Freak* project, Dann Huff was brought in to lend his monster guitar skills to rockers like "So Help Me God" and the title, track, "Jesus Freak." Dann's brother David Huff, a top-tier studio drummer, was brought in, too. David Huff is the drummer heard on the song "Jesus Freak" and several other tracks from the landmark album.

A few days after returning from Europe, dc Talk played a show at the Lawlor Events Center in Reno, Nevada with a duo named Heather & Kirsten. Made up of sisters Heather and Kirsten Ostrom, this duo of talented singers had been performing together since they were very young. Their album *Betcha Didn't Know* had been released in 1990. It garnered them a nice following and a lot of positive press. They eventually stopped performing together later in the 1990s, but Kirsten Ostrom still creates music and performs concerts.

With dc Talk's popularity increasing and sales starting to pick up, ForeFront felt that the group could leverage the experience they'd gained on the road into headlining their own tour. dc Talk had made significant headway since their trips with Michael W. Smith, and it seemed that a well-organized, well-marketed tour could help propel dc Talk's platform even further.

Plans were drawn up, full-page ads were taken out, the setlist was re-examined, and new musical partners were found. *Campus Life Magazine* agreed to sponsor the tour and put together free three-month subscription packages for attendees.

Joining the production as stage manager was a fixture from the CreationFest scene: Denny Keitzman. In an interview with Rona Pryor for the May/June 2001 issue of *Christian Musician*, Keitzman revealed that the fall outing with dc Talk was his first job ever as a tour manager. After running logistics at CreationFest for years, he'd originally been offered a job as stage manager for Amy Grant. Though he ultimately decided to turn down the gig, it wasn't long before dc Talk came along with an offer of their own. This time, he accepted. Keitzman ended up running dc Talk's tours for the rest of the band's career.

After different opening acts were considered for the tour, it was decided that Heather & Kirsten would be invited, as would a group called the Dynamic Twins. To round out the show, another little band, one called the Newsboys, would also be going out with them.

The Newsboys were originally from a town called Mooloolaba in Queensland, Australia. They were put together in 1985 during jam sessions in future front-man Peter Furler's garage. At the time that the fall 1991 tour was being put together, the Newsboys were on an uphill trajectory similar to dc Talk's. The fanbases of the two groups overlapped quite a bit. Additionally, the Newsboys were on the cusp of releasing their breakout album *Not Ashamed*, and dc Talk was on the cusp of releasing *their* breakout album, *Free at Last*. The groups were a natural fit for each other. The *next* releases from both groups, The Newsboys' 1994 album *Going Public* (which contained the mega-hit "Shine") and dc Talk's 1995 release *Jesus* Freak, would make both of them household names in the industry.

Though this would be the only tour that The Newsboys and dc Talk went on together (until the Jesus Freak Cruises), the groups would remain close friends for the duration of their careers. In the early 2000s, Peter Furler could often be found chatting with TobyMac at an event or sitting at Kevin Max's dinner table. He and Max even planned a short tour together. The tie between the groups became inseparable when in 2010, Peter Furler stepped down from The Newsboys and Michael Tait became the new lead singer in his place – a position that Tait still holds today.

Nu Skool Jam Tour

The Dynamic Twins was a Christian rap duo from New York made up of identical twins Robbie and Noel Arthurton. Their debut album *Word 2 the Wise* had just been released at the time of the tour. After their outing with dc Talk, The Dynamic Twins continued to make music well into the 2000s.

The show was titled the Nu Skool Jam Tour, and it kicked off on October 17th, 1991 at Anderson University in Indiana. For a month, the group traveled the country: first to the Midwest, then New England, and then down to Toby and Michael's hometowns near Washington D.C. and Lynchburg, Virginia. Lynchburg is home to Liberty University, but the group didn't perform at their alma mater – the show took place at the E.C. Glass High School. They also performed in Houston, Texas at First Baptist Church where former bandmate Vic Mignogna would later serve as a worship leader. After nearly twenty stops, the tour ended on November 20th in Spokane, Washington.

The dc Talk setlist for these shows wasn't *too* different from the concerts that they'd played up to this point, but the group had begun to experiment with some different material. The big change was a new encore piece. The new song was a cover of "Lean on Me" that they'd devised after playing around with the song at one of the old carnival karaoke booths. This very popular dc Talk cover of "Lean on Me" would be included on their next album, *Free at Last*.

Rap, Rock, and Soul

In late 1991, dc Talk released its first video compilation project to VHS. It was the fans' first in-depth look at all three members of dc Talk and included an assortment of music videos, interview clips, and performances. Called *Rap, Rock, and Soul*, the project still stands as a fairly comprehensive summary of their early work as a band.

Clocking in at thirty-two minutes, the video begins with a brief introduction to each member: the "Rap" (Toby), the "Rock" (Kevin), and the "Soul" (Michael). The "Nu Thang" music video is played, and then there's a spotlight on Toby where he gives his thoughts on rap music. He also talks about growing up in the suburbs of Virginia and having to travel to D.C. just to get hip-hop records, a story he later repeats in musical form on *Free at Last*.

After a few rehearsal and concert clips, the "I Luv Rap Music" video plays. It's followed by a spotlight on Kevin. He talks about the rock and roll records he used to listen to and gives a humorous anecdote about how he used to tell people that Rod Stewart was his stepfather.

After the "Walls" video, the Michael Tait spotlight dives into his family life (five sisters and two brothers) and his growing up around music. The viewer gets to see plenty of Toby and Michael's hats, too. The Tait spotlight ends with a clip of dc Talk performing "He Loves Me" at the 1990 Flevo Festival. Matching outfits are in full-force.

The March 1989 *Lightmusic* clip of "Time Ta Jam" is also included. The video takes place in a reality where if you get hungry enough, you just might need to rap until your server pays attention to you.

The most substantial part of the video is the segment before the "Heavenbound" video where the trio discusses the themes in their music and what living as a Christian means to them. Chatter that appears over the credits also provides some interesting tidbits. The viewer learns that Toby earned his name because his parents knew he was going to be born in October and his brother kept asking when "Tober" was coming.

The director of photography for *Rap, Rock, and Soul's* interview segments was Philip Alan Waters, a mainstay in the industry best known at the time for his work on music documentaries and horror films. No jokes about the video being so outdated that it qualifies as a horror film, please.

Passengers on the Jesus Freak Cruise in 2017 were treated to a unique photo opportunity when True Artist Management (dc Talk and TobyMac's management company) brought the sweaters that the group had worn on the cover of *Rap, Rock, and Soul*. Several fans tried them on and had fun trying to recreate the photo.

Rap, Rock, and Soul must've proven to the label that there was a market for dc Talk on video. After their next album came out, the machine behind dc Talk undertook a film project the likes of which Christian music had rarely seen: *Free at Last: The Movie*. Before we can discuss that, though, we have to dive into the album itself.

Free at Last (1992)

dc Talk had a little bit of downtime after the Nu Skool Jam Tour wrapped up. Thoughts began turning to their next album.

Toby caught up with Mark Heimermann in hopes that the *Nu Thang* producer could helm the new record with him. Heimermann and his production partner Chris Harris were in the process of finishing the debut project for an artist named Lisa Bevill, a Christian dance/pop singer with Sparrow Records. As Heimermann and Harris worked their magic, Toby ended up co-writing two of Lisa Bevill's songs with Heimermann: "Chaperone" and "It's Gonna Be Worth It." He also laid down a few rap tracks on "Chaperone" and a song called "I Took a Tumble." Previous dc Talk studio musicians Jackie Street, Jerry McPherson, and George Cocchini also contributed to the project.

The Lisa Bevill album, *My Freedom*, was released on April 16th, 1992. Heimermann jumped straight from that project to his role as the producer of Michael W. Smith's upcoming album, *Change Your World*. As this was happening, Toby guest-starred on a track for one of the most iconic Christian music albums of all time, Stephen Curtis Chapman's *The Great Adventure*. Released on June 19th, 1992, the seventh song on *The Great Adventure* features an endearing section where Chapman tries the rap to "Nu Thang" and decides that hip-hop just ain't his game. Toby appears later in the song, and Mark Heimermann joins in with some background vocals. It's a cute scenario that not many people could pull off, but somehow Chapman and McKeehan were the perfect team for it.

dc Talk made a few concert appearances, notably one at the Dove Awards where they performed "Nu Thang." They also got an early start on the summer festival season. In between concert dates, Mark Heimermann brought Toby into some of the Michael W. Smith sessions. The end result was a Smith / Heimermann / McKeehan collaboration called "I Wanna Tell the World." Toby even had vocal lines in the song. Michael Tait and Kevin Max were brought in to do background vocals on the Michael W. Smith song "Give it Away," too. Musicians like Jackie Street, Jerry McPherson, Dann Huff, and George Cocchini all appeared on the album.

As the preparations for the summer festival season *really* ramped up, Toby was able to spend enough time in the studio with Heimermann and guitarist George Cocchini to craft a new song called "Luv is a Verb." With Atlanta Fest and CreationFest coming up on the calendar, he was eager to try it out on a new audience.

The CreationFest team was excited about having dc Talk at their event. dc Talk had a special "in" because of their road manager, Denny Keitzman. The groups worked together to formulate a dramatic entrance for dc Talk's set. It was decided that the band would "land" on the stage somehow, perhaps by grappling down from the rafters. Someone came up with the idea of dc Talk landing in the crowd on a helicopter. That seemed the most exciting, so that's exactly what they did. On June 25th, 1992, dc Talk (wearing matching blue and purple-striped outfits) touched down in the middle of CreationFest. Amidst dramatic entrance music, they took the stage and hammered out the brand new song "Luv is a Verb" to an exuberant audience for the first time ever. CreationFest and dc Talk had no shortage of dramatic entrance ideas – just ask fans who saw the band riding up to the stage on motorcycles.

Heimermann was able to focus almost exclusively on dc Talk once Michael W. Smith's *Change Your World* album, which released on August 21st, 1992, was complete. Most of the team from *Nu Thang* was reassembled, some new additions were added, and Mark Heimermann continued sifting through almost two year's worth of Toby's song ideas.

With more mature songwriting and a sophisticated take on modern hip-hop, the *Free at Last* album was taking shape. Bandmates Michael Tait and Kevin Max Smith were given more room on this project. Many of the new songs emphasized their talents in ways the previous albums hadn't. Joe Hogue from the *Yo Ho Ho!* compilation was involved more, and the dc Talk team as a whole gave extra time and care to the recording process. The group was pulled away from time to time to do live performances, notably for a Christian Artists Music Seminar, a Missionary Alliance Conference, a one-off appearance with Petra, and Disney's Night of Joy, but they kept their eye on the prize. In September, Toby and Michael Tait took time out to appear on a compilation album for kids hosted by Jodi Benson, the voice of Ariel in Disney's *The Little Mermaid*. As the fall season was underway, Heimermann and McKeehan and crew put the finishing touches on *Free at Last*.

Hitting the shelves in the first half of November 1992, dc Talk's newest release was a major artistic leap for the group. Stuffed with seventeen tracks, *Free at Last* was more of a comprehensive "album" project than their previous efforts. Jumping effortlessly from contemporary hip-hop numbers to soulful ballads to interludes to pew-stomping gospel and rap-laced covers of yesterday's hits, *Free at Last* was the first time that dc Talk had taken a swing for the fence and had cleared it with room to spare. The trio was finally putting their best foot forward in the marketplace. And the marketplace responded.

Free at Last reached number one in the Christian music charts and sold over half a million units in less than a year. As the first single, "Jesus is Just Alright," pumped through radio speakers all over the country, it was immediately clear that dc Talk had turned a corner. Rarely had contemporary styles been harnessed so effectively for the Christian marketplace. The group's sound and style caused even mainstream audiences to take notice. In just a few years, "DC Talk and the One Way Crew" had gone from an "amusing" demo tape to industry titans.

In this book, full coverage of the first two albums was done mainly for the fans and for those wishing to know the origins of dc Talk. But it's here, with *Free at Last*, that the story truly begins.

Let's "take this mug for a ride!"

Free at Last Album, Track 01:
Luv is a Verb

"Luv is a Verb" takes dc Talk to the next level with a growling bass line and plenty of extra funk. Fans of the previous albums noticed the elevated musicianship right away. A more mature Toby McKeehan raps over thicker beats and more complex background harmonies while jazz hits punctuate the song and move it so effortlessly through strong vocal sections that it's hard to tell where choruses begin and end. The lyrics aren't *too* much more advanced than the material found on *Nu Thang* (they improve as the album goes on), but the production value and delivery are much stronger than before.

"Luv is a Verb" was influential, and not just because it was the first example of a newer, better dc Talk sound. It served as a strong opener to live shows, a good promo for radio markets, and a perfect template for the new style of hip-hop that Toby and Mark Heimermann were experimenting with. Catchy riffs and almost hummable bass lines were one of the dominant features of *Free at Last* (and even more so on the next album, *Jesus Freak*). Toby's rhythm-based style complimented these elements perfectly.

The co-writer on this track, George Cocchini, is famous in the music industry for the guitar work he's provided to several major acts from the 1980s onward. When it came to dc Talk and some of the other groups he worked with, Cocchini contributed far more than great-sounding studio tracks, though. Not only was he

Free at Last

credited as a co-writer for "Luv is a Verb," but he also helped write the *Free at Last* track "Time Is" and tracks on *Jesus Freak* and *Supernatural*, too ("Colored People," "My Friend (So Long)," and "Fearless").

"Luv is a Verb" has a robust horn section that's a big step up from the "Heavenbound" days. And not only did Michael and Kevin provide more dominating vocal performances, but dc Talk dancers Stacey "Coffee" Jones and Teron "Bonafide" Carter (who later went on to form the group "GRITS") were also featured in the background. *Nu Thang* album was big on sampling other songs, and *Free at Last* carried on that tradition. The same "Funky Drummer" breakbeat that was used so heavily on the previous album was used again during verses. As pointed out on *whosampled.com*, the introduction clip ("take this mug for a ride") came from a 1946 Bugs Bunny cartoon called "Racketeer Rabbit."

Single:
The song was released as a single toward the end of *Free at Last's* promotional cycle. It did fairly well, reaching number 15 on one of the Christian charts.

Alternate Versions:
Gotee Remix: In 1994, dc Talk released four new remixes on a project called *Free at Last Extended Play Remixes*. Featured on the disc was the "Gotee" version of "Luv is a Verb." The remix is quite a bit more chill than the regular version, with a few new elements added and an emphasis placed on the brass sections. The riff used on the main version doesn't make much of a showing, but a new, funky guitar loop repeats throughout. Swelling brass segments and a new solo at the end adds a great vibe. Toby's main vocals are processed through a "telephone" or "AM radio" type of an effect, and the "down with the dc Talk" portion is stripped of its background vocalists to make it a Toby-only affair.

The track is called the "Gotee Remix" because it was produced by Gotee Records, the new label/production company that Toby started during the *Free at Last* years with partners Todd Collins and Joey Elwood. The trio sometimes produced music together under the moniker "The Gotee Brothers," too. The only full album released by the Gotee Brothers themselves was a 1996 project called *E.R.A.C.E.* The label itself went on to become a major force in the Christian music industry.

Welcome to the Freak Show live track: The 1997 album chronicling dc Talk's 1996 *Jesus Freak* tour contains an electrifying rock version of "Luv is a Verb."

Intermission version: dc Talk's greatest hits album, *Intermission*, made a few edits to the original song. The "Yeah boy, haha!" was removed from the intro, and the guitar loop that was prominent in the "Gotee Remix" now plays throughout the entire track.

Accompaniment: An accompaniment/instrumental version of this song was available on cassette through "Street Trax." Portions of the instrumental can also be heard as background music for menus on the *Free at Last: The Movie* DVD. A drum-only version was released by Hal Leonard with a book containing sheet music for the song.

Live Versions:
"Luv is a Verb" made its live debut several months before it was released. The first time it was ever performed was at CreationFest '92. Toby was looking for something new to add to the show since the dc Talk setlist had changed very little since they'd last performed at summer festivals. He decided that it was the right time to introduce the first new song from the upcoming *Free at Last* album: "Luv is a Verb." The song made its debut against the dramatic scene of dc Talk arriving in a helicopter. For the rest of the summer, it was moved further back in the set and performed

Free at Last

after songs like "Can I Get a Witness."

"Luv is a Verb" was an integral part of dc Talk's show for the rest of the *Free at Last* and *Jesus Freak* years. As more electric guitars were added to their live arsenal, the song took on more of a rock flavor. The guitars doubling the bass riff added a *lot* of punch to the song. "Luv is a Verb" was also the piece they used to kick off their first ever Billy Graham Crusade performance on June 11th, 1994 in Cleveland, Ohio.

The Supernatural Experience Tour is the only concert series that didn't include the song at all. The first leg of the Solo Tour also did without it, but the second leg brought passages from the song back into the fold.

When it was sung on the Jesus Freak Cruise in 2017, the crowd went nuts for it. The scene repeated itself on the 2019 cruise, this time with the backing track getting some extra spins and scratches from DJ Maj.

Videos:
A concept video was never made for the song, but a music video was assembled using various candid clips and performance shots taken during the 1994 Free at Last Tour. The music video was included on the home video project *Narrow is the Road*.

An actual performance video from that same tour was included on *Free at Last: The Movie*, a long-lost dc Talk film released to DVD in 2002 to celebrate *Free at Last's* tenth anniversary.

The *Welcome to the Freak Show* VHS/DVD project included a 1996 rock-inspired performance of the song.

Free at Last Album, Track 02:
That Kinda Girl

dc Talk often set out to produce music with a message. To that end, "That Kinda Girl" is an exploration of the desirable character traits that an ideal mate should possess. "I Don't Want It," a later track on the album, explored some of the same themes.

With heavy beats, sparse instrumentation, nimble verses from McKeehan, and tight vocal passages that built on each other, "That Kinda Girl" has aged far more gracefully than most of dc Talk's early material. Everything that was groundbreaking about the hip-hop genre in the early 90's is found in spades on this track. Vocal harmonies are layered with surprising variations and feature great ad-libs from Michael and Kevin. Neither the bass, keyboard, nor guitar is overpowering – they're content to let the beat and the skill of the rapper/singers carry the song.

The interplay of the beat, rap, and vocals is a master class on how to effectively produce a song with stripped-down elements. Non-musicians and non-producers usually can't appreciate how challenging it is to make a song like this work so well. It's a rare combination: a track with a simple hook, unprocessed vocals, no grand riff, and a deceptively difficult spit-fire delivery. When these things are put together, they often sound basic and amateurish. Not with dc Talk. "That Kinda Girl" was the group's talent laid bare and one of the first examples of the band being able to hold their own artistically against anything else in the genre.

"That Kinda Girl" was never released as a single, though that's hardly surprising since the song didn't have any of the adult contemporary or rock elements that helped some of their other singles make the charts.

Alternate Versions:
The instrumental/accompaniment version released by "Street Trax" contains an intro that's not found on the album. Additionally, a drum-only track of "That Kinda Girl" was released by Hal Leonard to accompany the album's sheet music.

Live Versions:
The song worked so well thematically with "I Don't Want It" that the two were performed together as a medley during the *Free at Last* tours. The song disappeared during the *Jesus Freak* years, but DJ Form brought it back during his spotlight segment on the *Supernatural* Tour. DJ Maj followed his example during the 2017 and 2019 Jesus Freak Cruise performances.

Video:
Clips of the band performing the "That Kinda Girl" with "I Don't Want It" can be found on the VHS release *Narrow is the Road*.

Free at Last track 03: Greer
The first of many interesting interludes on *Free at Last* is "Greer," a prank phone message for "Joey E." (Joey Elwood of the Gotee Brothers, no doubt, and also Toby's cousin). The caller warns Joey about dc Talk's habit of lifting samples off of old recordings. The interlude occurs before dc Talk's cover of "Jesus is Just Alright," their most sample-heavy track on the album.

The name "Greer" means "alert, watchful" – a perfect handle for the character making the call.

Free at Last Album, Track 04:
Jesus is Just Alright

"Jesus is Just Alright," the lead single for the new record, was one of the most popular songs to come out of *Free at Last*. In subsequent years, it's officially become their most-performed song of all time (surpassing even "Jesus Freak" if solo shows aren't tallied) and one of the most recognizable Christian music tracks from the 1990s.

The chorus to the song was originally written by a musician named Arthur Reynolds. It first appeared in 1966 on the Art Reynolds Singers album *Tellin' It Like It Is*. There wasn't a whole lot to the song yet – subsequent cover versions by groups like The Byrds (in 1969) and the Doobie Brothers (in 1972) added much more to it.

No one added more to the song than Toby McKeehan did, though. Changing the theme of the song to "Jesus is **Still** Alright" and coming up with rap verses, dc Talk also added an infectious beat, great vocals from Michael and Kevin (along with background singer Joe Hogue), and a climactic rap breakdown from Toby that had concert-goers stumbling over words for almost ten years.

The bridge that originally appeared in the Doobie Brothers' rendition is nowhere to be found on the song itself, but dc Talk covered *that* portion of the song, as well. It can be found at the very end of *Free at Last* as Track 17. It's usually called the

Free at Last

"reprise" on dc Talk albums, but printings of the single call it the "blues bridge."

Samples abound in this song, so the warning from Greer turned out to be serious business. The "I've got the power" lick from the band Snap! is the most famous one. "Now we come to the payoff" comes from a track called the "Lesson 1 Pay-Off Mix" from the *Tommy Boy 1985* project by Double Dee and Steinski. "I gotcha" comes from a track by Joe Tex. The "squeal" sound in the background of Toby's third verse comes from Lyn Collns' "Think (About It)," a song that the group sampled from quite a bit on the *Nu Thang* album. Other samples used in *Nu Thang* from the James Brown song "Hot Pants" can also be found in the background. These notes and others can be found on whosampled.com.

Singles:
When the song was released to radio, dc Talk's first single from *Free at Last* came in at a respectable number two.

Physical CD promos were released to radio stations in the US and Japan. The cover photo on the promo is the same as the cover from the *Free at Last* album, but the color has a sharp yellow tint and more contrast to it. Several edits of the song are featured:

Track 1) Jesus is Just Alright (Album Version)
Track 2) Jesus is Just Alright (Funky, Wit Less Rap)
Track 3) Jesus is Just Alright (Still Funky, Wit No Rap)
Track 4) Jesus is Just Alright (With Original Blues Bridge)
Track 5) Jesus is Just Alright (Reprise)

The US version added "Yo Ho Ho!," an interlude from *Free at Last*, and a promo spot for the new album. The "Original Blues Bridge" mentioned above is, of course, simply the "reprise" from the end of the *Free at Last* album edited into the middle of the album version. Tracks two and three from the promo are mostly just the album versions with a lot of extra choruses repeated where the rap verses used to be.

Alternate Versions:
In addition to the alternate tracks found on the promo single, the following versions of the song also exist:

Retro Remix: Two remixes, both by Scott Blackwell, appeared on *Free at Last Extended Play Remix* project (a project we'll discuss in its own section later). Lasting for six minutes and thirty-seven seconds, the "Retro" version opens with a watery synth and breaks into a relentless beat with fantastic guitar work. The keyboard part and some great bass lines from the album version are given a spotlight. Michael Tait's "Alright with me, yeah" lick forms the foundation of the song. Some great synth strings, brass sections, and brass solos extend throughout the rest of it.

Techno Remix: Lasting five minutes and thirty-eight seconds, the "Techno Remix" is another interesting take on the song. The pulsating bass is the main feature. At the end, some vocals are spliced to make a new lyric.

"Live Bonus Cut": Store-bought CD versions of the "Jesus Freak" single contained an edited, mixed-down version of the group performing "Jesus is Just Alright" from the Detroit show of the 1994 Free at Last Tour.

"Switchback" Remix: On some pressings of the Japanese version of the *Jesus Freak* album, a version of "Jesus is Just Alright" called the "Switchback Remix" is included. It's a shame that it's so rare, because this modern take on the song is one of the best dc Talk remixes out there.

Welcome to the Freak Show: 1997's *Welcome to the Freak Show* album has an incredible live version of the song recorded from their 1996 tour. Its inclusion on the cd/cassette of this project is significant because it was one of the only songs *not* included on the video version. The track is exclusive to this release.

Intermission version: The greatest hits album contained a few edits from the original version, namely some missing bars at the beginning (cut for time) and some vocals from Michael and Kevin that were recorded during the original sessions but never included in the final track.

Accompaniment: The "Street Trax" version of the song opens with an extended vocal section that isn't present on the original album version. Additionally, a songbook was released by Hal Leonard that included the drum track.

Live Versions:
"Jesus is Just Alright" was a hit with live audiences right away. Along with "Luv is a Verb," the song was a mainstay in dc Talk shows throughout the early 1990s.

One of the most significant performances of the song was on November 12th, 1993 when dc Talk sang it on the *Jay Leno Show*. They'd transitioned to using live musicians at this point, though they still used a track for parts of several songs. This appearance was also notable for featuring a percussionist. dc Talk didn't bring one along for the 1994 Free at Last Tour, but they *did* include one in the line-up for the 1996 Freak Show Tour.

Another significant performance was in late April 1994 for the Dove Awards at the Grand Ole Opry House in Nashville, Tennessee. Even though dc Talk was in the middle of a tour, they were able to make adjustments to the song and fine-tune it for the special appearance. The tour version still relied on the backing track for thicker vocals and several different cues, but the group went 100% live for the Doves. "Jesus is Just Alright" won a Dove Award for Rock Recorded Song of the Year at the same ceremony. "Socially Acceptable" also won a Dove Award that year.

On these and other special occasions, the "reprise" portion of the song was performed in the middle. At longer *Free at Last* shows, it was performed separately as an extended jam piece. During the 1994 Free at Last Tour, "Jesus is Just Alright" was the big number before the show slowed down for the acoustic set. During this gospel-infused version of the "reprise," Michael and Kevin had extended parts, Toby had speaking segments, and the guitarist and keyboardist each got solos.

One of the fun things to listen for during any performance of "Jesus is Just Alright" is to see if Michael Tait remembers his cue during the third verse. This is where Toby delivers a mouthful of lines without taking a breath. Tait is supposed to cover the "for the dough" line to let Toby breathe, but occasionally he forgets and there's just the sound of Toby inhaling. On the 2019 Jesus Freak Cruise, Toby refused Michael's help and powered through by taking short, unnoticeable breaths between syllables.

The "reprise" was used as the opening song of the 1995 Jesus Freak Tour. The main song itself was performed right before the acoustic set, just like the 1994 tour.

The 1996 Freak Show version of the song is a fan favorite. It took every element from the original version that worked well and brought them into a rock environment. The B-3 organ sound stands in for the electric piano tone, and the clean sound of the electric guitars gave way to a lot more crunch. For this tour, the "reprise" segment was featured in the middle and given a climactic end that sounded better than previous versions. As with the Jay Leno performance, the percussionist added a lot of new texture to the rhythm section.

The Supernatural Experience Tour featured an all-new version of the song that was anchored by a pulsating riff strongly resembling the "Mission: Impossible" theme. Laden with DJ scratches, synth arpeggio hits, droning guitars, and an overall futuristic take, the song fit well with Toby's new bridge: "They say Jesus is all wrong for the new millennium. I'm here to let you know that Jesus is still alright!" The same version (with a little more rock and roll added) was performed during the Solo Tours.

In 2017, when the band reunited for the Jesus Freak Cruise, fans were dying to know what the opening song would be. When the lights went out and the drummer hit a few toms, it was clear: the "reprise" segment of "Jesus is Just Alright" was the opening number. The rest of the song followed. The same setup was repeated as the first number of the encore during the 2019 Jesus Freak Cruise. The cruise versions of the song resembled the original *Free at Last* version of the song, not the *Jesus Freak* or *Supernatural* tour versions.

Videos:
"Jesus is Just Alright" was the first music video created to promote *Free at Last*. It was shot in the desert with a sepia tone that was popular at the time. The group still had the hair styles seen on the album cover. The video, along with a few seconds of a live performance, was included on the *Narrow is the Road*.

Neither the *Welcome to the Freak Show* video nor the *Supernatural Experience* video contained live versions of the song, though the *Welcome to the Freak Show* audio CD/cassette *did* feature the track. Live performances from the *Free at Last* days can be seen on *Free at Last: The Movie* and a VHS project called "God's Late Night Show: The Works" which features a performance from dc Talk's first Billy Graham Crusade.

Free at Last Album, Track 05:
Say the Words

Lyrically, "Say the Words" is the least overtly "Christian" song on the *Free at Last* record. Considering that the overwhelmingly clear message of the New Testament is *love*, though, perhaps one could say that its efforts to boil down love to its purest form is one of the *most* Christian messages on the record.

dc Talk knew instinctively that their message of faith and positivity didn't need to mention the name of Jesus at every turn for them to remain legitimate. But their evolution in this regard—writing about universal themes through the lens of faith *without* having to meet any "quotas"—was a more precarious precipice than most fans probably realize. On some level, there was a struggle to transcend the label of being "Christian artists" and morph into being recognized as "three artists who are Christians." The difference is subtle, but that particular distinction decides which record store puts an album on which shelf. Even now, the "Christian artist" label carries connotations that prevent good music from reaching the mainstream market, though dc Talk was one of the first trailblazers to make headway against this. Through sheer popularity, quality, and of course—*sales*—dc Talk *was* able to step out of their industry's box and be recognized in the mainstream market. However, in some ways, they were penalized in both the mainstream market *and* in some facets of the Christian music industry for their so-called audacity in aiming for mainstream listeners. On one side of the fence, an artist who mentions "Jesus" in any capacity can be promptly sent packing back to the Christian book stores. On the other side of the fence, an artist who does *not* mention "Jesus" at every turn can be automatically lumped in with all kinds of unsavory stereotypes regardless of their actual message or body of work. During the *Free at Last* years, as dc Talk's success catapulted them through both worlds, these were some of the issues they dealt with. They were wisely able to stay the course. Their mission was validated by pointing to the Great Commission: "Go into all the world and preach the Gospel." It was unfortunate that there were judgments passed on the band as they lived this out. Of all the bad music, bad influences, inappropriate acts, explicit material, and general junk cluttering up the airwaves in the 1990s, the positive, faith-based message behind dc Talk's music really should've been the least of anyone's concern.

"Say the Words" seems to have existed in a rough demo form as early at 1991. One of the members of the Newsboys who was on the Nu Skool Jam Tour clearly remembers hearing a demo of the song. According to the Newsboys, the original demo had a much better groove than the final recording of the song – a rare occurrence after so many hours are spent fine-tuning, arranging, and recording a song in a professional studio environment.

The fact that the song had never quite lived up to its potential was one of the reasons that it was given to producer Matt Bronleewe in 2000 for remixing purposes. His new version of the song, called "Say the Words (Now)," used the original *Free at Last* vocals. It appeared on *Intermission*, dc Talk's greatest hits record. The remix turned out so well that it was used as the first track and lead single from that release. Since *Intermission*, the "Now" remix of "Say the Words" has become the preferred version even in live shows.

Single:
With its Christian message packaged up in universal language,

the original version of "Say the Words" was naturally offered up as a single. It made no headway in the mainstream market, unfortunately, but it rose to number two on the Christian charts.

Alternate Versions:
As mentioned above, this song got a significant reworking for the *Intermission* project. That version of the song is explored in-depth later on in the book.

An instrumental/accompaniment track was released through "Street Trax." The original drum track was available through Hal Leonard.

Live Versions:
In a concert that featured rapid-fire rhythms, a huge lighting rig, an increasing number of live musicians, and tightly choreographed dancers, "Say the Words" wasn't the most exciting song to play for audiences. The song found its niche during the Free at Last Tour as the opening song, though. Starting with almost two minutes of dramatic pads and synths to set the stage, dc Talk climbed onto the highest tier of their setup, stood in formation against backlighting, and kicked off the show with this mysterious and ethereal opening number.

After that tour, the original version of the song vanished from the setlist forever. After the "Say the Words (Now)" remix came out, the song was brought back for the Solo Tour in 2001. The "Now" version was performed again during the 2017 and 2019 Jesus Freak Cruises. The vocal harmonies were a bit different and quite a bit more intricate on the cruise versions, proving that even after all of those years apart, there was still magic in the three voices that make up dc Talk.

Videos:
Videos of the band performing the song appear on both *Narrow is the Road* and the *Free at Last: The Movie*. The movie version

has the full performance, while *Narrow is the Road* only features a brief clip.

Free at Last Track 06: WDCT
This interlude from Gotee's Joey Elwood simulates a late-night radio broadcast. For the 10th Anniversary release of *Free at Last*, "the E" continues to "flip that wax" for a new "WDCT" segment that introduces the bonus interview tracks.

For a couple of years, Joey Elwood wrote articles for the official dc Talk newsletter ("The Vibe Tribe") using that same character voice and vocabulary. So much time has passed now that some of the retro lingo and slang makes for articles that are almost indecipherable to modern readers!

Free at Last Album, Track 07:
Socially Acceptable

"Socially Acceptable" sums up several of the major themes of the previous album, including a loss of morality and the role of racism in the degradation of society. Not surprisingly, the message of treating some of these ills through a Biblical approach has become even *more* relevant in the twenty-five years since this song's release.

One of the best hip-hop songs of dc Talk's career, the instrumentation, chords, and beats in "Socially Acceptable" were top-notch artistry for the time period. The strings add a lot of tension to the song, the electric piano adds a layer of atmosphere that feels a little like "Say the Words," the organ grinds away in the left channel during climactic moments, the guitar adds the trademark "dc Talk funk," and the roving bass line generates a strong bottom end. Toby McKeehan once mentioned that it ended up being one of the tracks that he was most proud of on the album. This level of musical mastery wasn't achieved easily, though. On *Free at Last's* 10th anniversary release, Toby recounted one of the album's horror stories. He was in the studio mixing the track and getting frustrated with how thin the beat was sounding. At 2:30 in the morning, he dialed up producer and Gotee partner Todd Collins for help. The duo worked through the rest of the night to end up with a product they were finally happy with.

Kevin and Michael both have great moments in the song, but

Kevin Max really finds opportunities to outdo himself. The second verse is one of the smoothest tracks he's ever put down. For someone who generally gravitates toward genres other than hip-hop, his ad-libs at the end of the song are *clearly* the work of someone who enjoyed what he was doing.

The *Free at Last* 10th anniversary release also revealed how important the "let it go, T, let it go" section of the song became to dc Talk history. Toby, Todd Collins, and Joey Elwood were looking to start their own production company at the time of the recording so that they could do some work for a group called Out of Eden. They'd been struggling with what to call their new venture. During the recording session for the "let it go, T" part of "Socially Acceptable," the synergy of "let it go, T" and the goatee beard on Toby's face gave Mark Heimermann the idea of calling Toby's new company "Gotee." The name actually stuck, and the rest is history.

While the song "Word 2 the Father" has the most throwbacks to dc Talk's previous records with passages from "He Works" and "The King (Allelujah)," this song has a throwback, too: the section with "yo who's doin' it?" is taken directly from a segment on the title track of *Nu Thang*.

Single:
"Socially Acceptable" was released as a single right after the record came out. It did well, actually becoming dc Talk's first number one single in the Christian music charts.

A radio promo disc containing a slight edit to the intro of the song was sent to radio stations. The disc also contained the song "Stay Together" by labelmates E.T.W.

Alternate Versions:
The version on *Intermission* has a vinyl/static sound over the intro,

the result of it following an interlude that used the same effect. The song also seems to fade out quicker.

Mixdown remix: Released in January 2003, the *ForeFront Mixdown* cd was a compilation of brand new remixes by "Mooki," a producer and songwriter who also works under his real name, Michael-Anthony Taylor (not to be confused with the actor or other individuals of the same name). The project contained remixes of various songs from the ForeFront Records catalog. For dc Talk, Taylor chose to tackle "Socially Acceptable."

Taylor's take on the song brings the "background chatter" recordings (which were barely audible in the original version) way up in the mix. He also includes a Michael Tait lick near the end of the song that was recorded during the original sessions but never used on the album. You're able to hear Tait build up to his big ending more clearly, too.

At the time that this project was put together, Taylor had worked on TobyMac's debut album (*Momentum*) and Stacie Orrico's self-titled album, both released by ForeFront.

Early mix: Astute listeners will be able to hear an early, stripped-down instrumental mix in the background of one of the interview portions on the *Free at Last* 10th anniversary disc. This version has a guitar riff highlighted and a beat that sounds more like a *Nu Thang* track than a *Free at Last* track.

There was an instrumental/accompaniment version of "Socially Acceptable" available through the "Street Trax" line. It's an odd mix, as the drums are turned down and some of the instruments are mixed to be louder. A much better version of the instrumental was featured as part of the DVD menu on *Free at Last: The Movie*. A drum-only track was released on the Hal Leonard cd that came with the *Free at Last* songbook.

Free at Last

Live Versions:
The song was only performed during the 1993 and 1994 *Free at Last* tours. During 1994, it was reserved for the encore and even had a costume change for Toby. Kevin Max, known for his improvisational abilities on-stage, found several creative and incredible routes through the second verse.

Videos:
A brief (and edited) segment of dc Talk performing the song appears in *Free at Last: The Movie*.

Free at Last Album, Track 08:
Free at Last (song)

One of the bounciest songs on the album is the title track, "Free at Last." The formula is closer to something from *Nu Thang*, but execution-wise, it reflects the more mature style of the newer material.

Michael and Kevin get a lot of spotlight moments, but the busy background vocals are greatly enhanced by guest star Veronica Petrucci. Petrucci was best known at the time as one half of the gospel duo "Angelo & Veronica," an award-winning husband and wife act that launched their debut album *Higher Place* during the same year that *Free at Last* came out.

Also heard in the background is an assortment of other vocalists. This may be the only dc Talk song to feature two different choirs, too... a "bad" one and a good one. The "bad" one, a "congregation choir" featured in the intro, was a humorous touch.

The clip from Dr. Martin Luther King, Jr. served not only as the inspiration of the song, but its inclusion was used to drive home the song's connection between earthly freedom and spiritual freedom.

The track was never released as a single. Like other songs from the album, an instrumental was released on "Street Trax" and the drum track was featured on the Hal Leonard drum cd.

Free at Last

Live Versions:
One of the most memorable live performances of this song was on the *Arsenio Hall Show* when dc Talk sung it in honor of Martin Luther King, Jr. Day. Accompanying them was The Mighty Clouds of Joy, a gospel quartet with a history going all the way back to 1960.

The song quickly became part of the dc Talk set at the time of its release. It remained part of the show throughout 1993 and 1994. During the headlining tour in 1994, it was performed as the very last song of the show.

Videos:
A video of the group performing the song on the *Arsenio Hall Show* was recently uploaded to the internet. Live video clips of the song from the 1994 Free at Last Tour can be found on *Narrow is the Road* and *Free at Last: The Movie*. Unfortunately, the credits and other video clips interrupt both versions before they can finish.

Free at Last Album, Track 09:
Time Is...

Following in the footsteps of "No More" but outclassing it in nearly every way, this was *Free at Last's* big rock number. Opening with several puns and phrases related to "time," the intro ticks down until the song goes off like a bomb. The "time" references don't stop there, as the group got creative with the beat and used a ticking clock sound to spice it up.

It's hard to pick him out of the busy crowd, but one of the biggest treats is the inclusion of Michael Sweet on background vocals. Sweet was the main vocalist of the legendary rock band Stryper. He also wrote most of Stryper's music and often did lead guitar work for the band. Around the time of *Free at Last,* Sweet was in the process of making a solo record.

Single:
The song was released to Christian radio in 1993. It charted fairly well compared to dc Talk's earlier releases, coming in at number 12 on the main Christian Contemporary Hit Radio chart and number 22 on the Christian Rock chart.

Alternate Versions:
A high-energy live version from dc Talk's 1996 tour can be found on the album *Welcome to the Freak Show.*

An instrumental/accompaniment version of this song was released through the "Street Trax" line. The room-heavy drum track was on a Hal Leonard cd accompanying the sheet music.

Live Versions:
"Time Is" was an insanely popular performance piece for dc Talk in the mid-1990s. It was first presented in 1993 as part of a medley with "Walls." The songs remained paired together for the rest of their tenure on the setlist, often serving as a high-energy sendoff before the show's encore. Kevin Max, who usually sang from behind a keyboard prop for most of the 1993 shows, would even come out and participate in the choreographed dance moves.

During the 1994 tour, an increased budget for more smoke, lights, and staging made this a very rock and roll affair. Barry Blair from the opening band, Audio Adrenaline, would double the amount of noise on the stage by coming out and joining Brent Barcus on guitar. Just like the shows in 1993, the group would play "Walls" and then launch straight into "Time Is." The ending would be drawn out as long as they thought the crowd could take it. The synchronized dance moves from Toby, Michael, and Kevin were gone by this point, but the backup dancers still had plenty to do.

The medley was so successful that the group retained it for their worldwide Freak Show Tour in 1996. It was one of the only pre-*Jesus Freak* songs to survive. Still performed as part of a medley, "Time Is" was reserved for the end of the main show. The performance remained kinetic despite the Freak Show Tour dropping the backup dancers.

Videos:
A video of the group performing the song at a 1993 summer festival exists as a rare item among collectors. A clip of the song with a shortened ending can be found on *Free at Last: The Movie*. The *Welcome to the Freak Show* VHS/DVD project also features the "Walls" / "Time Is" medley.

Free at Last Album, Track 10:
The Hardway

"The Hardway," with its mournful brass, haunting pads and dramatic melody, was unlike anything dc Talk had ever recorded. While the group had dabbled in slower-tempo songs before ("He Loves Me" and even "Things of this World" and "Children Can Live (Without It)"), this was their first full foray into recording a pop ballad. They'd return to the style in the future as their work matured.

Toby has spoken often about the creation of the song, but his most poignant introduction to it was on the 2019 Jesus Freak Cruise. He explained how he'd typically worked with co-writers on dc Talk songs, but "The Hardway" was one of the rare times that he'd written a song completely by himself. After "The Hardway" became a hit, Toby had often told interviewers that it had been written with Kevin Max in mind. It was always a little ambiguous as to whether it was written for Kevin's *voice* or if it was on more of a personal level. The question became moot because on the cruise, Toby said that looking back, he probably wrote it more for *himself*, not Kevin, because of his *own* experiences having to learn things the "hard way." Regardless of who the song was for or why, there are times when it applies to *everyone*. Because the song taps into such a universal feeling, it's stood the test of time as one of dc Talk's most popular songs. Toby McKeehan, though he's created and produced hundreds of songs in his illustrious career, still says that out of all the songs he's written, "The Hardway" is still one of his favorites.

It's easy to see why. Though the song allows the listener to feel the full effects of their mistakes, it doesn't wallow in despair. There's not an explicit resolution, but there's still a feeling of hope and peace conveyed by the song... particularly in the lines "I have fallen, but you will forgive me." "The Hardway" is able to offer comfort, even if a mistake can only be resolved on a spiritual level. Toby would use the same approach on the next album for a track called "What If I Stumble?"

"The Hardway" has an ethereal quality to it, even when it's performed acoustically. Much like Michael W. Smith's hit song "Friends" or any other landmark song from an accomplished group, it's the kind of lightning that only strikes once or twice in someone's career (Toby would have a similar accomplishment many years later in his solo career with the song "City On Our Knees"). It was produced at the perfect time, too. There's a sense in each one of their voices that all three of them, in one way or another, are speaking from experience. Earlier in their careers, the lyrics wouldn't have carried the same weight because the trio hadn't lived long enough or had as many setbacks. Later in their careers, the message might've just sounded weary.

The muted trumpet (yes, that's a trumpet, not a saxophone) from John Mark Painter adds a lot of magic to the song. Painter, a world-class musician, formed a rock/pop duo with his wife Fleming right after the *Free at Last* album took off. He would go on to do a lot of work with dc Talk during the *Jesus Freak* sessions and work extensively with Kevin Max on solo projects in the 2000s. Another musician on the track, Anthony Miracle, is still in the music business. He's currently making electronic music under the name "Tony Miracle."

Single:
"The Hardway" hit the airwaves at the beginning of 1994. It did fairly well on the Christian Adult Contemporary chart. On the

Christian Contemporary Radio Hits listing—the most prestigious chart in the genre—it rose all the way to number one. dc Talk was finally finding the same level of success on the radio that they were experiencing in the rest of the marketplace.

Alternate Versions:
Video Mix: One of the first alternate versions of the song was the "Video Mix." This was merely an incremental improvement over the album version as far as new material went, but the new material *greatly* enhanced the song. The extra guitar work was added by John Mark Painter, the brass player on the original track. This new mix was first available on the *Free at Last Extended Play Remixes* CD. Since then, it's become the preferred version of "The Hardway" and included on almost every greatest hits package.

Welcome to the Freak Show version: The live performance of "The Hardway" from the 1996 Freak Show Tour was the most epic version put to tape. Starting off with a poem recital by Kevin Max ("Alas my Love," the secret track from the *Jesus Freak*), portions of the song were brought into a minor key and fleshed out far beyond the scope of the original. More tension was added to various parts of the song. It all built up to a climactic splash of light, sound, and drama.

2002 "Revisited" version: Before *Free at Last* was reissued for a tenth anniversary edition, there was a lot of talk about what kinds of bonus material to include. The big win for fans was the long-awaited release of the movie that had been filmed in 1994 and 1995. Flying a little bit more under the radar, though, was a complete re-recording of "The Hardway" with all-new vocals. The new track was spearheaded by Matt Bronleewe, the producer behind the successful "Say the Words (Now)" remix. The new version of "The Hardway" is worthy of its own chapter, so it's explored later on in the book.

Free at Last

Gold version live track: In 2003, a "gold disc" was released to promote the tenth anniversary of *Free at Last*. On this rare disc was an even *rarer* treat: a clean, studio-mixed live version of "The Hardway" from the 1994 Free at Last Tour. The inclusion of this exclusive track has made the 2003 gold disc one of the most sought-after dc Talk collectibles. While the recording is the same as the live clip featured on *Free at Last: The Movie*, the gold disc's audio is much cleaner and contains a longer introduction.

Instrumental/Accompaniment: For readers who don't have any luck tracking down the out of print "Street Trax" releases, there's some good news here: the instrumental of "The Hardway" is by far easiest dc Talk accompaniment track to obtain. The first way is indeed through the "Street Trax" releases, but it's easier to find it on a disc called *Open Mic Karaoke: dc Talk Volume 1*, a project released on June 10th, 2013 by ForeFront Records. If there's no even with that, the full instrumental can be heard as the background music to one of the DVD menus in *Free at Last: The Movie*. It should be noted that some of these instrumental offerings have a few background vocals intact, but others have none at all. The drum track by itself was released by Hal Leonard in conjunction with a book of sheet music for the album.

Live Versions:
During shows in 1993, dc Talk began performing stripped-down acoustic sets. On the 1994 tour, the acoustic set consisted of three songs, one of which was "The Hardway." It made for a raw, emotional moment in an otherwise loud, flashy show. During the 1995 Jesus Freak Tour, the group experimented with moving it to the end of the set as the first song of the encore. The placement worked, and during the 1996 Freak Show Tour, it became one of the most incredible moments at the close of the concert.

It was replaced by "Red Letters" on the Supernatural Experience Tour, but "The Hardway" was brought back for the second leg of the Solo Tour. In the late 90s, it was preceded by Kevin's "Alas My Love" poem. The Solo Tour's arrangement was similar to the Freak Show version but a little sparser.

On the 2017 Jesus Freak Cruise, "The Hardway" was used to slow everything down before the acoustic set. The instrumentation was similar to the Solo Tour. The song was completely refreshed for the 2019 cruise with new musical harmonies and a special appearance from John Mark Painter to recreate his muted trumpet solo from the original album recording.

Videos:
A music video was produced for the song in 1994 to promote the single. To enhance the song's theme with weighty visuals, the filming took place at a maximum security prison in Ionia, Michigan. Michael Tait's brother was also incarcerated at the time, making the scenery much more personal to Michael. In *Free at Last: The Movie,* the film crew followed Michael as he visited with his brother and showed him the video. A few other "making of" clips can be seen in *Narrow is the Road,* where the music video itself is also included. dc Talk performed a concert at the prison as a token of appreciation for everyone's help in producing the project. *Entertainment Tonight* ran a segment on the filming of "The Hardway." *Free at Last: The Movie* also contains a live performance of the song, as does the *Welcome to the Freak Show* VHS/DVD project.

Free at Last Track 11: 2 Honks & A Negro
This interlude, dated lexicon and all, was a mainstay of dc Talk shows at the time *Free at Last* was being recorded. When dc Talk appeared on the *Arsenio Hall Show* (a huge late-night show in the early 1990s), the host prompted them to sing something for the camera. The result was included as this interlude on *Free at Last.* The "give 'em something, give 'em a little something" is actually Arsenio Hall speaking.

Free at Last Album, Track 12:
Lean on Me

dc Talk and their team of producers/musicians were undeniably brilliant songwriters in their own right. Still, they weren't afraid to perform or record cover songs. While several of dc Talk's radio hits ended up being covers (songs originally written, recorded, or made popular by someone else), the group usually put their own spin on the tracks or added new verses. Examples of that include "He Loves Me," "I Luv Rap Music," "Jesus is Just Alright", and "Day by Day." Occasionally they went for a fairly straightforward rendition of the original artist's ideas (as with "Help" and, to a lesser extent, "In the Light"). The band's recording of "Lean on Me" took the best from both of these approaches.

The original version of "Lean on Me" was written by the singer / songwriter / musician Bill Withers in 1972. While Withers gets proper credit for writing the song in *Free at Last's* liner notes, the dc Talk version has a lot more in common with *another* cover of the song: a rendition of "Lean on Me" produced in 1986 by an R&B group called Club Nouveau.

In a bonus track on the *Free at Last 10th Anniversary* disc, Michael Tait explained that the idea to record "Lean on Me" came from a karaoke booth recording that he and Kevin did while they were on a road trip. The resulting private cassette recording was such a hit with the band's friends that they began including a performance of it in dc Talk shows as early as 1991. To bring it in line with music they were making at the time, Toby added a new rap verse to the mix.

It was as much a hit on the road as it had been in private listening sessions, so including it on *Free at Last* was a no-brainer. Michael W. Smith was said to have attended a recording session for the track to put down keyboard parts for the song, but nothing in the literature gives him any official credit. There *is* a throwaway line at the beginning that seems to reference "Smitty," though, which was Smith's nickname. Even if his tracks didn't make it onto the album, he *did* perform the song live with them at a one-off appearance in 1999.

Single:
Response to the song was overwhelmingly positive in both the live arena and on the radio. The single became dc Talk's best-performing radio entry yet, easily nabbing the number one spot on the main Christian chart and rising into the top ten on the Christian Adult Contemporary list.

dc Talk supported the song by releasing a comprehensive promo CD to radio stations. The disc was jam-packed with content—rare for a radio single—and included six configurations of a completely new Adult Contemporary mix, four versions of a slightly different Adult Contemporary mix, promo spots, intros from Toby, and a radio version of the original album track.

Alternate Versions:
The Michael W. Smith connection became more apparent through the radio promo, where the Adult Contemporary ("AC") mix is attributed to Bryan Lenox. Bryan Lenox is a legendary musician, producer, and engineer that's been involved in almost every aspect of the contemporary Christian music scene since the 1980s. Before *Free at Last*, he'd been heavily involved in the production of Michael W. Smith's *Go West Young Man* album. From being a background vocalist on Rich Mullins' "Awesome

Free at Last

God" to recording, mixing, and engineering dozens of major artists, Lenox is one of the talented people who is undeniably responsible for helping the contemporary Christian music industry thrive. Even after dc Talk had disbanded, TobyMac still enlisted Lenox for several of his solo projects.

The AC mix was the one that radio stations usually opted to play rather than the album version, probably because the promo single contained almost ten different configurations suitable for almost any broadcast situation. The AC version is a true gem from the *Free at Last* years for those who are only familiar with the original album: it contains some vocals that weren't included in the original mix, completely different instrumentation, and gives a fresh feel to a classic track that most dc Talk fans have already heard a thousand times.

Interestingly enough, most (if not all) of the official karaoke tracks made available of "Lean on Me" contain the backing track from the AC mix, *not* the album version. There were several releases, making it one of the easier accompaniment tracks to find, but the karaoke companies' preference for the AC mix has led to a lot of confusion for casual fans who don't even know that the AC version exists. The "Street Trax" version may contain the album version of the track, but production numbers were limited and it's rarely found in the wild often enough to test a working version. The Hal Leonard CD contains the beat track to the album version, but none of the instrumentation.

Live Versions:
This was the first song from *Free at Last* to ever be played live. "People just went nuts for it," Michael Tait said of these early 1991 performances. It was so popular that dc Talk used the song as an encore for the Nu Skool Jam Tour during the fall of 1991.

"Lean on Me" continued to be played throughout 1992, still

often used as an encore performance. It was also included in the Change Your World Tour that dc Talk embarked on with Michael W. Smith in 1993. It remained an important part of the show during dc Talk's headlining 1994 tour, moving to the middle of the set and serving as a pick-me-up after the group's mellow acoustic numbers.

During the 1995 Jesus Freak Tour that led up to that album's release, "Lean on Me" was still featured as a bridge between the acoustic set and the rest of the concert. This time, it kicked off a disco segment that heavily featured a cover of KC and the Sunshine Band's "That's the Way (I Like It)."

It was dropped before the 1996 Freak Show Tour and unfortunately, the song has stayed out of the main rotation for good.

The 1999 Supernatural Experience Tour featured an expanded disco set lasting nearly fifteen minutes. This was where dc Talk introduced each of the band members and gave each musician a solo. Every night, they did a gag where Kevin Max would pop up in place of Jason Halbert, the group's keyboard player. Max would play a few lines from the "Star Wars Theme" before turning the keys back over. While the disco set would've been the perfect opportunity to throw a little "Lean on Me" into the mix, the song was nowhere to be found… on *most* nights. At one of the performances, after Kevin Max popped up in Halbert's place, Michael W. Smith popped up in *Kevin's* place. The group went on to perform a few bars from "Lean on Me" to a rapturous crowd.

The song hasn't been included on any of the reunion cruise shows, but if reunions continue, it stands a decent chance of being brought back in some capacity.

Free at Last

Video:
A concept video of "Lean on Me" was never made, but a partial performance of the song from 1994 can be seen on *Free at Last: The Movie*.

Free at Last Track 13: Testimony
This brief interlude features Toby telling the story of how he was introduced to hip-hop. As he's taking turns rapping against himself, two lines frequently confuse folks of later generations: "Rapper's Delight was the ditty" and "No Scritti for my Politti."

"Rapper's Delight" was a landmark song by the Sugar Hill Gang, credited as the first hip-hop track to gain traction in major mainstream markets. "Scritti Politti" was a British band with an artistic, experimental catalog of mostly punk and pop. Anyone born around the same time as Toby would've certainly been exposed to both.

Free at Last Album, Track 14:
I Don't Want It

Did dc Talk just say the word "sex"? Indeed they did. Written as a direct response to a 1987 George Michael song called "I Want Your Sex," this song by Toby McKeehan, Mark Heimermann, and Kevin Max attempted to bring the concepts of patience, respect, and love back into the conversation. It wasn't intended to make parents blush; it was an important message for younger generations in an era where popular music seemed to be glorifying and commercializing promiscuity.

The verse melody is one of the nicest passages on *Free at Last*. The album version doesn't do it justice – it was brought out more during live performances by a guitar sound with a heavy chorus effect. Michael Tait tried some new things with his voice on the album recording, and he's joined by Gotee Brother Todd Collins on some of the backing tracks. Tony Miracle from "The Hardway" recording sessions teamed up with Toby for the drum programming.

Though it had a commercial sound to it, the song was never released as a single.

Searching for the song on internet video sites is a task only for the brave, as it leads to some very strange—yet "G" rated—entertainment. Modern interpretations of "I Don't Want It" are quite creative, as parody artists have introduced colorful costuming and enthusiastic dance routines.

Free at Last

Alternate Versions:
For some reason, the instrumental version from the "Street Trax" is very lackluster. Almost all of the edge is taken out of the beat because most of the center channel was eliminated for some reason. Some fans note that on the *Free at Last* album, the vocal processing on "I Don't Want It" sounds very different from the rest of the project. It's possible that the song was recorded with a different setup than some of the other tracks and that ForeFront didn't have access to all of the stem elements that they usually do when putting together a "Street Trax" release. In situations like this, sometimes "instrumental" versions are made by using phase cancellation methods on the center channel, while elements further to the left or right of the stereo spectrum are left alone. When this is done, most of the bass and percussion will be lost. This seems to be what happened. We obtained three different "Street Trax" cassettes to make sure that the odd mix wasn't the result of errors or tape degradation. They all sounded the same. Thankfully, the drum-only version available from Hal Leonard sounds fine. Patient fans can mash them together to get something serviceable.

Live Versions and Video:
"I Don't Want It" was performed during *Free at Last* tours as the second half of a medley with "That Kinda Girl." A partial video of a performance from 1994 can be found on *Narrow is the Road*.

Free at Last Track 15: Will Power
"Will Power" is a clever interlude that ties into the theme of "I Don't Want It" by spoofing a commercial advertisement.

"Temptation sold separately! Batteries not included!"

Free at Last Album, Track 16:
Word 2 the Father

"Word 2 the Father" is a love letter to classic dc Talk fans. It merges old styles and new styles, old sounds and new sounds, and even old lyrics and new lyrics. Unbeknownst to Toby McKeehan and Mark Heimermann at the time, the chord progression even sets up their next record—the blockbuster album *Jesus Freak*—by using the same underlying chord pattern as "So Help Me God." Both songs are built around the Cm7 / F major chord progression – a true classic amongst rock musicians. This chord pattern has also been used extensively in jazz, making a musical bed for "Word 2 the Father" that sounds both laid back and energetic. Having the *last* track of the third album have the same musical DNA as the *first* track of the fourth album, and on a song that emphasizes dc Talk's history, is next-level genius... even if the nod was the result of serendipity.

Toby's rap verses have a bit of a chorus effect on them. It gives them a more distinct, thicker quality. The instrumentation itself lacks some of the stereo separation that some of the other *Free at Last* tracks were designed with, so this effect helps provide a better illusion of space in the mix (especially for those listening with headphones).

The lyrics, probably intentionally, channel some of the sillier moments in dc Talk's earlier albums. "Jump on it like a hornet" is a fan favorite. The *main* throwback/tribute to dc Talk's earlier work arrives in the third verse, as Toby delivers a clever rap passage that integrates most of his old song titles into a fairly organic, coherent presentation. Vocal licks from "He Works" (*Nu Thang*) and "The King (Allelujah)" follow.

Some of the background musicians/vocalists should be pointed out. Billy Gaines, one of the background singers, was a notable recording artist for many years. He also recorded background vocals on "Socially Acceptable" and "Luv is a Verb." Ken Springs, better known to the music community as "Scat Springs," is still a performing musician. His group, the "Scat Springs Band," is based in Nashville and plays soul, pop and rock numbers.

Alternate Versions:
An instrumental/accompaniment version exists through the "Street Trax" series. A drum-only version was included in Hal Leonard's *Free at Last* songbook.

Live Versions:
"Word 2 the Father" was a lively showpiece on dc Talk tours. During the headlining shows in 1994 and 1995, it was performed after their hit "Luv is a Verb." Occurring early in the set, the song was also used as a brief band introduction piece.

In 1995, when most of the *Free at Last* tracks were dropped in favor of newly-minted *Jesus Freak* tunes, "Word 2 the Father" survived all of the cuts. It was performed in the same block of the show as "So Help Me God," its sister song on *Jesus Freak*.

Videos:
A clip of the group performing this song can be found on *Free at Last: The Movie*. A special live version (audio only) was also used as the background of the 1995 version of the movie's trailer.

Free at Last Album, Track 17:
Jesus is Just Alright (reprise)

The album ends with a little bit of the blues, as the missing bridge from the Doobie Brothers' version of "Jesus is Just Alright" is given its own legs to stand on. dc Talk forsakes its hip-hop roots for a moment to showcase Michael Tait and Kevin Max's vocal prowess and to give some of the greatest session musicians of the early 1990s some room to flex. This passage was discussed earlier in the book, but we can't turn the page on *Free at Last* without discussing the last interlude in a bit more detail.

Alternate Versions:
The interlude was included in the middle of "Jesus is Just Alright" in just one of the tracks on the promo single released in the United States and Japan. Its inclusion makes for a version that's a bit more similar to the Doobie Brothers' arrangement.

No instrumental or drum track has ever been made available.

Live Versions:
dc Talk often performed this "reprise" in the middle of their live "Jesus is Just Alright" performances. One of the best-known early examples of this was their appearance on the *Jay Leno Show* in 1993 and their Dove Awards performance in 1994. That setup was continued on the 1996 Freak Show Tour.

During the Free at Last Tour in 1994, it was performed at the *end* of "Jesus is Just Alright" as an extended piece that lasted for several minutes. Guitar solos, organ solos, a speech or two from Toby, and several spotlight moments for Michael and Kevin made for a moment where everyone had a chance to cut loose before the acoustic set.

In 1995, the "reprise" was used as the introduction to the whole show. During the *Supernatural* and *Solo* years, performances of "Jesus is Just Alright" took on a more techno / dance / rock feel. The organic "reprise" was dropped.

After being on hiatus for fifteen years, dc Talk used the "reprise" as the opener of their long-awaited reunion show on the 2017 Jesus Freak Cruise. Fans could hardly contain themselves when the distinctive tom hits and seventh chords began playing and dc Talk finally stepped out onto the backlit stage. Twenty-two years after it had been used as the opener in 1995, the group sounded just as limber as they ever had. The song appeared again to start off the encore on the 2019 cruise.

Video:
A video clip of dc Talk performing an extended version of the "reprise" can be found on *Free at Last: The Movie*.

Free at Last Era:
I Luv My Neighbor

Jodi Benson, the voice of Disney's *The Little Mermaid*, lent her name and vocals to a project called *Jodi Benson and Friends Sing Songs from the Beginner's Bible*. Released on September 21st, 1992, the project contained a song called "I Luv My Neighbor" that featured none other than Toby McKeehan and Michael Tait.

This wasn't a mere guest appearance: it's practically a dc Talk song. Toby raps every verse, Michael Tait sings every chorus, and the "goofy" voices are performed by some of the same folks who worked on other dc Talk projects.

Despite the kid-oriented lyrics, it's a pretty good track. The beat has a strong shuffle, the modern-sounding brass hits swing competently under the chorus, and Michael Tait gives the melody his all (especially toward the end). One of the weirdest things to ever happen on a dc Talk track, though, is the Robin Williams impersonation ("Good morning Mrs. Barber" instead of "Good morning Vietnam"). "dc Talk" isn't explicitly credited as contributing to the album, perhaps because the sillier, kid-friendly approach would've taken some of the edge off the upcoming November release of their serious contender, *Free at Last*.

There were two versions released of *Jodi Benson and Friends Sing Songs from the Beginner's Bible*. One of them contains the dc Talk track, and the other one doesn't. When purchasing, take care to ensure that Track 7 is "I Luv My Neighbor."

Free at Last Era:
We Three Kings

It's a shame that this track isn't more widely available. This 1994 take on "We Three Kings" is one of the best Kevin Max / Michael Tait duets ever produced. It's a low-key, loop-based take on the classic Christmas track from the mid-1800s with new lyrics in the form of Toby McKeehan rap segments throughout. A gospel choir joins in halfway through.

There are two versions of this song. Both feature the same dc Talk elements, but they differ in how heavily the choir is featured.

"We Three Kings" was featured on various Christmas compilation albums in the mid-1990s, most notably a November 1994 release called *Joyful Christmas*. The compilation also included tracks from Eddie DeGarmo, Patti LaBelle, and others.

The CD releases were the only places it could be heard. The track was never put out as a single, and there's no record of it ever being performed live.

Free at Last EP (1994)

Before discussing the *Free at Last* concerts, it's worth looking at another mid-90s release: The *Free at Last Extended Play Remixes* project. dc Talk had always been popular at concert venues, but it wasn't until the end of 1992, with the release of their third album, that stores were having trouble keeping up with the demand for dc Talk records. By 1994, two years had passed without any new material from the group and vendors had nothing new to sell. To tide fans over until dc Talk could get back into the studio, their label devised a remix project.

Released in 1994, the *Free at Last EP* featured a collection of remixes from some of their most popular songs: "Jesus is Just Alright," "Luv is a Verb," and "The Hardway."

Jesus is Just Alright (Techno Remix)
The disc had two remixes of "Jesus is Just Alright," both created by Scott Blackwell. A DJ well-known to the club scene in Florida and New York in his early years and later in Southern California (especially Los Angeles), Blackwell focused on gospel-based techno and dance music. He also ran the labels MYX Records and N-Soul Records. One of his big claims to fame during the *Free at Last* years was an event called "Scott Blackwell's Gospel Rave House" in Southern California. Later, he became best known for the "Nitro Praise" series of remixes and compilations.

The "Techno Mix" of "Jesus is Just Alright" hits a little harder than the album version, applying the pressure with breakbeats equalized to various parts of the sonic spectrum. At the end, Blackwell creates some new lyrical moments by splicing together portions of Toby's rap verses.

Jesus is Just Alright (Retro Remix)

The groove created for this mix sounds contemporary even today. The track features extended brass solos and a heaping helping of Tait's "Alright with me, yeah" vocal phrase. Clocking in at six and a half minutes, this is the perfect version of the song to listen to if the album version leaves a listener wanting more.

Luv is a Verb (Gotee Remix)

The "Luv is a Verb (Gotee Mix)" was a way for Toby and the co-founders of his new label to work with material they were already familiar with. This version of the song has a very laid-back 1990s feel to it with some extra brass and a prominent guitar loop that later became part of the core song. As opposed to the original recording, which had Toby's verse louder and the chorus quieter, here the verse is mixed down and the chorus is more prominent over the sparser instrumentation. Gotee would come back again to try their hand at the next release's title track, "Jesus Freak."

The Hardway (Video Mix)

There was very little to improve upon with "The Hardway," so rather than a complete remix of the song, this version was simply an enhancement of the original with additional guitar parts from John Mark Painter.

dc Talk's *Extended Play Remixes* sold moderately well. The idea was commercially viable enough for ForeFront Records to expand the effort to some of its other artists. One of the other projects to get the remix treatment was the *Don't Censor Me* album by dc Talk's future opening band, Audio Adrenaline.

Change Your World Tour

Special thanks to Bert Gangl for contributing to these and other concert history sections.

dc Talk's successful 1991 outing with Michael W. Smith opened the door to a repeat of the opportunity in 1993. The synergy was expected to be even *more* powerful a second time, as Smith and dc Talk had spent the past two years sharing producers, musicians, and even syncing their album release / touring schedule.

On January 23rd, 1993, dc Talk debuted their new music video, "Walls," and performed at a "Racial Unity Rally" in Pulaski, Tennessee (the mayor even named it "dc Talk Day"). A week later, they opened for Michael W. Smith's "Change Your World Tour." dc Talk drew most of the material for their nine-song set from their brand new *Free at Last* record.

New material meant a new approach. In the past, dc Talk had relied heavily on backing tracks for their live performances. With a bigger stage and a larger budget, they'd begun shying away from that. Live musicians were now an essential part of their performances, though the band still played on top of backing tracks to some extent. With world-class musicians, enthusiastic backup dancers, lively songs, and the natural talent of the group, the popular set was quite energetic.

Change Your World Tour

Since the release of his *Go West Young Man* album, Michael W. Smith had enjoyed phenomenal success in both the mainstream and Christian markets. Now dc Talk, his opening act, was replicating the feat. The group's elevated production values and ability to hold a large audience for nine songs went a long way toward convincing management, the label, and other stakeholders that dc Talk was perhaps ready to headline a major tour of their own.

The Change Your World Tour went all the way through May. After it was over, dc Talk took a few weeks off and then went straight back out on the road for a busy summer festival season. In September, they played their first show with label-mates Audio Adrenaline, a group that they'd eventually take on tour with them. dc Talk played a couple more shows with Michael W. Smith in Washington State that month, and they booked a few more fall dates. On November 12th, 1993, they performed "Jesus is Just Alright" on *The Tonight Show with Jay Leno*.

Michael W. Smith's set from the Change Your World Tour was made available on a VHS release but unfortunately, none of dc Talk's performances were included.

Free at Last Tour (1994)

Free at Last had cemented the group's success. In some ways, though, the success was relative. The group still wasn't receiving as much radio play as they'd hoped for, and though they'd made appearances on some of the biggest television shows in the country, they'd made few inroads into the mainstream music community.

It was time to capitalize on what dc Talk did best: putting on a live show. The group's stints with Michael W. Smith, the Nu Skool Jam Tour, and their widespread acceptance at festivals had proven that the group was finally worthy of their own spotlight. They were ready for their own tour.

This was going to be a completely different animal from 1991's Nu Skool Jam Tour, though. Larger venues, over forty cities, stops in major markets, and a bigger and better lighting rig would help dc Talk take their material to the next level. Their world-class dancers and musicians added polish to the show. It was a massive undertaking, the likes of which the group, management, and even the label had never quite dealt with before. The rock band Audio Adrenaline (the group's ForeFront labelmates) was selected as the opening act. The length of dc Talk's setlist was practically doubled. More effort was put into the set's production. The marketing machine worked overtime. To make the trek even *more* intense, it was decided that a documentary film crew would travel with the band and film the excitement as it unfolded.

Free at Last Tour

To keep the stressful undertaking from coming undone, road pastor Michael Guido was hired to accompany the group in their travels. Guido applied his Scripture-based counsel and no-nonsense style to a group that needed it more than ever as the tour catapulted dc Talk further into the public's consciousness. Guido became an essential member of the dc Talk tour and remained with the band for several years.

The Free at Last Tour went from February to May, with time carved out for detours like the Dove Awards. That particular detour was time well-spent, as dc Talk took home two awards at the ceremony (one of them for "Jesus is Just Alright," the song they'd performed that night. The other was for "Socially Acceptable").

Shows on the Free at Last Tour were a thing to behold. They began with a smoky, mysterious version of "Say the Words" as the silhouettes of dc Talk climbed onto a high-rise platform and each performed their respective sections of the song. Stage lights flickered to life and the dancers joined the fray as "Say the Words" gave way to "Luv is a Verb," a setlist choice that Kevin Max later pointed out as the "answer" to "Say the Words," almost making the opening of the show into a narrative. Band introductions were given at the beginning of "Word 2 the Father," and the hip-hop element took over the show with a medley of "That Kinda Girl" and "I Don't Want It" that explored the intersections of love and wisdom in a sophisticated way.

The crowd was always on their feet for dc Talk's high-energy take on "Jesus is Just Alright." Following that was the reprise, "Jesus, He is My Friend," which gave the musicians, vocalists, and even the dancers a chance to inject as much drama into the show as they could.

New to the dc Talk experience in the *Free at Last* days was a stripped-down acoustic set. The band delivered softer, more thoughtful versions of "The Hardway," Larry Norman's "I Wish We'd All Been Ready," and U2's "40" to the crowd. At special shows in 1994, music legend Larry Norman himself joined the band on-stage.

"Lean on Me" and "Nu Thang" brought the energy level of the show back to 11, and an extended version of the "Walls" / "Time Is" medley that was so popular during the 1993 concerts nearly brought down the house before the band could even play its final song of the main set, a jazzy version of their first hit, "Heavenbound."

A slow-tempo medley of "Things of This World" and "Children Can Live (Without It)" were played as part of the encore during early shows in the tour, but it seems this was dropped to improve pacing. After a quick wardrobe change, the group delivered "Socially Acceptable." In typical Kevin Max fashion, no two verses were ever the same.

If the audience clamored for more, and they always did, Michael Tait owned the spotlight with an abridged, piano-based version of "He Loves Me" from the debut album. If concert-goers were paying attention, they'd notice that only *one* song from the new album hadn't been performed yet. The title track, "Free at Last," was a celebratory send-off to an incredible night with Christian music's rising stars.

A month after the Free at Last Tour ended, dc Talk was invited to perform at Cleveland Stadium for a Billy Graham Crusade. The group (sans Toby because of a prior engagement) had met with Graham at his home earlier in the year. The legendary evangelist spoke about the disconnect between his generation and the newer ones, and he later expressed a desire to use dc Talk as a "translator" of sorts to help his message reach the youth of the country. dc Talk's appearance at the Billy Graham Crusade in Cleveland, which also featured Michael W. Smith, was a success. It led to a partnership between Billy Graham and dc Talk that lasted the rest of the band's existence. By the time they'd disbanded, dc Talk had performed at nearly twenty Billy Graham Crusades.

The year kept getting busier. Between concert appearances, dc Talk won several more awards. In addition to a Grammy for *Free at Last* and numerous Dove Awards, the group also won a Billboard Music Video Award for "The Hardway," a Billboard Contemporary Christian Album award for *Free at Last*, and Billboard's Contemporary Christian Artist of the Year for 1994.

Free at Last: The Movie

Few Christian bands had ever achieved what dc Talk was achieving. Naturally, there were stories to be found. What better way to find them than to capture their first major headlining tour on film in real-time?

For over two dozen stops on the Free at Last Tour, a documentary crew followed the group's every step. The shows, the crowds, the behind-the-scenes drama, the tense moments, the ups, the downs, the rights, the wrongs, the triumphs, and the troubles were *all* caught on film. The end goal was to take the raw footage to the editing room and find a way to craft a documentary that could be released to movie theaters nationwide.

Free at Last: The Movie, as it was called, would show the ins and outs of how a diverse group of people handled the stress of the road, the pitfalls of sudden success, and how these things were approached by a group who looked at them through a Christian lens. Helming the project was director Ken Carpenter, a relative newcomer to the field back in 1994. After this project, Carpenter went on to direct and/or produce over forty long-form projects, many of them in the Christian music industry.

Some of the more meaningful filming days were at Liberty University and the boys' home base in Franklin, Tennessee. Scenes at various landmarks and tourist stops along the way made for several candid moments, too. A wide range of material was shot even *after* the tour wrapped up. One of the filming days even included a "Jesus Freak" recording session. As the principal photography finished in 1995, a film pro named Eric J. Smith began cutting and editing the footage together. A release date was set for September 17th, 1995.

Narrow is the Road
To tide fans over until the film's release—and to find a use for footage that would most likely be cut—a home video project called *Narrow is the Road* was released to VHS on September 23rd, 1994. In addition to several candid scenes and some backstage footage, it contained a montage music video for "Luv is a Verb," portions of several live performances (including "Jesus is Just Alright," "Say the Words," and "Free at Last"), and the music videos for "Jesus is Just Alright" and "The Hardway." A live segment called "Back 2 the Basics" expanded on *Free at Last's* "Testimony" to include band solos. A live medley of "That Kinda Girl" and "I Don't Want It" was also featured, as was the complete performance of "I Wish We'd All Been Ready."

Narrow is the Road performed well in the marketplace, selling enough copies to be certified Gold by the RIAA less than two and a half months after it came out.

The Release of Free at Last: The Movie
As September 1995 drew nearer, *Free at Last: The Movie* suffered numerous issues on both the film *and* distribution side. Movie trailers were produced, but they were left largely uncirculated as the future of the project became murkier. Promotional materials were drawn up, but as the release date approached, the marketing efforts were caught in a holding pattern.

September 17th, 1995 came and went without a dc Talk film in movie theaters. According to volume six of the official dc Talk newsletter, the film was held up by "unforeseen technical and legal difficulties." When dc Talk's *Jesus Freak* album was released two months later and proved to be even *more* of a game-changer than *Free at Last*, the film was finally shelved.

And there it remained—unreleased—for years. It wasn't until December 17th, 2002 (exactly seven years and two months after its originally scheduled release date) that fans got to finally see the film.

Launched on DVD to commemorate the tenth anniversary of the *Free at Last* album, the long-awaited movie was released exactly as Carpenter, Smith, and the rest of the crew had left it: coherent and cohesive, but incomplete.

The film is a must-watch for dc Talk fans. But coming out so many years later, after so many chart-topping hits and world tours from the group, the movie's value is not in its narrative but in what it offers for posterity. As a documentary, the story lacks the conflict or crux a moviegoer needs to make it interesting for outsiders. There's no hero and no villain. Instead, there are remarkable examples of teamwork – many different individuals living on a bus amongst cereal boxes and bunk curtains and somehow coming together to make it all work on stage. It would be easy to call the movie a time capsule, a film of bygone days that can entertain viewers who go for the nostalgia of backup dancers, oversized clothing, and the last gasp of an earnest brand of hip-hop. It's clear that the team didn't really end up with the movie they had wanted to make, but that's not a bad thing. The film isn't about a band who had *arrived*, but of a band who had just *begun*. It's obvious in the footage, as there's a unique energy surging in every interview and every performance. What they ended up capturing was not the rip-roaring success of *Free at Last*, but the bedrock and formation of one of music's most influential albums: *Jesus Freak*. From the hotel room meeting with Brennan Manning that graces the beginning of *Jesus Freak's* "What If I Stumble?" to a recording session of "Jesus Freak" itself, the movie is less a celebration of *Free at Last* and more the story of three young men shedding their matching stage outfits and reaching for something beyond them. This was the era during which they began putting forth their own unique styles, voices, and perspectives and *using* those perspectives to form an unprecedented platform.

In a May 2016 interview provided by United Christian Broadcasters in the UK, Toby McKeehan was asked if there would ever be a documentary about the dc Talk story. He reminded the audience that there already *was* a movie that told the dc Talk's coming-of-age. This is *the* dc Talk movie. While the other chapters of their career are noteworthy in their own ways, there was never a time in dc Talk's history more important to capture than the transition between *Free at Last* and *Jesus Freak*. Amazingly the management, label, and band had the foresight (or simply the good fortune) to put it to film. In *Free at Last: The Movie*, the story of dc Talk is all there in glorious black and white.

The Jesus Freak Era

Free at Last had been a sensational hit by any standard. It earned Platinum certification from the RIAA on July 14th, 1995 for over one million copies sold.

dc Talk was everywhere now. The Grammy Awards. Magazine covers. Radio interviews. Headlining sold-out concerts. Some of those concerts were part of a lengthy international touring schedule that, between the end of the 1994 summer festival season and the first couple months of 1995, took them everywhere from Washington, D.C. to New Zealand. There was no time to rest on their laurels; the Free at Last Tour had catapulted them to stardom. Still, Toby McKeehan somehow found time to marry his college sweetheart *and* to begin crafting lyrics for the next record. As dc Talk's exhausting touring schedule took them to the other side of the world, Toby was putting the finishing touches on the song that would define his career.

The last few lyrics to a fledgling version of a song called "Jesus Freak" came together on the other side of the world in Johannesburg and Port Elizabeth in the week of February 10th, 1995. On the January and February dates in Australia, New Zealand, and South Africa, early versions of the song were played live for the first time ever. To craft this new experiment, Toby had taken the best elements of several successful dc Talk tracks: there were the rap-over-rock guitars a la "Walls," slow and hypnotic verses like "Say the Words," a wordy but high-concept hook like "The Hardway," and a live-concert high-energy approach to the performance like "Heavenbound" and "Luv is a Verb."

The crowds were enthusiastic about this new song, but many in the dc Talk camp had reservations. Was it was for the group to veer away from the fortress of laid-back beats they'd built with *Free at Last*? This move to overdriven, aggressive, guitar-oriented alternative rock was surely foolish in light of the type of music they'd produced up to this point. dc Talk's hip-hop style had sold nearly two million records... so why risk their audience? But Toby was dead-set on this experiment. And that's what it was... an "experiment." If the marketplace wasn't receptive, he could always pull back and return to hip-hop. dc Talk's road manager, Denny Keitzman, explained it best in a November 18th, 2015 article by Gabriel Jones on *decentchristiantalk.com* called "Jesus Freak: 20 Years Later": "Toby put 'Jesus Freak' out as a single before the album was even finished. He basically tossed it out like a frisbee to see what would happen. If it would have gone out and bombed, he would have time to change the direction of the whole album."

The South Africa shows were the end of the road for a while. While dc Talk continued to perform sporadically, the group carved out some time before the summer festival season for some much-needed R&R. Toby McKeehan, finally settling into a new home and a new life, continued to craft song ideas for the upcoming album. He wrote with his bandmates, management, the label, and producers like Mark Heimermann and Todd Collins. As the lengthy pre-album sessions for *Jesus Freak* went on, some drastically different ideas began to emerge.

There could've been several reasons for Toby wanting to shift gears. By 1995, the hip-hop genre had reached a strange turning point. In the general public's eyes, there was negativity and even a culture of violence that had usurped the sound. And the genre became based more than ever on the esoteric and hard-to-decipher credibility factors of the rapper rather than the credibility of his or her lyrics. A clean-cut Toby McKeehan might not have been able to operate in that space as convincingly or legitimately as he once had. By this time, McKeehan was a world-class record producer with his finger on the pulse of every trend in every corner of the music industry. He must've been aware of these things.

While listening to music in their leisure time, the members of dc Talk as a whole had been enjoying the new wave of alternative rock that had become so popular in the early 1990s. Michael Jackson's *Dangerous*, the epitome of the style and production elements that records like *Free at Last* had aspired to, had been knocked clean off the charts by Nirvana's *Nevermind* – an event seen as a turning point for the music industry. dc Talk was influenced by these changes even as they performed their signature hip-hop show night after night. No longer fringe players in the music industry or mere observers of the culture at large, dc Talk had won a Grammy for *Free at Last* and had become firmly entrenched in the musical culture of the mid-1990s. Their sensitivity to the changes around them was even evident in the grunge-style wardrobe worn by the band during the Free at Last Tour in 1994. When Nirvana frontman Kurt Cobain passed away while dc Talk was on tour in 1994, the group was visibly shaken by the news. They had just toured Washington State in Bellingham, Seattle, Kennewick, and Spokane a week or two before his death. These were some of the areas where Nirvana's sound had been formed.

While some of the approaches that Toby, Michael, and Kevin were discussing for the new record were a radical departure from what they'd done before, the core of their work remained the same. The wild success of *Free at Last* and their keen awareness of the music industry may have given the group more experience and more resources, but it didn't change their message. Toby's lyrics still offered a faith-based solution to society's problems. If anything was different in his words, it was that this time around, he wrote from a more personal standpoint. "The Hardway" had been one of his first attempts at this. For the new record, songs like "What If I Stumble?" and "Between You and Me" were elaborations of this. The new songs were pages taken from his own life, lyrics forged from the pressures he faced and the challenges of touring and the new responsibilities he had as a husband and a founder of his own production company.

Even in late 1994, when the album was in its earliest stages, the potential in the new material was obvious. As Todd Collins explained in an interview with *CCM Magazine's* Justin Sarachik for a January 15th, 2016 article titled "'Jesus Freak' at 20, Part Two," the songs were unmistakably solid even in just their raw, unadorned form. The label, understandably wanting another record in the mold of *Free at Last* and probably a little apprehensive about deviating from a winning formula, wasn't quite *as* enthused. But as summer approached in 1995, it was time to commit to the new direction. More musicians were brought in and more studios were booked. Many of the usual suspects were already participating and some of the country's best studios were available. Even so, the group needed more room to work. Experimentation in a recording studio is an expensive activity. They needed space to figure out their new sound without the time limits imposed by renting commercial facilities.

House of Insomnia
Nu Thang and *Free at Last* had been put together piecemeal in various studios around town based on touring schedules, availability, and other factors beyond the group's control. Time and resources were sometimes flat-out wasted, like the months

spent recording *Nu Thang* with live players. In many ways, the records had suffered from the traditional "record company" approach. This time, it would be different.

In April, dc Talk performed "The Hardway," "Jesus Freak," and a cover of Charlie Peacock's "In the Light" (with Charlie Peacock himself) at a Gospel Music Association's songwriter's showcase. The group felt emboldened by the responses that "Jesus Freak" and their "In the Light" covers were getting. Toby and company went all-in that summer, purchasing a small house in Franklin, Tennessee to convert into their own creative space and recording studio. By July, the halls had been filled with effects racks, microphones, preamps, mixing decks, musicians, producers, and engineers. The space sprung to life, with every corner of the house working feverishly on the new record. The studio was appropriately dubbed the "House of Insomnia," as sessions could last well into the morning hours (at least on nights that the group wasn't playing for their softball team).

The *Free at Last* documentary crew was invited back to capture some of this inspired time. Many of those involved in this effort have described these months as the best time in their lives. Even the older couple next door, initially annoyed at the late nights and the loud music, learned to look back fondly at their time with "the boys." A cordial team of musicians, including well-known names from the past, collaborated in this space on the many different arrangements, mixes, vocalizations, and experiments. Hit after hit was crafted in this tiny house. The new record started to take shape.

Jesus Freak
One of the first hits to be finished, of course, was "Jesus Freak." As dc Talk had to start spending more time on the road in 1995 to fulfill summer festival engagements and to perform at another Billy Graham Crusade, they were able to bring something new

The Jesus Freak Era

along: a disc made to look like an old 45 rpm record containing their new song.

The rest of the album was riding on the public's reception to this lead single, "Jesus Freak." Though dc Talk had ventured into rock and roll with "Walls," "No More," "Time Is," and even "The King (Allelujah)," this was an all-in kind of an approach. To help ease the transition, dc Talk included a hip-hop-oriented remix of "Jesus Freak" on the single. If the public didn't like what they were offering, this remix could become the version used on the next album.

The transition wasn't fully felt by summer audiences yet, as most of the show contained the familiar rap and pop tunes from *Free at Last*. The crowd's response to the new songs still mattered quite a bit. Even more than that, Toby wanted to continue to gauge Michael Tait and Kevin Max's thoughts. He was making a conscious effort to involve his bandmates more in all aspects of the operation. By all accounts, Michael and Kevin were excited by the new sound. Not only were both interested in making a rock record, but the group had grown to the point where they didn't want their music to sound outdated as quickly as some of their past work had. dc Talk, Mark Heimermann, and everyone involved were of the same mind in that regard. As Mark Heimermann explained in an interview by Deborah Evans Price for the liner notes to the 10th anniversary edition of the *Jesus Freak* album, the new material was approached with the goal of giving the project legs and producing something that the band could perform for years to come.

After a busy summer, the *Jesus Freak Single* was released to the wide market in August. The response was exactly what Toby had hoped for – people loved it. There was no need to change direction. After a few concerts in August, the next several weeks were spent really nailing down the rest of the album. Their eye was on a November release date. It was finished not a moment too soon; dc Talk was slated to take off on a fall tour with over two dozen stops throughout October and November. The new material was going to be given a trial by fire. While songs like "In the Light" had been tried out already, audiences were going to get their first tastes of "So Help Me God," "What if I Stumble?", and "Day by Day." Thankfully, the tour went well and the reception for the new songs was overwhelmingly positive. Hip-hop or no hip-hop, the crowd loved dc Talk.

Jesus Freak came out on November 21st, 1995. The album made its debut at #16 on the Billboard charts, sold over 85,000 copies, and smashed the record for a best-selling album released by a Christian artist. It sold half a million copies in a matter of weeks... a wildly brisk pace for *any* artist in *any* market.

Through the commercial success and artistic merit of *Jesus Freak*, dc Talk became one of the voices of their generation. And unlike many of their contemporaries and the aforementioned Nirvana, the members of dc Talk used their voices to explore hope, not hopelessness. They still explored pain, as their peers did, but they offered love and peace at the end of it. They looked at the deep interpersonal and relationship struggles that every person faces, and they showed how to approach it as part of a Christian walk.

The record was used to speak directly to a world that needed to hear its message. Their previous projects had devoted plenty of space to praise and worship, but *Jesus Freak* focused more on dissecting complex issues. The questions of what to do after jeopardizing friendships, how to manage the shame of messing up in a public way, and how to handle the struggle for forgiveness were themes that were analyzed from the standpoint of people who faced those positions daily. "When we were in school, the Bible was a textbook that we looked to for answers on our tests," Toby McKeehan explained many years later on the first

The Jesus Freak Era

Jesus Freak Cruise. "Life on the road taught us how to live it. We chopped things up and learned along the way."

A lot had changed in the three years since *Free at Last*. The *Jesus Freak* album was an insightful understanding of the Christian faith set to music and translated for a modern audience. It's not hyperbole to say that the record has had a lasting influence on the lives of hundreds of thousands of people. The value of dc Talk went beyond the well-oiled machinery of the record companies, the flawless choreography of the live shows, and the effortless harmonies on-stage. If there were any doubts that *Free at Last* was a fluke, this new material was proof that these three were true artists on an inspired mission.

dc Talk and their groundbreaking album *Jesus Freak* have withstood the test of time. It was one of the first "Christian" albums to truly transcend industry walls and connect with audiences on a worldwide level. And it continues to speak to every generation who hears it.

Jesus Freak Single

Before the internet was widely adopted, news traveled a bit more slowly. Even with all of the press surrounding dc Talk, there was no way for fans to keep track of the band's every move in real-time. When it came to the new rock and roll incarnation of dc Talk, it was primarily the record store where fans got their first hint of the new direction.

Placed unassumingly among the band's earlier material, the little black and blue CDs and cassettes enticed fans with the simple title "Jesus Freak." Those who hadn't been out to see dc Talk on the road lately had no idea what to expect. Fans who *had* seen them in concert over the summer had been given a chance to purchase a special version of the single: a "festival version" which had artwork resembling an old 45 record with 1970s typography. The festival version was no doubt a callback to the era when the word "Jesus Freak" had been used as a derogatory term for Christians. The record store version not only had additional material, but it had artwork that was much sleeker and more modern. It was designed by Toby and his sister, Kerri. The same style that Toby and Kerri came up with for the single was also used for the pre-release version of the actual *Jesus Freak* album.

Starting on August 1st, 1995, fans could spend a few dollars and take home their first taste of what was to come. Both the festival and the record store version of the single included the brand new song, a remix, and a cut from their 1994 tour. The record store

Jesus Freak Single

CD version contained an extra live track. With technology that was relatively new at the time (but never really caught on), CD owners could place the disc in their computer's optical drive to access a few videos of the band.

For anyone who had been a dc Talk fan from the early days, hearing the new single for the first time was probably one of the most confusing and exciting times ever had while listening to a dc Talk project. Nearly three years had elapsed since *Free at Last*, and most listeners had moved on from that brand of hip-hop. As the fans' musical tastes changed, lo and behold, it seemed dc Talk had changed along with them.

Track 1 was the full rock version of "Jesus Freak," but Track 2 was a remix of it with some of the old *Free at Last* style. Perhaps the band hadn't strayed far from their roots after all, listeners wondered. Track 3 was a live version of the apocalyptic ballad "I Wish We'd All Been Ready," a Larry Norman cover introduced during their 1994 tour. The bonus track, a live version of "Jesus is Just Alright," was safe and soothing ground for anyone confused by all of these changes. Both of the live songs were recorded at an April 9th, 1994 show in Auburn Hills, Michigan.

Response to the rock version of "Jesus Freak" had been good on the road, but success on the road didn't always translate to success in the marketplace. dc Talk nervously waited to see how the single would perform, both in stores and on the radio. They were knee-deep in their new album and had already committed a lot of energy toward changing course. There was still time to turn back, as the album wasn't slated to be released until the end of the year, but the dice had been rolled. Not only were they in unfamiliar waters, but they had to prove themselves in a new genre. Along with that came the understanding that some fans and institutions would be reluctant to accept such a secular sound for a "Christian" band. The hip-hop remix was a "safety net" of sorts, though... an insurance policy that reassured any nervous consumers that dc Talk could still churn out hip-hop, too.

Whatever worries that anyone had about the single failing turned out to be unjustified. The rock version of the song was an instant hit. The single moved briskly (partially due to a clever marketing strategy where thousands of free discs were sent out to youth leaders across the country), and it even gained mainstream attention. dc Talk had taken the leap and had landed solidly on their feet.

For all that's been written about the *Jesus Freak Single* and its significance, one of the most remarkable things about the transition was that the band had intentionally dropped a known, winning formula to undergo a complete metamorphosis – and they'd survived to tell about it. Truly, most artists who attempt these types of transitions are heckled back to their regular stomping grounds. The phenomenon of dc Talk's evolution says quite a bit about the group, their talent, their willingness to take calculated risks, the goodwill they'd built up with fans, and their understanding of the where the music industry was at. This wasn't a group of people who would ever be content to rest on their laurels. Apparently, their fans wouldn't be, either.

Notes About the Different Versions

A quick summary of some of the changes mentioned earlier: the festival-only version (the print that looks like an old record) contained "Jesus Freak," the "Jesus Freak (Gotee Bros. Freaked Out Remix)," and a live version of "I Wish We'd All Been Ready." The retail version (commonly called the AVCD version) had the same three tracks plus a live version of "Jesus is Just Alright." Video interviews of the band were available if the listener placed the CD into a computer. The retail cassette version had the same tracklisting as the festival-only version, but it had some exclusive artwork on the inside folds.

Jesus Freak Single Track 01:
Jesus Freak (song)

If the first few seconds of a chewy acoustic guitar, amp noise, and the songwriter saying "Jesus Freaktus" wasn't a good enough clue that dc Talk had changed a bit, then the wall of distorted guitars punctuated by a catchy Kevin Max vocalization certainly was. This was rock and roll. "No More" and "Time Is" had tried this formula before, but neither had been standout tracks... nor had they just completely *gone for it* the way that "Jesus Freak" did. Luckily, just as some fans were wondering if there was something wrong with their cassette player, the verse brought everything back to familiar territory. The song's hypnotic beat and Michael Tait's voice carried that traditional dc Talk vibe, and by the time the rock guitars flared up again and Toby McKeehan's rap cut through the madness, most listeners were up to speed. dc Talk had effortlessly made the transition from hip-hop stars to alternative rockers, and they were executing the style as if they'd owned it for years. The main riff and the bridge solo are among some of the best segments of rock ever produced on any album by any band, and the bridge (repeated almost as a chant) provided a catchy phrase that rivaled the chorus itself.

"Jesus Freak" was the first shot fired in dc Talk's alternative revolution. Much more will be said about "Jesus Freak's" chart performance, impact, and legacy in the chapter on the album itself, so for now, we'll skip our CD players to Track 2: the "Gotee Bros. Freaked Out Remix."

Jesus Freak Single Track 02:
Jesus Freak (Gotee Bros. "Freaked Out" Remix)

During the *Free at Last* era, Toby McKeehan started a record label called "Gotee Records" with his colleagues Joey Elwood and Todd Collins. Originally only a production outfit to help launch the group Out of Eden, the label continued to grow and began to house several acts. Today, Gotee counts among its alumni the group GRITS (who started as dc Talk's backup dancers), Zilch (who started as dc Talk's backup band, later renamed Sonicflood), Reliant K, Family Force Five, the Katinas, and many others.

Like his early work with dc Talk, much of Toby's early work with Gotee was in the hip-hop genre. GRITS' first album, *Mental Releases*, was being put together at the same time as the *Jesus Freak Single*, and the two projects even came out on the same date. It was natural for the Gotee Brothers (McKeehan, Elwood, and Collins) to take a stab at "Jesus Freak" as well, especially considering that Collins was doing production work on the new album and the Gotee Brothers had remixed "Luv is a Verb" for dc Talk's *Free at Last EP* project.

The Gotee Remix was a smart inclusion; it was placed on the single almost as if to prove to consumers that yes, believe it not, that *was* actually dc Talk that they'd just heard. The market could enjoy dc Talk's hip-hop phase just a little bit longer if they chose to do so.

Jesus Freak Single

The "Jesus Freak" remix was much more effective than their "Luv is a Verb" remix. The track took the haunted feel of the verses and extended that mood throughout the entire song, while the impressive guitar riff was replaced by an equally impressive bass riff. New vocals were peppered throughout, including an exclusive rap verse from Toby during the bridge. It was hard to tell, but it sounded like the chorus was thickened out with new vocals from the Gotee Brothers themselves.

Live Versions:
During the introduction portion of 1996 Freak Show concerts, Otto "Sugar Bear" Price played the bass riff from the Gotee Remix and Toby performed the remix's exclusive rap verse. On the next major concert series, 1999's Supernatural Experience Tour, Toby and Otto "Sugar Bear" Price again performed the segment together, though this time Otto was McKeehan's hype man instead of his bassist for that part of the show. They also performed throwback verses from "Heavenbound" and "Nu Thang."

Jesus Freak Single Track 03:
I Wish We'd All Been Ready (live)

dc Talk's extended stage time on the *Free at Last Tour* had included an acoustic set. While "The Hardway" and "40" were beautiful moments in this new part of the show, "I Wish We'd All Been Ready" was by far the most solemn moment of the night.

Written by pioneer Christian artist Larry Norman for his 1969 album *Upon This Rock*, Norman's version of the song had been received well but had never reached its full potential. In a scene on *Narrow is the Road*, Norman explained to the band that he was sometimes too emotional to perform the song because of the frighteningly realistic possibility that all of it could come to pass. Norman noted an appreciation for the version dc Talk's sang, as they were able to end the song with a more positive message of hope for the future instead of the finality of the end times.

A video of the band performing the song was included on *Narrow is the Road*, and the clip was subsequently played on television shows covering the Christian music industry. It became one of dc Talk's most popular cover songs.

To repay the band for their support, Larry Norman covered "Jesus Freak" at the Flevo Festival in the Netherlands in 1998. His version was even edgier than dc Talk's, with a bridge solo that took some interesting turns and verses rapped by Norman himself.

Jesus Freak Single

Larry Norman, a "Jesus Freak before there were Jesus Freaks" as Kevin Max once put it, passed away on February 24th, 2008 at the age of 60. To celebrate his legacy, Kevin Max is in the process of creating a much-anticipated tribute album.

Other Live Versions:
At a few concerts in 1994, the band performed the song with Larry Norman himself. One of the most significant of these was at the American Christian Music Awards. A video can be found online.

During 1996's Freak Show Tour, the song remained part of the show's acoustic set.

It doesn't seem to have been played again until 2017's Jesus Freak Cruise, during which Kevin Max gave a crushing performance during the bridge. It was also brought back for the 2019 cruise.

Jesus Freak Single Track 04:
Jesus is Just Alright (live)

Simply titled "Live Bonus Cut" on the disc jacket, this high-energy fan-favorite was the perfect song to round out the single. While most of the disc is dedicated to moving on and evolving, this cut gives the project a firm foot in the past.

It's difficult to say if this exact recording is unique to this release, as a live version of "Jesus is Just Alright" can be found on the *Free at Last* movie, too. The movie version references San Jose in the middle of the song, but some of the underlying tracks and vocal takes seem to have come from this particular recording. Only purists and collectors will care about such things, but this recording does appear to be mostly unique. It's been heavily edited in a few regards, though, and the "strike a pose" segment was shortened.

Many of the performances of "Jesus is Just Alright" from this era still had the backing track. The various tracked elements and vocals are obvious in this recording. To hear a straighter performance of the song from the same tour, check out the "Jesus is Just Alright" clip from the 1994 Dove Awards on internet video sites, as it contained only live vocals.

Much more about "Jesus is Just Alright" can be found in the *Free at Last* chapter.

Jesus Freak (album)

At this point, there was little doubt that *Jesus Freak* would be a success. The single was doing well. The new material was getting a warm reception on the 1995 fall tour. As the year was wrapping up, it was time for dc Talk to take their new sound to the masses.

Jesus Freak was released on November 21st, 1995. The album was an instant smash hit. As *USA Today* noted in Ann Oldenburg's "DC Talk Blessed With Success" article on December 4th, 1995, it had "the biggest first-week sales for a Christian album ever." To compare, Michael W. Smith's 1995 album had sold just over 50,000 and Amy Grant's 1994 project *House of Love* had moved 55,000. *Jesus Freak* sold over 85,000.

As the weeks went by, sales continued to mount exponentially. They totaled over half a million in a matter of weeks, allowing the album to achieve Gold status on January 17th, 1996. Before 1996 was over, *Jesus Freak* had gone Platinum (Double Platinum was achieved in less than five years, awarded on October 25th, 2000). This album was not only dc Talk's best-selling project, but it was also one of the most commercially successful Christian music records of all time.

Jesus Freak's success led to a mainstream distribution deal with Virgin Records. Thanks to this partnership, dc Talk's new singles achieved widespread radio play for the first time ever. It also earned the group a 1996 award for Billboard Contemporary

Christian Album, garnered two Billboard Music Video Awards, a Grammy for Best Rock Gospel Album, seven Dove Awards, and numerous other accolades.

The following pages explore this pinnacle of dc Talk's career. The creation of the album, the musical nuances, the live expressions of the songs, the rare and alternate versions, and the market's reception to each of these masterpieces will be examined in-depth. As they say on "So Help Me God," let's go for a ride!

Jesus Freak Album Track 01:
So Help Me God

Jesus Freak was a very different animal from previous dc Talk albums. If the single released over the summer hadn't convinced the public that the landscape was changing, "So Help Me God" left absolutely no doubt.

The mellow guitar arpeggios at the beginning of the album might fool a listener into thinking that it's going to be a quiet journey. It's not. And when Toby announces "I've got something for you man" and the wall of distorted guitar riffs comes up, it's clear that the band indeed *does* have something for you.

The song begins with a very "Kevin Max" vocal motif and a rap verse from Toby through a grungy telephone effect. A mid-tempo rock beat drives the Minor Tonic - Subdominant chord structure... a fancy way of saying that the music has the same backbone as many of the old jazz and boogie-woogie standards. Here, the chords are harnessed by rock guitars and overdriven solos. While the riffs and the melodies sharpen a modern edge, Mark Heimermann's B-3 organ maintains some of the throwback feel.

Music buffs familiar with the band's work (or readers who have made it through the chapter on *Free at Last*) might notice that the main chord progression for "So Help Me God" is the same as *Free at Last's* "Word 2 the Father." Is it a coincidence that the *last* main song of the third album and the *first* song of the fourth album share the same key and underlying musical structure? Or is it an incredible display of continuity between albums, the like of which is rarely seen even amongst the most meticulous artists? It doesn't matter. The songs work so well together that during the fall 1995 shows, they were placed in the same block. Performing them this way probably made the group's transition between styles a bit more palatable for those who were reluctant to give up their hip-hop and move into mid-90s alternative rock.

Apparently, the original demo of the song wasn't nearly as powerful as the final product. Todd Collins had this to say in Justin Sarachik's January 15th, 2016 *CCM Magazine* article titled "'Jesus Freak' at 20, Part Two": "This was not one of the first songs we demoed... [The final album version] sounds vastly different than the demo, which was a lot more intimate." It was Dann Huff and his monster guitar riffs that turned "So Help Me God" into the high-octane powerhouse that allowed the band to steer away from the *Free at Last* sound and plant their flag somewhere new. Huff earned a co-writing credit for his trouble.

One of the neatest "dc Talk artifacts" made available to guests on the 2017 Jesus Freak Cruise was the actual notebook that Toby used while he was writing the lyrics to "So Help Me God." Scrawled on its pages were dozens of unused lyric fragments and several unused verses. There were also ideas for songs and different titles that have never been finished or released, as well as general thoughts for the record and sample tracklistings. Other mementos from the band's storied career were on display, too, but this was by far the crown jewel. Some fans, given full access to this item for the first time ever, went as far as photographing every single page.

Single:
"So Help Me God" was released as the band's first single of 1997. It did well in the Christian Rock charts, making it all the way up to number 3. It was considered a good showing, as the album

had already been out for a year and the band had finished touring for it.

Alternate Versions:
A live version of the song from dc Talk's 1996 tour can be heard on the *Welcome to the Freak Show* album.

The *Jesus Freak 10th Anniversary Special Edition* contained a remix of the song called the "Savadocious Junk Yard Mix 1974." The piano-based remix was created by producer / musician Jeff Savage. It emphasizes the chord progression's rich roots from older rock and roll numbers. Before remixing tracks for the *Jesus Freak* re-release, Savage had done a lot of production work for TobyMac's first two albums and had co-written the TobyMac song "Atmosphere," a song remixed by dc Talk in 2004 during one of their rare post-break-up collaborations.

Another interesting take on the song appeared on the 2006 *Freaked!* tribute album, a project produced by Toby McKeehan's Gotee Records to celebrate the tenth anniversary of the *Jesus Freak* record. The disc consisted of various artists under the Gotee label trying their hands at covering dc Talk tracks. The cover of "So Help Me God" was recorded by a metal band called The Showdown.

Live Versions:
This rousing, high-energy number was a mainstay on the 1995 and 1996 tours, but it's only been performed a few times since. On the 1995 fall tour, it was played during the opening moments of the show after the group had performed the "Jesus is Just Alright" reprise. On the 1996 Freak Show Tour, the band opened the show with a cover of the Beatles' "Help!" and again led straight into "So Help Me God." The live version of the song was pure rock and roll with a modern lighting and video effects rig added to appeal to younger audiences.

A great version of the song, including the full *Jesus Freak* album intro, was performed during a Billy Graham Crusade on October 25th, 1997 in Oakland, California. Toby had trouble remembering the lyrics to the first verse, but he improvised his way out of a tough spot so convincingly that even the most die-hard fans wondered if he'd composed a new verse just for that show.

As the 2017 Jesus Freak Cruise was coming together, many fans were hopeful that "deeper cuts" would appear on the setlist – songs that had sat on the shelf collecting dust during the group's final tours in the late 1990s and early 2000s. "So Help Me God" was one of the fanbase's most-requested songs, and the noise may have done some good. "Help!" and "So Help Me God" were performed in tandem on the cruise as the band's encore piece as a nostalgic throwback to the opening of dc Talk's greatest tour. On the 2019 cruise, the performance was repeated, but this time at the *start* of the show. When the lights went down and the musicians roared to life, dc Talk rose onto the stage via a large platform elevator just as the first chords of "Help!" were played.

Video:
A live performance from 1996 can be seen on the *Welcome to the Freak Show* VHS/DVD release.

Jesus Freak Album Track 02:
Colored People

This earnest track about racial equality spotlights Kevin Max like never before. It was co-written by George Cocchini, a musician who also played guitars on the track and had co-written songs like "Luv is a Verb" and "Time Is" for the previous album.

Jesus Freak is known for its great riffs, and the distorted guitar passage that kicks off "Colored People" is one of the best examples. A little known fact about the song: the chord progression for the verses in "Colored People" is actually the same chord progression used for the verses in "Jesus Freak" – it's just modulated five half-steps higher. What a difference in tone though, as the verses in "Jesus Freak" are like a slow hypnotic stare and the verses in "Colored People" are folksy and inspiring.

While "So Help Me God" still featured Toby McKeehan at the front of the group with a rap influence, "Colored People" was a major shift in balance. McKeehan, who remained the principal songwriter of the group, revealed in interviews that the shift in duties was an intentional move on his part. With the change in sound on *Jesus Freak*, he wanted to showcase Michael Tait and Kevin Max a lot more than he had in the past.

"Colored People" was also significant to dc Talk because the group, since its inception, had strived to exemplify the idea of "living integration." Made up of different cultures, nationalities, and diverse backgrounds, dc Talk and their crew were never shy about tackling the conversation about race in America head-on. Like "Walls" from *Nu Thang*, this song served as an anthem that reflected their desire to explore important social issues. The mainstream market had pegged them as evangelists, but obviously, there were many *more* layers to dc Talk's message. "Colored People," like many of dc Talk's songs, was much more than a religious statement.

Single:
A mainstream, radio-ready sound and a well-crafted music video catapulted "Colored People" to the top of *almost* every Christian music chart. The song rose to the top of the usual Christian music rotations *except* for the Christian Adult Contemporary chart where it just barely missed nabbing number one.

A physical promo single was sent out to radio stations. It contained a shorter edit of the song and a ten-second "call out research hook" (used by broadcasters to gauge how recognizable a song or band is). The cover art on the promo featured a rendering of four hands, each a different color, reaching out and holding onto each other. The same design was reproduced in the background of the music video, too.

Alternate Versions:
The "Groove Mix" and "Organic Mix" are very rare, stripped-down versions of the song that offer a sublime, intimate take on "Colored People." Containing only vocals, acoustic guitars, strings, and some very basic percussion and bass, these incredible mixes are almost impossible to find on the collector's market. It's well worth the trouble to find at least one of them, though, as most fans prefer these to the album version.

The "Groove Mix" was featured on a micro-sized CD promo released by ForeFront Records called *three and three-forths* [sic], the overall name referring to the disc's smaller size and the "forths" misspelling referring to the name of ForeFront Records. In addition to the "Groove Mix," the disc also contained tracks by Rebecca St. James and a brief introduction by dc Talk for radio stations to use as a liner. The "Organic Mix," a similar track, was included on a very rare promo disc shipped with early copies of the *Welcome to the Freak Show* VHS. It's a little easier to find than the "Groove Mix." If neither can be located, a decent substitute can be found on internet video sites that list dc Talk's 1997 Dove Awards performance of "Colored People." It had much of the same instrumentation and feel.

A note for collectors: the only difference between the "Groove Mix" and the "Organic Mix" is that the "Groove Mix" contains a subdued version of Toby's bridge rap and the "Organic Mix" eliminates the passage entirely.

On the 2006 *Freaked!* Gotee tribute to *Jesus Freak*, the "Colored People" cover was performed by Ayiesha Woods and John Reuben. In a *very* rare appearance, the Gotee Brothers themselves were also featured.

Live Versions:
"Colored People" was added to the setlist during 1996's Freak Show Tour. Since then, rarely has a dc Talk show been performed without it. Throughout every tour, the band has had a tradition of sharing their experiences and beliefs related to overcoming racism before performing the song.

One of the best performances was at the 1997 Dove Awards where the group delivered a stripped-down version of the song. Michael Tait gave a rare exhibition of his acoustic guitar skills while a violinist accompanied him. An interesting concept played out on-stage while the trio sang the song: the prolific artist and Ragamuffin band member Jimmy Abegg painted a work of art on a giant canvas in real-time right behind the band as they performed.

During 1999's Supernatural Experience Tour, the song was capped off with the chorus from John Lennon's "Give Peace a Chance." During the summer, the group reunited with Michael W. Smith and played an acoustic version of the song to a crowd in Kansas. Both legs of the Solo Tour also featured the song, as did the shows on the Jesus Freak Cruises.

One of the best parts of seeing "Colored People" performed live is witnessing the improvisational style that Kevin Max takes with the verses. Despite singing the song hundreds of times in his life, rarely are any two takes ever exactly the same.

Videos:
The concept video was straightforward and effective, scrolling through a diverse cast of people with simple but evocative words and imagery behind them. The video won a 1998 Dove Award for Short Form Music Video of the Year.

A live video performance of the song can be found on the *Welcome to the Freak Show* VHS/DVD project. The DVD version also includes the music video.

E.R.A.C.E Foundation:
"Colored People" represented more than a belief system for all of dc Talk and the support staff around them. To further live out these beliefs, dc Talk was instrumental in creating an organization called the E.R.A.C.E. Foundation. Standing for "Eliminating Racism and Creating Equality," the E.R.A.C.E Foundation was the result of years of discussion, reflection, and efforts to promote healing and partnerships in our communities. According to literature released by the group in 1997: "Priorities for the foundation include increased communication among historically

divided groups and the healing of long-standing social rifts. Targeted for the 15-25 year-old age group, E.R.A.C.E. programs include campus outreach, a series of issue-oriented public service announcements, special events and an Internet website."

In 1996, TobyMac participated heavily in the creation of Gotee Record's *E.R.A.C.E.* album, a project that examined cultural issues through music. It featured contributions from many dc Talk, Gotee Records, and ForeFront Records alumni. The project is hard to track down, but any dc Talk fan will find it to be an artistic triumph worth the pursuit.

Jesus Freak Album Track 03:
Jesus Freak (song)

One of the greatest guitar riffs of all time kicks off the title track of dc Talk's best-selling album, *Jesus Freak*.

As mentioned previously, the verses share a chord progression pattern with "Colored People," but the similarities end there. On "Jesus Freak," the progression is forged into a spacy, pulsating rhythm with just a slight undercurrent of aggression. It gives way easily to a guitar-laced rap delivered with an unbridled enthusiasm that hadn't been seen from McKeehan since he shamelessly shouted the words to "Heavenbound" in what seemed like a lifetime before.

During the verses, the words turn inward on the narrator. During the raps, the song tells the stories of "Jesus Freaks" from yesterday and today. The chorus gels things together with lyrics that rise defiantly in a proclamation of faith. "Jesus Freak" is both an unapologetic stand for Christianity and an embrace / rebranding of a term that once had negative connotations. In four minutes and fifty seconds, the years of social persecution are reframed and redefined.

Just as the lyrics defy the cultural status quo, the guitar solo over the bridge defies conventional music theory. Which is probably why it works so well. One of the song's most masterful flourishes is the staccato vocal lick from Kevin Max that punctuates the track throughout. It's become so intimately identified with "Jesus

Jesus Freak

Freak" that those simple two or three monotone notes can bring an entire arena to its feet with anticipation.

"Jesus Freak" is a stand against persecution, an anthem for the unflinching, and a tribute to the expression of Christian faith. It's all-inclusive – from the everyday person on the street to extreme expressions like the martyrdom of John the Baptist. It's a battle cry for those who wish to stand up. These weren't new concepts for dc Talk, but they had never been packaged together so passionately.

Perhaps some of the spirit of this song came from the place that the final lyrics were written. Toby McKeehan had finished the song in South Africa. With the political climate and effects of apartheid felt across the area, some of the energies of persecution may have inspired these powerful, uncompromising words.

The band Nirvana was also a huge influence on the song. dc Talk has openly discussed Kurt Cobain's influence on them during this time. The wool cardigans, the grunge flavor to their music, and even Kevin Max's look took cues from the trail that Nirvana had blazed. The verse's chords in "Jesus Freak" were almost identical to Nirvana's "Heart-Shaped Box." Later in the song, the outro lyrics served as both a tribute and an interesting twist to one of Nirvana's last songs: the "What else can I say? Jesus is the way" phrase is an inversion of Nirvana's "What else can I say? Everyone is gay." Since "Jesus Freak" was often described as "unapologetic," how interesting it is that McKeehan included a brief parody of Nirvana's "All Apologies" at the end of the song. In live performances, this parallel was emphasized quite a bit more with the band performing *several* bars from the Nirvana classic. Fans who own a deep collection will find that their bootleg copy of the "Jesus Freak" performance at CreationFest 1996 was the best example of this.

"Jesus Freak" won a Dove Award in 1996 for Rock Recorded Song of the Year. dc Talk performed the song at the same ceremony.

Single:
Discussed earlier in the book, the single released in August 1995 was a game-changer for the band. When Virgin Records reached out and tried to bring dc Talk to the mainstream market, another single promo disc was produced for radio stations. The disc contained the album version, an edited version with the bridge shortened, and a brief "call-out" research hook.

The song easily captured the number one spot on the Christian Rock charts and very nearly charted on Billboard's Top 100 mainstream singles chart. The number of awards and accolades that "Jesus Freak" has received could fill a book of their own, but one of the honors worth mentioning is that it was ranked as the second-best Christian music track of all time by *CCM Magazine*. On their ranking, "Jesus Freak" is sandwiched between Rich Mullins' "Awesome God" at number one and Michael W. Smith's "Friends" at number three. That's pretty good company.

Alternate Versions:
The intro portion to the album version of the track (the part with the tinny guitar and Toby singing the chorus) appears to be some kind of original demo for the song. A few more seconds of it can be heard in a trailer for *Free At Last: The Movie*.

The 1995 "Gotee Remix" has been discussed already, but a 2006 remix of the song has not. When *Jesus Freak* was re-released for its tenth anniversary, a new remix by Jeff Savage was included. His version dropped the electric guitars for dirty, aggressive drum samples and tight, springy piano chords.

Covers of "Jesus Freak" are far too numerous to mention, but notable ones include the two on *Freaked!* (Gotee's tribute album):

the compilation included a cover by 4th Avenue Jones and one by the group Chasing Victory. Another notable cover is the Newsboys version that appeared on 2010's *Born Again* – the first Newsboys record with Michael Tait as the lead singer. What better way to bridge the gap between the two bands than by covering "Jesus Freak"? The rap on that version was performed by artist KJ-52. Interestingly, several songs on the *Born Again* album were co-written with former dc Talk dancer Juan Otero, a talented songwriter who went on to have tracks recorded by several well-known artists.

Live Versions:
"Jesus Freak" was quickly introduced to the dc Talk setlist once it was written, and it's remained there ever since. It's one of the only songs to survive the demise of dc Talk, too, since it's usually the only dc Talk song performed at TobyMac, Newsboys, and Kevin Max solo concerts. Each member puts their unique stamp on it, of course. Michael Tait seems reluctant to perform the rap parts. Kevin Max used to be, too, but in recent years he's had no qualms about it. The "Jesus Freak" rap even turns up in unexpected places when his band riffs and jams to other songs. More recently, Michael Tait has invited pre-selected audience members on-stage to perform the song *with* him, making for once-in-a-lifetime experiences for many hardcore dc Talk fans.

"Jesus Freak" was typically performed during dc Talk's encore. The 1999 Supernatural Experience Tour had an interesting voiceover introduction: "Some, no doubt, will find this record amusing. Some will find it a novelty. No doubt, some will find it repulsive and bordering on heresy. It is not intended as such."

The *Supernatural* concerts also featured a segment before the guitar solo where the music would drop out and the band would freeze for over half a minute. It was an eerie effect that TobyMac later repeated at solo performances. At some *Supernatural* shows, the crowd was so enthralled by the band's performance that dc Talk came back out and performed "Jesus Freak" a second time.

Along with "Jesus is Just Alright" and several tunes from the *Jesus Freak* album, the song has appeared at almost every dc Talk show since it was recorded.

Videos:
For the music video, dc Talk sought out a director named Simon Maxwell. Maxwell had achieved widespread recognition for his work with the secular group Nine Inch Nails. He was hired to bring the same aesthetic over to the "Jesus Freak" video.

The video features new voiceovers and film clips with religious symbolism, much of it related to persecution. Several scenes feature the band in what appears to be a dark jail cell or an interrogation room. The imagery is bold and thematic. While modern audiences can clearly recognize that it was made in the 1990s because of its style, the video has aged much better than dc Talk's earlier work.

If the goal was to create something that would cause people to sit up and take notice, it worked. For starters, the choice of Simon Maxwell as director proved to be a controversial one because of his background with mainstream musical acts. Also, many in the Christian music industry were turned off by the dark, haunting imagery of the video. A November 11th, 1995 article by Brett Atwood in *Billboard Magazine* called it "one of the most progressive religious music clips ever released," but not everyone on the evangelical side saw that as a good thing. dc Talk stood by their choices and they stood by Maxwell, stating that their goal had always been to "push the envelope" – not with what they could "get away with," but by leaving their comfort zone and meeting the culture where it was at.

The negative reaction must have been disappointing, especially since the video contained no ambiguity about its message or the beliefs of the band. Simon Maxwell did a tremendous job of coming up with visuals to match the spirit and intensity of the song. The video looked as good as anything else on the mainstream marketplace, a simple fact that should have taken nothing away from the message that dc Talk was trying to convey. In that same *Billboard Magazine* article, the director took the controversy in stride: "There will obviously be some people who miss the point entirely or who interpret this differently," he said. "But you can't please everybody. That would be completely bland."

Controversy gave way to triumph as other Christian artists followed dc Talk's example and a wave of more progressive music videos hit the airwaves. dc Talk's approach was validated further when the concept video for "Jesus Freak" won a Dove Award for Short Form Music Video of the Year in 1997.

Two other video projects related to "Jesus Freak" exist. One is a videotaped performance of a show from the 1996 US tour. The other is a music video featuring a compilation of clips from the 1996 European tour. Both can be found on the *Welcome to the Freak Show* VHS/DVD project.

Jesus Freak Album Track 04:
What If I Stumble?

dc Talk had been affected by their rise to fame, but not in the same ways as most newly minted celebrities. "What If I Stumble?"—the most nuanced and vulnerable entry in dc Talk's entire discography—showed where their true concerns were. Were they doing this for money or for God? Would they make a mistake and alienate people from Christianity? As more and more young people looked to them as role models, the road became narrower and their fears were amplified to the same degree as their platform.

The quote at the beginning was an inspired choice: "The greatest single cause of atheism in the world today is Christians who acknowledge Jesus with their lips then walk out the door and deny Him by their lifestyle. That is what an unbelieving world simply finds unbelievable." It described the penalty of failure in real terms. The words were spoken by Brennan Manning, one of the most fascinating authors and evangelists of the modern era. Chapters of Manning's life include a stint as a priest in Pennsylvania, a job as a college professor, six months in a Spanish desert living in a cave, a prison sentence in Switzerland, and several years among the poor in Alabama. During the time of 1994 Free at Last Tour, dc Talk had a chance to spend time with him in New Orleans. The "What if I Stumble?" quote was captured as Manning fellowshipped with the group in prayer and communion.

Like a true examination of any real moral conflict or base fear, "What If I Stumble?" is better at *asking* questions than at *answering* them. Earlier work by dc Talk would've simply offered a theological solution right away. In "What If I Stumble?" the questions linger much longer. The song works through the toll of relationships and public perception regardless of the spiritual answers that can be found. Every statement in the chorus can be followed by a question mark. After exploring these feelings for almost a full five minutes, Toby offers a resolution: "You are my comfort and my God." This one line is the only reassurance that the song is able to provide.

Apart from the universal fears that the song taps into, "What If I Stumble?" resonates so well with audiences because its quiet, acoustic setting really showcases the magic of dc Talk. The loud drums, distorted guitars, and electronic effects are nice, but they're not always necessary. Like the "Colored People (Organic Mix)" and the *Jesus Freak Single's* "I Wish We'd All Been Ready," the track is a raw, unfiltered look at the true talent and cohesiveness of the dc Talk sound.

Even critics agree. In 2006, "What If I Stumble?" was ranked #31 in *CCM Magazine's* list of "100 Greatest Songs in Christian Music."

Single:
"What If I Stumble?" was released to Christian radio as a single in 1996 (less than a year after it had made its debut on the *Jesus Freak* album). Reaction was strong. It went number one on the main Christian chart for six weeks and it peaked at number three on the Adult Contemporary chart.

Alternate Versions:
An instrumental of the song (with a few backing vocals) can be found on a rare karaoke cassette release that was distributed in

the late 1990s. The haunting, "living-room" live version of "What If I Stumble?" can be found on 1997's *Welcome to the Freak Show* disc.

On the *Jesus Freak 10th Anniversary* project, a remix by "DoubleDutch" (musicians Josiah Bell and Robert Marvin) gave the chorus a much more positive musical theme. The melancholy riff of the original song doesn't appear until the bridge.

Sarah Kelly provided the piano-based remix of the song for the Gotee Records *Freaked!* tribute album. Around the same time, Kelly was releasing her album *Where the Past Meets Today*. The project received great accolades, charted on the Billboard Top 200, and earned her a Grammy nomination. She released one more record with Gotee before changing careers a bit and becoming the worship leader at a church near Houston, Texas. Live videos of her performing "What If I Stumble?" can still be found online.

Live Versions:
"What if I Stumble?" has been a mainstay of dc Talk's acoustic set ever since its introduction at the 1995 *Jesus Freak* shows. It was shortened a bit and a bass riff was emphasized for the 1999 Supernatural Tour.

One of the nicer performances was during the first leg of the Solo Tour. Toby gave a lengthy introduction to the song that explained how he should've titled it "What *When* I Stumble?" since for human beings, failure is inevitable. The song was also performed on both of the Jesus Freak Cruises, with the 2019 version sounding a bit different by blending the best elements from both the Freak Show Tour and the Supernatural Experience Tour.

Jesus Freak

Video:
Video from a live performance of the song can be found on the *Welcome to the Freak Show* VHS/DVD project.

Jesus Freak Album Track 05:
Day By Day

"The song we wrote in our sleep," as Kevin Max famously described it at several concerts during the era. "A song about baby steps."

Even behind all of the distorted guitars, fans of the 1971 musical *Godspell* by Stephen Schwartz and John-Michael Tebelak will recognize it as soon as the chorus starts up. Covered by everyone from The 5th Dimension to Andy Williams to even Homer Simpson, "Day by Day" is a pop-culture gem that actually originated as a 13th Century prayer by Saint Richard of Chichester. It's survived the centuries to become a widely appreciated, radio-friendly hit.

"Jesus is Just Alright" and "Lean on Me" had been popular on *Free at Last*, so covering songs from a couple decades back wasn't anything new for dc Talk. Though producers and album personnel have made reference to having been less than enthusiastic about including it on *Jesus Freak*, "Day by Day" became one of the most enjoyable songs on the dc Talk setlist for many years.

Much of that is due to the new verses written by Toby and Kevin Max. Building around a classic is never an easy task, but the verses are so solid and timeless that they sound like they've always been there.

Jesus Freak

The roster of musicians on the album recording sessions included some familiar faces from the road: Otto "Sugarbear" Price and Brent Barcus from dc Talk's touring band joined the fray on bass and guitar. Mark Heimermann got to bust out his B-3 organ skills for the track, while Todd Collins of the Gotee Brothers used percussion and loops to enhance David L. Huff's drums. *Jesus Freak* studio pros Oran Thornton and Dann Huff added rock guitars to this and several other tracks on the record.

Single:
"Day by Day" was released as a single in 1997 (over a year after *Jesus Freak* had been on the market). It charted well on Christian Rock listings.

Alternate Versions:
"Day by Day" was the only song to not have a remix, live version, or instrumental featured on the second disc of the *Jesus Freak 10th Anniversary* project.

House of Heroes, one of the longest-running alternative rock groups in the Christian market, covered the song on the *Freaked!* tribute album. It was a pretty straight-forward cover aside from a new riff introduced halfway through the intro and some faster guitar work during the last half of the chorus.

Live Versions:
"Day by Day" was an exciting part of both the Freak Show and Supernatural Experience tours. The song was a mainstay at crusade and festival dates, though it was conspicuously absent from the 2017 Jesus Freak Cruise. On the 2019 Jesus Freak Cruise, it made a triumphant return as the final song of the band's encore. If dc Talk never takes the stage again, it'll be the last song that they ever performed together as a trio.

Video:
During a lull in dc Talk releases before their next major album,

Supernatural, the group recorded a concept video for "Day by Day." The video features a man toiling away by himself in gritty conditions with only a single lightbulb and a rodent (who gets way too much screen time for most people's tastes) to keep him company. Individual shots of the band members are peppered throughout. The angles and color saturation are typical 1990s. Toward the end of the video, the subject washes himself and breaks the lightbulb as he exits.

Perhaps because it was made in an "in-between" year, the video for "Day by Day" doesn't appear on most of dc Talk's music video collections.

Jesus Freak Album Track 06:
Mrs. Morgan

dc Talk's new studio, The House of Insomnia, was located in a fairly residential strip of Franklin, Tennessee. Naturally, they had next-door neighbors: an older couple named Richard and Katherine Morgan.

For some of the *Jesus Freak* sessions, dc Talk employed live drummers: Aaron Smith, Scott Williamson, Shawn McWilliams, Todd Collins, David L. Huff, and even Will Denton (their touring drummer) contributed live drum tracks for the album. Live drummers are loud, especially when they're only a few walls and a small yard away.

After receiving a couple of complaints from the Morgans, dc Talk and the Gotee Brothers went out of their way to be neighborly. Once the late-night drumming sessions were toned down, the Morgans warmed to them. When promotional items for dc Talk's album and concerts were shot on the studio's property, the Morgans were even good sports about it and allowed themselves to be recorded for the *Free at Last* movie, the Freak Show Tour promo video, and the *Jesus Freak* and *Intermission* albums.

The charm of the "Mrs. Morgan" track isn't in the intergenerational conflict, nor is it because of the "rapping grandma" gag that was so popular in the 1990s (see Adam Sandler's *The Wedding Singer* for a classic example). The draw is that her Tennessee charm and newfound affection for these unruly neighbors comes through in her story. Mrs. Morgan's inclusion on the *Jesus Freak* record definitely brought her "15 minutes of fame," as she later called it, and she was a well-loved addition to dc Talk fandom. It wasn't hard to figure out where dc Talk's studio was, so fans who found themselves in Franklin, Tennessee often stopped by Mrs. Morgan's house to say hello. Many got their picture with her. There used to be a social media account that collected these but sadly, the account and its content have been lost.

Jesus Freak Album Track 07:
Between You and Me

The members of dc Talk were close, but the stress of living together, touring together, and creating art together for so many years could sometimes take its toll. Being in business with anyone is tough, and it's even tougher when so much time is spent on a small bus, in a cramped studio, or hitting the stage together with unresolved conflicts. In that kind of environment, battle scars are unavoidable.

The song "Between You and Me" came out of these difficult situations. Written by Toby McKeehan and Mark Heimermann, it's a song about the basic need to love someone enough to break through someone's own sorrow, anger, and ego. As Toby explained on the 2017 Jesus Freak Cruise, once the three members of dc Talk had left college and hit the road together, the Bible ceased being a "textbook" and it became a living example of how to treat each other. Fans had always known that the song was born out of various conflicts that members had over the years, and some of those conflicts were made public, but the particulars are irrelevant in the grand scheme of the song. The song is about working to make amends. Toby often cites Ephesians 4:26 when discussing his inspiration, which reads, in part: "Do not let the sun go down on your anger."

One of the strongest tracks on the album both musically and lyrically, "Between You and Me" is one of dc Talk's most radio-friendly hits. It served as a major mainstream breakthrough track for them, thanks largely to a partnership with Virgin Records. In the secular market, Michael Tait was often mistaken for Seal (a popular recording artist at the time). dc Talk had met with Seal in 1995, so perhaps Tait was a fan or was even influenced by his vocal style in some capacity.

In addition to receiving widespread Christian and mainstream airplay, the song won Best Pop / Contemporary Song of the Year at the 1997 Dove Awards. It ranked highly on the mainstream *Billboard* chart – the only dc Talk single to do so. By these metrics, "Between You and Me" can be considered the most successful song of dc Talk's career. It's a nice legacy, as the song is one of the greatest testimonials to forgiveness and brotherly love that's ever been written.

Single:
Numerous physical promos were released: some on cassette, some on CD, and even one on vinyl for jukeboxes. Some of the promo discs were released by ForeFront and some by Virgin Records. The Virgin singles seem to be quite a bit rarer in the collector's market.

The bridge of the song, certainly the most esoteric moment on the album, is usually cut for radio play. This created an interesting backlash at the time, as the bridge was the only section of the song where God is explicitly mentioned. Because of these edits, dc Talk was accused of secularizing their music for radio play. There was no nefarious intent, though. The song was simply much too long for radio, and cuts had to be made where possible.

The song charted *everywhere*, even rising up to number twenty-six on the mainstream Billboard ranking. When a video was produced, it achieved heavy rotation on MTV and VH1.

Alternate Versions:
Aside from the radio edit, an official karaoke version was released sometime in the early 2000s.

On the *Freaked!* tribute, artists Paul Wright and Ayiesha Woods tackled the cover for "Between You and Me." A cover by Reliant K was also included. Paul Wright went on to work on some of TobyMac's early solo records, but he eventually left Gotee and now releases music independently. Ayiesha Woods is still with Gotee. She's led a successful career and has even scored a Grammy nomination. Reliant K, well-known to most readers, is a titan of the Christian music industry. Though they're no longer with Gotee, Matt Thiessen, one of their founding members, continues to collaborate with TobyMac from time to time. Mark Lee Townsend, a longtime member of dc Talk's touring band, has worked closely with Reliant K for years as a producer.

A new remix of the song called the "fab Remix" was featured on the *Jesus Freak 10th Anniversary* bonus disc. It was created by Christopher Stevens (producer of several TobyMac records) and featured guitar work from Justin York. York was a member of Michael Tait's solo band in the early 2000s, a contributor to TobyMac solo records, a touring guitarist for Reliant K, and is the son of Sparrow Records executive and Capitol Christian Music Group president Peter York. His brother is Taylor York, the main guitarist for the rock band Paramore.

Live Versions:
Despite "Between You and Me" being dc Talk's biggest crossover hit, it wasn't played at every concert on the Freak Show Tour. When it *was* played, it was during the first part of the show near other *Jesus Freak* tunes like "Like It, Love It, Need It" and "Colored People." During other festivals and concerts of the era, "Between You and Me" was featured regularly. On 1999's Supernatural Experience Tour, the song served as a transition

between the *Supernatural*-heavy first act of the show and the extended acoustic set. At the end of the song, Toby read passages about love from a modern Bible translation while the musicians set themselves up on a smaller stage in the center of the arena for the acoustic songs.

"Between You and Me" didn't show up during the Solo tours, but the band gave extended introductions and touching performances of it during both Jesus Freak Cruises.

Video:
A concept video was created to help promote the single. In the video, the camera follows a young man with a nondescript box. As he carries this burden through the streets, he's pursued by two men in dark clothing. He eventually ends up in a laundromat populated by dc Talk and an odd character or two. The laundromat—a place where something dirty goes to get cleaned—inspires him to leave the box behind and be free. At the end, dc Talk gathers around the box and takes a peek inside. Much to fans' dismay, the video ends just before the viewer can see the box's contents.

The video is included in various dc Talk DVD projects. Another clip of "Between You and Me"—a live performance from the Supernatural Tour—was featured as an after-credits bonus video on the *Supernatural Experience* VHS/DVD release.

Jesus Freak Album Track 08:
Like It, Love It, Need It

Album reviewers often describe "Like It, Love It, Need It" as "filler" – a song included to flesh out the rock feel of the album and hit a predetermined track count. That couldn't be further from the truth. "Like It, Love It, Need It" earned its rightful place on the album through incredible riffs, brilliant yet simplistic musical dissonance, and another solid reminder toward the end of Toby's penchant for rapping his way out of any situation.

This was one of several songs that Kevin Max co-wrote with Toby for the record, and Kevin's lyrical prowess is evident. In many ways, Max played Lennon to Toby's role of McCartney, adding poetic turns of phrase that greatly enhanced McKeehan's "everyman" pop sensibilities. The duo's writing style was perfectly suited for this song. The colorful phraseology and 90s playfulness with words like "care-o" rhyming with "despair-o" made for quite a fun time.

Toby's voice is perfect for this style of music. He gets two verses all to himself – a rare thing with talents like Michael Tait and Kevin Max around. It's a shame that TobyMac rarely tackles the rock genre from this angle anymore in his solo career. The single "Gone" from his second solo album was a great track and was the closest he's ever gotten to recreating the feel of "Like It, Love It, Need It."

Despite the song's heavy reliance on guitars, the synth parts shouldn't be overlooked. Whether they're whooshing by during the verse, shimmering in the background during the chorus, or pulsing underneath the bridge, the synth sections are some of the many touches that elevate dc Talk's music to another dimension. Mark Heimermann and the other studio wizards should be commended for their production values on these records. All of the elements fall into place nicely: Will Denton's drums hit in unexpected places, the guitars dodge and weave wildly, the bridge is architected to sound like an impromptu splurge, and the listener is treated to what almost amounts to a false ending. The song has a fun factor that helps take the edge off of some of the lyrically heavier tracks. If that makes it "filler" to the critics, then so be it. The "fun factor" is part of what made these dc Talk records such a solid listen. While songs like "Jesus Freak," "Between You and Me," and "What If I Stumble?" can be life-changing, an album needs room to breathe.

Speaking of some of the session musicians, Mark Heimermann is credited as the "finger cymbal" player on the track. That, to be sure, was at a noise level even Mrs. Morgan could approve of.

Single:
"Like It, Love It, Need It" was released as a single fairly early in the promo cycle and reached number one in the Christian Rock charts. The single version can be found on a radio disc called the "Jesus Freak Alternative Rock Sampler."

Alternate Versions:
The *Jesus Freak 10th Anniversary* project contained a remix by TobyMac's bandleader Dave Wyatt. The remix also featured TobyMac's guitarist Tim Rosenau.

The *Freaked!* tribute album contained a cover by a band called Fighting Instinct. The group was only with Gotee for a couple of years in the mid-2000s. They attempted some independent work after their time with Gotee, but they folded when lead singer TJ Harris left to join a band called Decyfer Down in 2008.

Live Versions:
The song was only played on the Freak Show Tour. Though it hasn't aged as well as other entries from *Jesus Freak*, it would make a welcome addition to any future dc Talk reunion shows.

Video:
A video of the band performing the song can be found on the *Welcome to the Freak Show* VHS/DVD project.

Track 9: Jesus Freak Reprise:
"Like It, Love It, Need It" was a bit of fun before the serious business of "In the Light" and the even weightier message of "What Have We Become?" But if "Like It, Love It, Need It" wasn't quite fun *enough*, then the "Jesus Freak (Reprise)" was just the ticket. Sung by Todd Collins over a sampled loop (during what must have been a very late night at the studio), the "Jesus Freak (Reprise)" is simply the sort of thing that happens when a producer has been working on a record too long and has been hearing the same chorus a thousand times.

dc Talk didn't include such interludes in their *Supernatural* album, which was quite a bit more straight-laced, but *Free at Last* and *Jesus Freak* luckily still left the door open for sillier moments like this one.

Jesus Freak Album Track 10:
In the Light

"In the Light" was written and recorded by Charlie Peacock for his 1991 album *Love Life*. Peacock was originally a jazz pianist, but Christian artist Russ Taff began calling on him for his songwriting and production abilities. Over time, Peacock and his musical partners Jimmy Abegg and Aaron Smith found themselves drawn more and more into the contemporary Christian music genre. Charlie Peacock found incredible success there, becoming an industry leader in just a few short years with hit songs, best-selling albums, and a Grammy Award nomination.

By the time the *Jesus Freak* sessions were underway, dc Talk had already collaborated with Charlie's cohorts Jimmy Abegg and Aaron Smith. Abegg is a noted musician and painter. He created artwork for a 1994 Kevin Max poetry project and was later called on to do a live painting during dc Talk's 1997 Dove Awards performance and to paint the cover for dc Talk's single of "My Will" and Michael W. Smith's *Exodus* project. Aaron Smith is a legendary drummer known for his work with The Temptations, Ray Charles, and Rich Mullins. Abegg, too, had worked with Rich Mullins. Charlie Peacock himself was also on dc Talk's radar because of a song he'd written and recorded called "In the Light." Toby McKeehan loved the song so much dc Talk had begun performing a cover of it during acoustic performances in 1995.

dc Talk's acoustic rendition of the song fit so well into their universe that it was a no-brainer to add it to the *Jesus Freak* record. While Peacock's original version was inspired by South African pop music that featured synth arpeggios and strong downbeats, Toby and Mark Heimermann experimented with a Latin flair and syncopated rhythms. Drummer Aaron Smith, who had played on Charlie Peacock's original recording, was brought in to record drums for dc Talk's version. He was assisted by percussionist Terry MacMillan. Charlie Peacock himself was invited to record vocal passages for the outro. McKeehan and dc Talk's live band musicians put their own stamp on the song by editing out several of the original lyrical passages and writing a completely new bridge.

With an incredible beat, amazing guitar work, and an uplifting string section, "In the Light" became one of dc Talk's most successful recordings ever. It's been included in nearly every concert, greatest hits record, or dc Talk retrospective that's come to market since its original release. In the modern era, downloads and play counts on social media and streaming services have tallied up to seven figures. While much of the song's success is clearly due to Charlie Peacock's inspired writing, dc Talk's repackaging and presentation of it took the song to even greater heights.

Single:
dc Talk's version of "In the Light" was released as a single to radio in 1996. It performed incredibly well, securing the number one spot on the Christian charts and becoming one of the most talked-about releases in the industry.

A CD promo single was also released. The disc, with its bright white cover and stunning typography, was one of the better products that dc Talk offered during the *Jesus Freak* era. It contained the original album mix, an alternate mix with a different outro and slightly different instrumentation levels, and a third track that was completely instrumental. The instrumental version was also included on the *Jesus Freak 10th Anniversary* bonus disc.

Alternate Versions:
Charlie Peacock's original version of the song is a highly recommended listen, as are subsequent recordings he's created that feature some of dc Talk's additions.

One of the highlights of the *Freaked!* tribute record was StorySide:B's "In the Light" cover. The group, signed to Gotee Records in 2003, decided to disband a few years later when their bass player, Ron McClelland, tragically passed away from an undiagnosed heart condition at the age of 33.

Live Versions:
"In the Light" started working its way into the acoustic portion of dc Talk sets before the *Jesus Freak* album was even released. It was during these shows and rehearsals that Toby and dc Talk's live band formulated the bridge that contained the lyrics and instrumentation not found in Charlie Peacock's original.

During 1996's Freak Show Tour, a rousing version of "In the Light" was featured during the acoustic set. Subsequent shows in the late 1990s saw dc Talk moving it to a stand-up acoustic number. By the time the *Solo* tours rolled around, it had transformed into a rock song. The Solo Tour version usually began with a call-and-response of "daylight come and me want to go home" – a line from Harry Belafonte's "Banana Boat Song."

"In the Light," as one of the group's most recognized staples, was sometimes played at TobyMac, Kevin Max, and Tait/Newsboys shows throughout the 2000s. During the Newsboys' 2010 *Born Again* tour, the band played an acoustic version for VIP ticket-holders.

Jesus Freak

On September 24th, 2005, all three members of dc Talk happened to be in the same location at the same time at Overlake Christian Church in Redmond, Washington. They performed "In the Light" and "Jesus Freak" to a *very* enthusiastic audience. Toby stepped aside and let Kevin Max sing the second verse, after which Kevin remarked: "I never get to sing that part!"

"In the Light" was performed on the 2017 and 2019 Jesus Freak Cruises. Rather than singing "daylight come and me want to go home" during the intro, Toby instead led with Hues Corporation's 1974 line "rock the boat, don't rock the boat baby" (except for one show during the 2019 cruise when Tait brought back the "daylight come and me want to go home" call).

Videos:
Despite it being a huge hit for the group, dc Talk never made a concept video for "In the Light."

A live version from the Freak Show concerts can be found on the *Welcome to the Freak Show* VHS/DVD project. Another live version, recorded a few years later, can be found on *Creation Festival: The Movie*.

Jesus Freak Album Track 11:
What Have We Become?

This is the "deepest" album cut on *Jesus Freak* – an underappreciated masterpiece with the sharp commentary of a Jonathan Edwards sermon and the dynamic range of a Beethoven symphony. Emotional verses and a thundering bridge are only the beginning. Rap passages perch on the listener's shoulder and whisper worldly thoughts into their ears, flutes mourn society's lost values, and transfixing drum loops drive repeated vocal phrases that feature Kevin Max better than almost any dc Talk record to date.

On the *Nu Thang* and *Free at Last* records, the group had written several songs about societal problems and issues of the day. Most of the commentaries were fairly broad, like "Things of This World," "Talk it Out," or "Socially Acceptable." "What Have We Become" had the potential to go that way too, but unlike the other songs mentioned, the verses included some very pointed examples. From a preacher going against his brother's interracial marriage to a girl driven to suicide on Christmas Day, these vivid anecdotes go darker than any dc Talk song had gone before. Kevin Max's influence as co-writer of the song is obvious in some of the more poetic phrases, while the McKeehan/Heimermann duo work their magic to create yet another complex, richly textured masterpiece with a heavy (yet approachable) universal message.

Both Kevin Max and Michael Tait have been approached with the idea of doing a tour backed by a full orchestra. While the show would undoubtedly focus on standards, a symphonic rendition of "What Have We Become?" would be epic.

Single:
"What Have We Become?" reached number one on the main Christian charts and broke the Top 40 on the Christian Adult Contemporary charts. It was the last single released from the *Jesus Freak* record when it the market sometime in 1997.

Alternate Versions:
A remix of "What Have We Become?" was featured as the sixth track on the *Jesus Freak 10th Anniversary* bonus disc. The remix was overseen by TobyMac's bandleader Dave Wyatt and featured additional guitar work from TobyMac's live guitarist, Tim Rosenau.

The *Freaked!* cover was performed and put together by Victor "Liquid Beats" Oquendo, a production artist who had done remix work for TobyMac and Gotee. Some of the vocal work was performed by Toby's good friend and Diverse City bandmate Gabriel "Gabe Real" Patillo.

Live Versions:
"What Have We Become?" was only played live during select shows of the Freak Show Tour in 1996. Along with "Between You and Me," it was often dropped from the setlist. *Unlike* "Between You and Me," the song has yet to resurface.

Jesus Freak Album Track 12:
Mind's Eye

The final main track on the *Jesus Freak* record is a playground for the imagination. Driven by percussion loops, rounded out by aggressive guitars, thick with synths, and designed to capitalize on Michael and Kevin's incredible vocal range, "Mind's Eye" is yet another solid hit that has stood the test of time.

The lyrics speak about the invisible nature of God and our mind's ability to capture that reality. Driving the point home is an inspiring quote from Billy Graham. The clip of Graham speaking was captured in June 1994 during the first Crusade that dc Talk was invited to play for.

The acoustics of the recording sound a little different from other *Jesus Freak* tracks. In 2016, Todd Collins (one of the producers of the record and the "Mind's Eye" percussionist) told *CCM Magazine's* Justin Sarachik that the song was recorded in another recording studio, not at dc Talk's House of Insomnia.

Single:
Like every other track from *Jesus Freak*, "Mind's Eye" was released to radio as a single. And like many other tracks from the album, it captured the number one spot on the main Christian music charts.

Alternate Versions:
Despite *Jesus Freak* being one of the most influential Christian

music albums of all time, very little demo or alternate material from the studio sessions has ever surfaced. That makes the studio demo version of "Mind's Eye" featured on the *Jesus Freak 10th Anniversary* release one of the rarest gems to ever escape the archives. The demo version features a much more subdued backing track in a major key, a guitar introduction with a heavy chorus effect and a slight tremolo, an early version of the lyrics, and a special vocal appearance by producer Mark Heimermann on the second verse in lieu of Kevin Max. The disc jacket subtitles the demo "A Swing and a Miss," which is a reference to songwriters Toby McKeehan, Michael Tait, and Mark Heimermann being unhappy with the overall feel of the demo at the time it was recorded. "Mind's Eye" was obviously reworked quite a bit – the final version of the song has a much harder edge. But this little piece of history was a very welcome release for fans. There's hope that more early tracks and unreleased demos will eventually find their way to market.

The *Freaked!* version of "Mind's Eye" was a cover performed by Family Force Five. They were one of Gotee's newest acts at the time. Family Force Five only released one album on Gotee, though they continued to release critically acclaimed records for several years afterward in both the Christian and secular markets. Despite the song losing over two minutes of running time, their cover of "Mind's Eye" was received well.

Live Versions:
"Mind's Eye" was introduced to live audiences during the 1996 Freak Show Tour. With its mysterious, extended intro, the song was the perfect way to transition from the low-key, sit-down acoustic set back to an on-your-feet rock show. Before even a single note of the distinctive intro could be heard, the projection screen in the background featured a surreal hurricane animation that clued in repeat concert-goers that the song was about to be played.

"Mind's Eye" was left out of the next couple of tours, but it returned as the first song of the Solo Tour's second leg (a run titled "An Evening with dc Talk"). The drama and mystique of its intro, along with verses that highlighted each member's incredible talents, made for a memorable opening to the final dc Talk tour.

It was also performed during the 2017 and 2019 Jesus Freak Cruises accompanied by the original 1996 Freak Show projection video. On the cruises, Toby McKeehan took a few more vocal parts than he used to, and the outro of the song became a platform for Kevin Max to really showcase his ageless talent.

Video:
No concept video was made for "Mind's Eye," but a live video of it can be found on the *Welcome to the Freak Show* VHS/DVD project.

Jesus Freak Album Track 13:
Alas My Love

Kevin Max has a way with words. Whether it's poetry, lyrics, an autobiography, a sweeping epic about fallen angels, or simply social media posts – art flows freely from his pen.

A year before *Jesus Freak* was recorded, Max released a spoken-word cassette and book project called *At the Foot of Heaven*. With art by Jimmy Abegg (Rich Mullins band member and frequent dc Talk/Kevin Max collaborator), *At the Foot of Heaven* was an impressive debut project from one of the most creative and competent young poets of the 1990s. The themes of love, spirituality, romance, vanity, abandonment, ambition, and more were explored through Max's thoughtful, revealing, and compassionate words. Many of those themes were revisited for a 1995 poem and *Jesus Freak* recording called "Alas My Love."

The first stanzas of "Alas My Love" are more universal, but they soon zoom out to observe the crucifixion and resurrection of Christ. An incredible arrangement of strings, percussion, and guitar masterminded by John Mark Painter light a path for the listener as Max uses only fifteen powerful, efficient lines to tell the evocative story of a showdown with darkness.

"Alas My Love" was the "secret track" – an audio gem that some *Jesus Freak* owners didn't even know they had. It could only be heard if the CD was left running for a few minutes after the guitar arpeggios on Track 13. Listeners who wondered why their CD was still spinning were eventually surprised by those swelling, somber strings that began the secret track. Max's poem on the next album, *Supernatural*, was much easier to find.

Live Versions:
Toward the end of the high-energy Freak Show setlist, the band would slow down and allow the crowd to collect their thoughts with a sparse, mellow instrumental segment. Kevin Max recited "Alas My Love" as the group geared up to perform the first of their big closers: a heavy, soulful rendition of "The Hardway." The live version of "Alas My Love" can be heard on *Welcome to the Freak Show*.

During the next major concert series, 1999's Supernatural Experience Tour, Kevin Max had a spotlight moment to perform a traditional version of "Greensleeves" and "What Child is This" which, coincidentally or *not*, began with the phrase "alas my love."

The 2002 leg of the Solo Tour was an interesting show because dc Talk would play a few songs together, leave the stage and let a member do a solo set, come back and do a few more songs together, then repeat. After the Tait band and TobyMac solo spots, dc Talk reconvened on stage for an acoustic set. "Alas My Love" was the first song performed during that segment of the show. Just as in the Freak Show Tour, it was followed by "The Hardway."

Jesus Freak Era:
Carried Away

Despite *Jesus Freak's* status as a landmark album of the 1990s, relatively little has been publicly revealed about its inception. How many songs were written? What happened to the ones that didn't make the cut? How many tracklists were tried out?

Some of the answers were found when one of Toby's notebooks was available for perusal on the 2017 Jesus Freak Cruise. The pages showed that even at an early stage of recording, Toby was agonizing over which songs to include on the album. There were lyrical snippets and song titles that were never heard from again outside of that notebook.

One of the songs that we *know* was written for the *Jesus Freak* record was a little tune called "Carried Away." The song was written in 1995 and slated for the album, but it was ultimately cut and shelved. In 1998, during the recording of *Supernatural*, the song was worked on again. Once more, it failed to make the cut. When dc Talk went "solo" around 2000, the song finally found a home on Michael Tait's debut album, *Empty*.

"Carried Away" is a straight-up rock song that would've been right at home on *Jesus Freak*—the lyrics even proclaim the singer to be a "full-on freak display"—but it worked well as a Tait piece, too. The song is about the different ways that the devil can sneak around. Ultimately, his efforts are in vain because the singers are already "carried away."

A Fan's Guide to dc Talk

The lyrics were written by Toby McKeehan and Michael Tait. The music to the original version was by Kevin Max and Michael Tait. While getting the song ready for *Empty*, Tait's bandmates Chad Chapin and Pete Stewart came up with a fitting bass riff and outro to cap off the song. Most of the arrangement ideas were probably from dc Talk's original version, but all of the vocals and instrumentation were completely re-recorded. Michael Tait sings the song solo, but if you're familiar enough with dc Talk's work, you can figure out where each of the three members would've taken their turn at the mic.

Jesus Freak Era:
Can't Get Away

Hearing a *Jesus Freak*-era dc Talk song without dc Talk at the microphone isn't an ideal situation, but if anybody has to be chosen to fill their shoes, the legendary John Schlitt is an excellent choice. As lead singer from 1986 to 2005 for the landmark Christian rock band Petra, Schlitt is one of the most influential and recognizable voices in the industry.

"Can't Get Away" is an early track on *Unfit for Swine*, Schlitt's second solo album. The song—an aggressive mid-tempo rock piece—is more "Jesus Freak" than *half* of the *Jesus Freak* album itself. Written by Toby McKeehan and Mark Heimermann, the track also features dc Talk's studio musicians Dan Huff (guitar player on the *Jesus Freak* record and others), Jackie Street (long-time dc Talk bass and guitar player), George Cocchini (long-time guitar player and co-writer of songs like "Luv is a Verb"), David Huff (*Jesus Freak* session drummer), and Terry McMillan (one of dc Talk's percussion players).

Mark Heimermann produced both the dc Talk album *and* the John Schlitt album within the span of a year, so there was bound to be some cross-pollination. The same thing would happen again between dc Talk's *Supernatural* and Jaci Velasquez' self-titled album that Heimermann produced. It's hard to say, though, how complete this song was before it was brought over to *Unfit for Swine*. According to hardcore Petra fans, the most likely scenario was that the music and structure were written during the

1995 dc Talk sessions, mostly by Toby, and the lyrics were written or completed by Heimermann in 1996.

"Can't Get Away" is a fantastic song. The verse progression harkens back to the "Colored People" / "Jesus Freak" chords before pulling back a bit and swelling up to a splashy chorus and a hard-hitting guitar riff. It's a shame that Heimermann didn't get to produce more rock albums during this era – his sound and style during the mid-1990s was incredible.

The rest of *Unfit for Swine* (the title of the album is actually taken from a line in "Can't Get Away") is a great listen, but "Can't Get Away" seems to be the only dc Talk artifact on the project.

On August 11th, 2019, Kevin Max and John Schlitt performed together as part of a group of Christian music luminaries called the "CCM All-Star Review." The performance, which took place at in Alberta, Canada at the No Greater Love Festival, included "In the Light" and "Jesus Freak." Though "Can't Get Away" links the two performers in a way that both of them have probably already forgotten about by now, the song did not appear in the set.

1995 Jesus Freak Tour

Again, special thanks to Bert Gangl for assisting with research that went into the concert history sections.

dc Talk scheduled two dozen tour dates for the six weeks leading up to *Jesus Freak's* release. The outing was much more low-key than the Free at Last Tour and afforded the group some room to experiment a little with some of their new material. Kicking off on October 7th in Colorado Springs at the United States Air Force Academy, dc Talk and openers GRITS and Christafari played for over two hours to an enthusiastic crowd. They continued throughout the rest of October, adding the band Sozo for one of the dates and playing a Billy Graham Crusade on October 21st in Sacramento, California. The week after the Billy Graham Crusade, openers Christafari were dropped for the Christian alternative band Hoi Polloi (their record had been produced by John Mark Painter, one of dc Talk's studio musicians and producers). GRITS stayed on the schedule and Hokus Pick was brought in to replace Hoi Polloi for the final dates in November. The last tour stop was at Indiana University on November 17th – four days before the *Jesus Freak* record hit the shelves. Immediately after the tour was over, dc Talk made several appearances at record stores to promote the album.

The setlist was a mix of old and new, bearing quite a bit of similarity to the upcoming 1996 tour but also retaining much of the *Free at Last* setup. It opened with the reprise from "Jesus is

Just Alright," a move that would be repeated twenty-two years later on the first Jesus Freak Cruise. "So Help Me God" from the new album was next, followed by the Free at Last Tour tag-team of "Luv is a Verb," "Word 2 the Father," and "Jesus is Just Alright."

The acoustic set resembled the upcoming 1996 tour closely, as "I Wish We'd All Been Ready," "What If I Stumble?", and "In the Light" were performed. Just as they'd done during the 1994 shows, they used "Lean on Me" as a pick-me-up, and this jammed into a disco set that worked as an early version of a medley they'd perform a few years later on their 1999 *Supernatural* tour. Rock and roll took center stage again as "Day by Day" from the upcoming album was played and the "Walls" / "Time Is" medley returned.

The encore was a dry run for the upcoming 1996 tour; a melancholy stand-up version of "The Hardway" and a heavy version of "Jesus Freak" as the big closer.

Freak Show Tour (1996)

dc Talk's 1996 Freak Show Tour was every bit as loud and historic as the record it was supporting – a worldwide spectacle that surpassed almost anything the Christian music industry had ever produced. Over sixty tour stops took the band everywhere from sunny Irvine, California to a groundbreaking show in conflict-torn Belfast, Northern Ireland. The group won Dove Awards along the way, a Grammy Award, and filmed a show that would earn them yet *another* Grammy the next year.

Out were the dancers and the hip-hop show elements. In were stacks of guitar amps, overdrive effects, distortion, a giant projection screen, mosh pits, strobe lights, lava lamps, and even a row of living room furniture. Several songs from *Free at Last* were still in the show, but the listener would almost never know that they were originally loop-based hip-hop songs. The new arrangements were pure rock and roll. From the acoustic opening cover of the Beatles' "Help" to the last thunderous chord of the encore closer "Jesus Freak," the energy in the show was off the charts.

The Setlist
After dc Talk's version of "Help!", they launched straight into "So Help Me God" from *Jesus Freak*. A rock-laced version of "Luv is a Verb" came next, followed by an extended take of "Like It, Love It, Need It." The band talked with the crowd a bit before launching into "Between You and Me" (though it should be noted

that the song was often dropped to make the set tighter) and "Colored People." A hyped-up rock version of "Jesus is Just Alright" finished off the first part of the set.

As the lights dimmed, the group gathered in the center of the arena to lounge on living room furniture. An acoustic version of "What If I Stumble?" was performed, followed by "I Wish We'd All Been Ready" and a passionate version of "In the Light."

On most shows, "Mind's Eye" drew the crowd out of the acoustic set (a few fans have noted that "What Have We Become?" was the first song after "In the Light" in the earliest Freak Show concerts). An extended version of R.E.M.'s "It's the End of the World As We Know It" served as a band introduction, allowing each musician to perform a solo. Toby took the opportunity to deliver the rap verse from the "Gotee Remix" of "Jesus Freak" during this segment. By all accounts, "Day by Day" always followed the band intros, though a few paper setlists have turned up with "What Have We Become?" listed as coming next at some shows, if it hadn't already been performed or dropped entirely. The band experimented with dropping the "Walls" / "Time Is" medley at first, but it was hard to keep a good thing down and the medley was incorporated back into the show almost right away. Along with the opening chords of Jimi Hendrix's "Purple Haze" and a finale with Steve Miller Band's "Fly Like an Eagle," the performance was powerful enough to close out the electric set.

dc Talk's encore began with Kevin Max reciting "Alas My Love" over softer instrumentation. The group moved into an emotional version of "The Hardway" set in a minor key. The song featured a crescendo moment where a large mirror ball bathed the entire arena in light. "What Have We Become?" was still the forgotten step-child of the album, but if it was slated to appear and had not already done so, it could be played after "The Hardway." Then came the moment the crowd was waiting for: "Jesus Freak." Booming through the arena (and extended with extra lines from Nirvana's "All Apologies"), the song was an imposing, majestic end to one of the greatest rock shows of all time.

At the end of every concert, after the noise had died down and the musicians had left the stage, Toby McKeehan took advantage of the transfixed crowd by standing in the spotlight alone and testifying about his experience as a Christian.

Tour Dates
After the 1995 fall tour had wrapped up, dc Talk made appearances at record stores to promote the new album. After a few days off for the holidays, the group began refining their show for the upcoming tour. Audio Adrenaline, their opening band for the Free at Last Tour, was invited once again to come along.

On February 2nd, 1996, dc Talk was slated to perform at the Mercury Lounge in New York City. A little over a week later, they performed at a "True Love Waits" rally with Michael W. Smith and The Newsboys. After a rehearsal period for the tour, the Freak Show kicked off on February 22nd at the UC Irvine Bren Events Center in Irvine, California.

dc Talk and Audio Adrenaline performed almost nightly for the next several weeks – not an easy feat, as they often stayed up until the early morning hours signing autographs, taking photos, and ministering to concert-goers. As far as scheduling, they did what they had done on the Free at Last Tour and carved out a block of time around the Dove Awards so that they could attend, perform, and hopefully come back with a few new trophies. They ended up playing a slightly more subdued version of "Jesus Freak" at the show. That worked out well, because it happened to win a Song of the Year award that night. They also won the coveted Artist of the Year distinction. As the tour rolled on, the accolades kept coming and they Grammy Award for Best Rock Gospel Album, as well.

The US leg of the tour officially wrapped up on May 21st at the Peoria Civic Center in Illinois, but that was hardly the end of the road. Three weeks later, they were hitting the summer festival circuit hard: the group played shows at Alive Fest, Atlanta Fest, Creation Festival, Spirit Song, Jesus Northwest, Worldfest, Disney's Night of Joy, Connection Festival, the Alliance Festival, and more. They performed at a Billy Graham Crusade in Minnesota with Michael W. Smith on June 22nd. A week later, they got to reunite with Audio Adrenaline for a show in Springfield, Massachusetts. August 9th was another show with Michael W. Smith – this time at the Wisconsin State Fairgrounds. As the summer came to an end, they played at a Billy Graham Crusade in Charlotte, North Carolina.

The European leg of the Freak Show Tour picked up in October. dc Talk played shows in Norway, Sweden, Germany, the Netherlands, Switzerland, the UK, and more. Michael W. Smith was along for some of the shows, and there was even a Kevin Max solo performance in Brazil at one point. The most inspiring concert from this period was at Ulster Hall in Belfast, Northern Ireland. This region of the world had been the scene of political violence, religious conflict, and civil strife for many years. It was a major event to have dc Talk perform there.

Apart from an appearance at Dallas, Texas' KDGE FM Christmas Party with Sarah McLachlan, Leah Androne, and Gravity Kills, the rest of 1996 was spent recuperating. Kevin Max stayed in Europe for a while, and they all spent time processing the incredible events of the past eighteen months.

Welcome to the Freak Show

dc Talk hadn't released anything new to the market in quite a while. To capitalize on the success of the Freak Show Tour, ForeFront Records hired a professional film and sound crew to capture some of the last concerts of the North American tour.

Audio was recorded at the Portland and Tacoma shows on May 10th and 11th, 1996, while video was grabbed at those two shows and also at the Kennewick, Spokane, Bismark, Fargo, Ames, and Peoria shows. Clips of the European leg of the Freak Show Tour were shot later and also included in the final product. To fill out some of the audio segments that didn't quite hit right, a few snippets and re-recordings were put to tape at a studio in Nashville.

The video was directed by Ken Carpenter (who had also helmed *Free at Last: The Movie*) and Erich Welch. Welch is a director who mostly works with music videos, but he recently directed a drama called *Beautifully Broken*. He was also tasked with directing and filming dc Talk's *next* longform video, and he also edited footage from the Jesus Freak Cruise for promotional ad spots. He created the projection-screen videos used on the Freak Show Tour and the Supernatural Experience Tour, too.

The VHS video version of *Welcome to the Freak Show* was released first, hitting the market on June 17th, 1997. Early packagings of it came with a bonus audio disc that included a live version of "In the Light" (the track has a few more bars than the one that would be released later in the summer), a live version of "Day by Day," the rare "Colored People (Organic Mix)," and the album version of "What Have We Become?"

The audio CD came out on August 26th, 1997. It featured two tracks that weren't included on the VHS tape: the "Jesus is Just Alright" and the "It's the End of the World As We Know It" covers. Both the video and the audio versions of the project did extremely well in the marketplace. The video was certified Gold by the RIAA on March 2nd, 1998 and the audio version won a Grammy Award for Best Rock Gospel Album. It was certified Gold on October 25th, 2000. The audio release also climbed halfway up the Billboard 200 chart.

Welcome to the Freak Show was released to DVD on October 21st, 2003 – about a year and a half after dc Talk had ceased touring together. The DVD included the music videos for "Jesus Freak," "Between You and Me," and "Colored People" as bonus material.

My Will (1998)

dc Talk had been going non-stop for several years, and 1996 may have been their busiest year yet. 1997 was much quieter. It was the first time in eight years that dc Talk didn't have an album release or a major tour scheduled. The band still performed several shows (mostly Billy Graham Crusades, benefit concerts, some summer festivals, and an E.R.A.C.E show), but they had relatively few outings. TobyMac kept busy with Gotee Records, Kevin Max married his girlfriend Alayna Bennett in August, and Michael Tait experimented with writing new material (some of it for other bands).

One of the songs Michael worked on was called "I'm a Believer" (later titled "Into Jesus"). He set it aside for dc Talk's eventual follow-up to *Jesus Freak*. dc Talk took one of their rare concert appearances in October as a chance to try the song out. A very early version of "I'm a Believer" was sung to a crowd in Oakland, California at a Billy Graham Crusade.

Another song that Michael worked on, a track called "My Will," was an upbeat acoustic number with a couple of toes dipped in the worship genre. Toby McKeehan, Joey Elwood (Toby's cousin and Gotee Records partner), and Daniel Joseph (co-writer with Toby for "What If I Stumble?") also worked on the song, and it too was set aside for the next dc Talk album. Fun fact: Michael would work with Daniel Joseph again a couple of years later on the songs "Talk about Jesus" and "Unglued" for his solo band's debut album, *Empty*.

While ideas and demos for "My Will" and other songs were still being drawn up for the next dc Talk album, the group got a call from Michael W. Smith. Smitty was in the process of putting together a compilation album called *Exodus* for his Rocketown Records label. Given the band's history with Smith and their enthusiasm for his projects, dc Talk was eager to participate. They happily donated "My Will" to his effort.

According to a talk Toby gave on the 2019 Jesus Freak Cruise, Michael Tait was the guiding force behind the track's recording sessions. Michael W. Smith and the famed producer/songwriter Bryan Lenox also worked hard to bring the track to fruition (Bryan Lenox, back in 1994, had produced the AC remixes for dc Talk's "Lean on Me"). It was still a "dc Talk" track, even though it was going on a compilation helmed by Michael W. Smith, so vocal duties were shared amongst Tait, Kevin Max, and Toby McKeehan like always. In fact, one of the strengths of "My Will" is that it gives each member of dc Talk a verse that's perfectly suited to their unique talents. And at the end of the song, the melodies swell into a mashup of two sing-along vocal phrases that could sometimes be recreated with different sides of the audience at live shows. It's also notable for being the only dc Talk song to feature bagpipes (performed on the track by Bryan Lenox).

While "My Will" would've gained a lot of exposure on dc Talk's next record, the *Exodus* album was no slouch. Released on May 16th, 1998, it went on to sell nearly 500,000 copies. It also won a Dove Award in 1999 for Special Event Album of the Year.

"My Will" is consistently ranked in top ten lists of dc Talk tracks. Judging by comments made by members of the band over the years, it resonates with *them* just as much as it does with fans. It

My Will

certainly holds a special place in Michael and Toby's hearts: at the end of a trip home to see his parents for Christmas in 1997, Michael took his father in for medical tests. His dad, Nathel Tait, was diagnosed with prostate cancer. After two very difficult months, Nathel Tait passed away. "My Will," barely even finished at the time, was sung at the funeral. When Toby McKeehan's father passed away in 2015, "My Will" was again sung at the service. In early 1998, Michael Tait opened up about the difficulties he faced with his father's passing to *Christianity Today* in a piece by Mark Moring called "My Dad, My Hero."

Single:
This was the first dc Talk single released in 1998. It performed spectacularly on the Christian music charts by reaching number one wherever it was eligible. The market had been hungry for more dc Talk since *Jesus Freak* had taken the industry by storm, and "My Will" was the perfect appetizer for the upcoming dc Talk record.

A physical release of the single was produced by Michael W. Smith's Rocketown Records. The cover was painted by Jimmy Abegg (prolific artist, musician, member of Rich Mullins' band, member of Charlie Peacock's band, and the artist who had painted live during dc Talk's 1997 performance of "Colored People" at the Dove Awards). In a brief conversation that we had with Toby about "My Will," he revealed that the original painting from the cover of the single is still on display in the McKeehan household.

Alternate Versions:
A few karaoke versions exist. Only official releases by ForeFront contain the original backing tracks.

Live Versions:
With the single performing so well and the group looking to revamp the acoustic portion of their show, "My Will" was a no-

brainer for the 1998 festival circuit. Other songs from the upcoming album also made appearances, but "My Will" was the only new song that audiences would've known.

It was carried over to the 1999 tour and served as an uplifting, prayerful segway between the bold declarations of "Into Jesus" and the more pensive "40."

The song served the same purpose during the 2001 Solo Tour, where "40" was moved to the very end of the show and "My Will" was the pick-me-up between very serious renditions of "What If I Stumble," "Awesome God," and the rock portion of the show. The 2002 Solo Tour featured an expanded dc Talk setlist where "My Will" again appeared after "Into Jesus."

The song was used as the closer to dc Talk's acoustic set on the 2017 Jesus Freak Cruise before the big finish of "Jesus Freak" and the encore of Help!" and "So Help Me God." At each of the three shows, fans noticed that Toby would look at Mark Townsend for approval before starting his verse. It looked like his muscle memory wanted to wait for the guitar solo before singing, but since the solo was taken out, Toby needed a little extra cue from Mark before jumping in. On the 2019 Jesus Freak Cruise, "My Will" occupied the same position in the set, but this time the guitar solo was put back in and Toby had no trouble finding his way.

Toby and Michael have included "My Will" in TobyMac and Newsboys shows at various times over the years. Michael and Kevin also sang it together at a private event in 2017.

At almost every live performance of "My Will" in 1999, Toby recited the fruits of the Spirit from Galatians 5:22-23: "love, joy, peace, long-suffering, gentleness, goodness, faith, meekness, temperance."

My Will

Video:
The group never produced a music video for "My Will," but the performance from the 1999 Detroit show is included on the *Supernatural Experience* VHS/DVD project.

Supernatural (1998)

The band has frequently used the words "shell-shocked" to describe how they felt after *Jesus Freak's* success. The Freak Show Tour had been a surreal experience, too. After the lights had dimmed and the fog had cleared from the arenas, what would their next move be?

The 1997 release of *Welcome to the Freak Show* bought them a little time to take several weeks to themselves, but it wasn't long before they were headed back in the studio. The question was... how does a band follow up a career-defining hit record like *Jesus Freak?*

According to multiple interviews given by the group, they did it the only way they knew how: by just rolling up their sleeves and putting together the best songs they could. Over sixty of them, in fact. And since only a third of the new tunes went beyond the demo stage, fans still dream of a mythical day when the vaults are cleared out and dozens of unfinished dc Talk tracks can be heard in their embryonic, unfinished glory.

The internal and external pressures to create the new record must have been far more intense this time around. The lead-up to *Jesus Freak* had been nerve-wracking because the new shift in styles had been such a gamble, but in a sense, the band didn't have as much to live up to. This time, the pressure was up and all eyes were on them. The group dealt with the challenge by

Supernatural

coming together and ensuring that the new album was much more of a team effort. Since earlier dc Talk records had been masterminded by Toby McKeehan, Toby had shouldered the bulk of the duties in the studio. He'd been the only member agonizing over every note and every beat. And while he was still the one spending the long nights in the producer's chair, the other two members of the group were given equal say and equal voices on the new record. For the first time, every song being finalized and recorded for the follow-up album featured all three members of dc Talk as co-writers.

Mark Heimermann was there too, just as he'd been since *Nu Thang*. Heimermann guided the ship through choppy waters and contributed his own considerable songwriting talents to the mix. The result of this collaborative spirit was a record that truly reflected *all* of the voices, creativity, and personalities that made up dc Talk. The whole of this band has always been greater than the sum of its parts, and more than any dc Talk project before it, the new record had bottled the magic. It was appropriately titled *Supernatural*.

Released on September 22nd, 1998, *Supernatural* smashed onto the Billboard Chart at number four and sold over 100,000 copies in its first week. A bit more subdued than *Jesus Freak*, *Supernatural* was a musically rich, mature, measured effort that easily lived up to its hype.

To promote it, a major North American tour was put together for the beginning of 1999. The album continued to fly off the shelves as its early singles received considerable airplay.

Supernatural was certified Platinum on February 21st, 2002. Like most of dc Talk's work, it remains one of the best-selling Christian music albums of all time.

Supernatural Album Track 02:
It's Killing Me

Just like the stormy waves on the back cover of the album, the swelling synths and a rising phaser announce the beginning of dc Talk's final studio album. "Supernatural... supernatural..." Toby whispers on Track 1 as the hint of a chord fills the stereo spectrum. Just as the digital effects reach their peak, they break into Track 2. Digital noise quickly gives way to the woody sound of an acoustic guitar.

"It's Killing Me" starts with Michael Tait alone against a single strummer. In a track that bucks the loudness war of the 90s by opting for more traditional dynamics, the arrangement starts to build as the verse melts into Kevin's reserved but crystal clear complementary tones.

Toby takes over on the chorus, which arrives as an eruption of distorted guitars and pitch-bends in the upper half of the fretboard. After the chorus, the guitars back off and the song settles into a groove that rivals anything on *Free at Last* or *Jesus Freak*. The vocalists each take another turn, then a musically rich bridge with chords voiced in a rising stair-step pattern begin the scale from E minor to C. Toby blasts through another chorus, then the chords turn around and head back in the other direction – stair-stepping down by half-steps as the vocalists finally let loose on one of the most aggressive rockers of their career.

The lyrics of the song are more opaque than fans were used to.

Supernatural

The meanings of this and other *Supernatural* tracks were a bit more malleable as the group cast a much wider lyrical net. With "It's Killing Me," Kevin Max explained in a social media post that it began as a song he wrote from the viewpoint of a character trapped in a tortured romantic relationship. After he brought the song to the rest of the group, Toby McKeehan was the driving force behind pepping up the chorus and reorienting it to describe the pains of wrestling a friend whose lack of faith was frustrating the protagonist. The result was a more universal song. Dealing with people on any level will eventually trigger the feelings that "It's Killing Me" describes.

Single:
The song was released as a single toward the very end of *Supernatural's* promotional cycle. It peaked at number four on the Christian Rock charts.

Alternate Versions:
The live performance of "It's Killing Me" from the 1999 Detroit show was included on the limited-edition Australian gold disc release of *Supernatural*. Only 5,000 of these discs were produced. They were individually numbered and featured signature prints of the band.

Live Versions:
According to a fan, one of the concerts in 1998 began with this song as the opener. The live arrangement *really* hit its stride during the 1999 Supernatural Experience Tour. In keeping with dc Talk's late-90s tradition of including Beatles songs in their set, they performed the first several bars of "Hello, Goodbye" as a prelude. Concert-goers were treated to a mid-song surprise interlude from DJ Form where he did his best to explain the difference between a turntable and a sewing machine. Once the audience was adequately informed, the DJ cut the sound and the audience sat in a blanket of silence until, after several seconds of anticipation, the lighting rig and the band roared back to life for

the song's energetic ending.
After the 1999 tour, "It's Killing Me" was never performed again. It's one of dc Talk's best songs, so one can only hope that a future cruise or tour will bring it back.

Video:
A music video was never made, but a taped performance of "It's Killing Me" is one of the highlights of the *Supernatural Experience* video package that was released after the tour ended. It's fun to compare the *Supernatural Experience* version against the raw feed of the same show that dc Talk released to internet video sites in 2018. To the credit of all performers, "It's Killing Me" had the fewest overdubs, fixes, tweaks, and polish applied to get it ready for VHS/DVD release.

Supernatural Album Track 03:
Dive

In a clever transition, the outro of "It's Killing Me" melts seamlessly into "Dive." A fun arena jumper with a strong visual theme, "Dive" borrows heavily from the *Free At Last* era's style of drum machines, rock guitars, thick pads, and keyboard samples to create a dc Talk track that sounds both classic and new.

The mystique of the verse recalls "Say the Words" and "Things of This World" before breaking into a bouncy, TobyMac-led chorus. Parts of the song may sound slightly familiar, as the record was made in an era where bands weren't afraid to expose their roots. dc Talk was channeling The Police in between watery synths, phased vocals, and sonar pings.

Listen closely to the lyrics about the "corporate man" who sounds to be at the end of his wits. He finds release by jumping into the arms of his Savior... metaphorically, of course. The passage wasn't always so sunny. In a chat a few years ago, Kevin Max revealed that the lyrics originated as a tale about suicide... a rather dark subject, but one with heavy lyrical possibilities. The fact that this idea could be spun into such a "throw your hands up" pounder is simply another incredible example of dc Talk taking a nugget of an idea and successfully putting a positive, mass-market spin on it. Though admittedly, now that the origins of the song are known, even the upbeat chord progression of the chorus can't shake some of the darker undertones.

A Fan's Guide to dc Talk

"Dive" won a 2001 Dove Award for Modern Rock Recorded Song of the Year. It was the lone track from *Supernatural* to win a Dove.

Single:
"Dive" was given to radio over a year after *Supernatural* was released. Rumors were already swirling about dc Talk's break-up, but the gossip didn't seem to affect the song's performance. It reached number four on the main Christian music chart and number nine on the Christian Rock chart. These slightly lower numbers were to be expected for an album track that had already spent so much time on store shelves.

Alternate Versions:
"Dive" is the only dc Talk track that has the distinction of having two *possible* alternate versions which may or may not even exist.

The first lead comes from a fan who claims that he used to own a special collector's edition gold disc of *Supernatural*. The album apparently came in a brushed metal case and contained a live version of "Dive" from the 1999 Detroit show. Unfortunately, nearly twenty years of in-depth conversations with other collectors has turned up no trace of this rare collectible or any additional information on it. It's entirely possible that it exists, though: a rare version of the *Free at Last* album in a collectible brushed metal case was produced in very low quantities at one point, and several imports of dc Talk albums contain rare, exclusive tracks. Not all of the overseas imports have been accounted for. It's also possible that the fan was mixing up a few of these collectibles and was referring to gold *Supernatural* discs that were produced in Australia that *did* contain live tracks from the 1999 Supernatural Experience concert in Detroit. None of them contained "Dive," though. Hopefully, a collector out there will clear this up.

The second possible alternate version of the song comes from

Supernatural

the rumor that "Dive" originally featured a rap segment. In a rather conspicuous move, the *Supernatural* album was missing one of the key ingredients that had always been present on dc Talk albums: rap. It's the only major dc Talk project to not feature any hip-hop or rhyming from Toby McKeehan. Even the new songs on 2000's *Intermission* and the 2002 single "Let's Roll" had rap sections. According to fan rumors that have persisted over the years, "Dive" had spoken-word passages that were cut before the album was finalized. On the pre-release version of *Supernatural*, nothing about "Dive" is different from the final market version, though. We were able to ask Kevin Max about this rumor, and he didn't recall any rap verses... though he commented that Toby and Mark Heimermann often littered the cutting room floor with experiments known only to them.

Live Versions:
"Dive" was chosen as the opener for 1999's Supernatural Experience Tour. The band's array of instruments, stage lights, and projection screens was on full display as the song swelled from its whispered beginnings on the arena's mini-stage to the unbridled roar of its chorus on the main stage. It was the perfect first step into the night's "journey to the great unknown."

Though it was one of the most memorable parts of the tour, "Dive" has yet to resurface in any other dc Talk show. Because of its "water" motif, there was much debate in dc Talk fandom over whether the song would be performed on the Jesus Freak Cruises. It didn't make an appearance. While that may have been because of the song's thematic material, the most likely explanation is that it simply didn't make the cut. The cruise sets haven't dipped too deeply into the *Supernatural* album. As a small consolation to "Dive" fans, the ocean-based spoken-word track from *Supernatural*, "There is a Treason at Sea," was performed during the Kevin Max set.

Video:
A live performance of the song can be seen on the *Supernatural Experience* VHS/DVD release.

Supernatural Album Track 04:
Consume Me

Beautiful and esoteric, "Consume Me" is a sincere, passionate mid-tempo masterpiece with fire for vocals and heavenly harmonies. Few can listen to it song and deny the Divine Providence that brought dc Talk together.

The lyrics offer one abbreviated passage after another of simple, profound declarations of all-consuming commitment. While at first, some listeners may mistake it for another 90s pop love song, the message is too bold and sweeping to be sung about another human being. This is the type of love that can only be shared between a Creator and His creation.

The driving force in the rhythm section is the bass, which steers the track by bouncing between two notes at a time. The pads are full but not overpowering, and the stringed instruments know when to sustain and when to go for broke. A brief guitar solo, introduced by a soaring vocal phrase from Michael Tait, uses a rare octave pitch effect to great success. The song is a musical masterpiece, a golden feather in the caps of Mark Heimermann and the members of dc Talk.

"Consume Me" was the perfect choice to bat "cleanup hitter" on the album. A high point of dc Talk's career, the song has been featured on greatest hits albums and top ten lists everywhere since its release.

A Fan's Guide to dc Talk

Singles:
"Consume Me" was dc Talk's first single of 1999 and their third off of *Supernatural*. It held the number one spot on both the main Christian music chart and the Adult Contemporary version of the chart. Though it certainly had the potential to break through, it failed to make it onto Billboard (though the organization did honor dc Talk with an award for the song's music video).

Several radio singles and promo discs were produced – too many to name or keep track of. There were three different pressings and configurations of the US release *alone*. More for overseas. Most of these discs contained minor radio edits, but one particular UK dc Talk single released around this time had a very special acoustic version of the song.

Alternate Versions:
The "acoustic version" of "Consume Me" is actually a rare *Supernatural* demo track. It's a very rough take with handheld percussion, a pair of acoustic guitars, unprocessed vocals, incomplete lyrics to the first verse, and a few ideas that were still being worked on. It's raw. But as everyone knows, dc Talk is often at their best under such conditions. Hearing this version of the song is a special experience, and any collector who finds it will certainly keep it amongst their treasures.

Live Versions:
Coming right after the new "Give Peace a Chance" coda to "Colored People," "Consume Me" was a dramatic moment on the Supernatural Experience Tour. Michael Tait's voice had rarely sounded so ready-made for a live song. Kevin Max, along with busier-than-usual vocal assistance from the talented Mark Townsend, filled in multiple harmony parts while Toby delivered strong lead lines. As the first verse made a crescendo into the chorus, a mirror ball splashed fractured light across the entire arena.

Supernatural

Unfortunately, the live number was left off of the *Supernatural Experience* VHS/DVD package in favor of the MTV-ready music video for the song. But fifteen years later, dc Talk's management released a raw feed of the 1999 Detroit performance onto internet video sites. It was shortly followed by a complete transfer of the entire 1999 Detroit show, an act that certainly made up for leaving the live clip off of the original VHS/DVD.

"Consume Me" has not been performed since 1999. In 2017, a video was released of dc Talk's backing band rehearsing the song for the Jesus Freak Cruise, but the song was cut during rehearsals.

Video:
Most of dc Talk's early videos were flashy, stylized pop montages that reflected the sensibilities of the era in which they were made. Not "Consume Me." The film was a compelling visual narrative of a fictional population tethered to the safety breathing masks. In a climactic moment, one of the citizens takes a leap of faith by ripping off the device. Others are inspired to follow.

The futuristic video was filmed in an airport. Outdoor scenes were shot at a high elevation in a freezing, biting wind. The memory of those temperatures probably makes the band and crew shiver to this day. In the video, Kevin's hair is dyed a dark red because of a movie part he was auditioning for at the time.

The video won the 1999 Billboard Award for "Best Contemporary Christian Video." It was also the last concept video that dc Talk filmed together.

Supernatural Album Track 05:
My Friend (So Long)

None of dc Talk's work embodies the late-90s progressive rock sound better than "My Friend (So Long)." From the walking octave-capped verse riffs to the jangly seventh chord callback and the lead-guitar-driven chorus, it was exactly the type of song that mainstream audiences could rally behind.

It's both an experiment for the group and a tribute to the rock of ages. As a tribute, the backing track to the bridge matches the chord progression and tempo of Pink Floyd's song "Time" (the "home, home again" reprise) almost note for note, but the passage is brought firmly into the realm of dc Talk when an extended sample of the "Jesus Freak" chorus floats in. Music theory buffs might note that overall, what sounds like an E Major piece settles into the D Major scale. The modulation is part of its effectiveness as a rock song.

Some of the music's interesting qualities can be attributed to the surreal circumstances under which the song was conceived. The song was written while the group was attending a writer's retreat in a genuine French castle. Sometime during their stay, they were paired with legendary musician Mark Hudson—best known for his work with Ozzy Osbourne and Ringo Starr—and "My Friend (So Long)" was born.

The lyrics deal with the imaginary scenario of dc Talk breaking up and one of the members going on to achieve mainstream

Supernatural

success. Note the word "*imaginary*." It was speculated for years that the lyrics were about a specific person, but the band has tirelessly explained that the situation was hypothetical.

Still, the demise of dc Talk and mainstream success of one or all of its members' solo careers was always a very possible scenario. Kevin had expressed interest in doing a solo album since the *Jesus Freak* days and had even performed some shows by himself. Michael Tait had begun singing with "Curious George," a cover band composed of friends with mega musical chops. Each of the three members had the talent to do it. Would they? And if so... as Michael sometimes says, would they take the "Cross over" when they made their "crossover"? How would it feel to the other two if they saw a former member going on to achieve success outside of the group?

It was probably a thought process that every major musical act at the peak of their success has struggled with. But despite this being far from a universal situation, dc Talk again managed to tailor the lyrics for mass appeal. Between the left-field song idea and the track's unusual musical beginnings, "My Friend (So Long)" somehow came together as one of the strongest tracks on the *Supernatural* album.

A bit of trivia: no one knows what's being said in the spoken word track after the bridge. Toby claims that it was late at night, they'd been working in the studio for hours on end, and the words were just gibberish.

Singles:
This was the second single released from *Supernatural*. It entered rotation on September 1st, 1998, which was just a few weeks before the album's release. Though the title track came close, "My Friend (So Long)" was the only single from *Supernatural* to nab a number one spot on the Christian Rock chart.

A Fan's Guide to dc Talk

Several CD and radio promo singles were produced in various countries. An intrepid collector can find up to seven different versions if they set their mind to it. Most of them contain only minor edits of the song, but one edit cuts it down to only two and a half minutes. One single contains brief, answer-only interview tracks from the band. Most contain the "call-out hook," which is a six-second portion of the chorus used by the industry to gauge the popularity of a song by tracking how quickly listeners recognize the artist. Like "Consume Me," a rare UK single contained an unplugged demo of this song.

Alternate Versions:
The demo found on the UK single is another "acoustic version," and it sounds like it was recorded during the same session and with the same equipment as the "Consume Me" demo. The writing is complete from both a musical and lyrical standpoint. With each member panned to their own space, dc Talk is joined by two acoustic guitars and various hand-based and subdued percussion elements. The demo has the same pep as the album version but none of the studio polish. And that's a good thing. dc Talk's talents are best appreciated when the effects loops are taken out, the amps are turned off, and there's nothing between the band and their listeners. Even without the benefit of overdubs, retakes, and splicing, it's a solid performance. Enjoy it, because given their long hiatus and the rock-oriented nature of the song, it's doubtful that they'll ever attempt an acoustic version again.

Live Versions:
The live performances in 1999 hit just as hard as the studio version did. Unfortunately, the live track was left off of the *Supernatural Experience* VHS/DVD in favor of the music video. Fans who didn't blink during dc Talk's later "Intermission" television special *did* get to see a few seconds of a 1999 concert performance, though.

Supernatural

Many dc Talk fans finally got to see the song live on the 2017 Jesus Freak Cruise. "My Friend (So Long)" was one of only two songs from *Supernatural* featured in the setlist, but it sounded just as good as it had in 1999. The minor choreography after the bridge with the Rockettes-esque leg kicking was still featured, though the kicks weren't quite as "eye-high" as they were in 1999. The performance was repeated on the 2019 cruise.

Video:
The music video for the song was coming together just as the album was about to be released. It was a busy time in dc Talk's lives: the summer festival season was coming to a close, Billy Graham crusades were on the schedule, and the group had various album release duties to fulfill. As they carved out time to film a music video for "My Friend (So Long)," something else happened: Toby's wife Amanda was about to give birth to the McKeehans' first son, Truett. Schedules and locations were rerouted to the Nashville area so that Toby could be with his wife when their son was born.

The music video heavily features a recently-abandoned hospital location. The story follows a miscellaneous rock star, played variously by each of the three members of dc Talk, as he suffers a terminal medical event. The event is symbolic of the "death" of the band member to his former friends and faith. Groupies and record executives look on as the medics struggle to save the subject's life. There's a pensive waiting room scene before the video erupts in a runaway 1930's musical film fantasy with feather dancers, Kazotsky kicking, and sweeping visual shots. It ends on a quiet note, as each member's spirit rises up from the hospital bed, looks around inquisitively, and leaves.

Both the "Consume Me" and the "My Friend (So Long)" videos were directed by Tyran George, a 30-year veteran of the film industry best known for cosmetic and fashion television spots.

Supernatural Album Track 06:
Fearless

A solid transition track between the rock sound of "My Friend (So Long)" and the ballad "Godsend," "Fearless" is one of the nicer "deep cuts" in dc Talk's discography. It was co-written with George Cocchini, who had also contributed to "Colored People," "Luv is a Verb," and others.

The song featured guitar work from Grammatrain's Pete Stewart. Grammatrain was on the same label as dc Talk, so Stewart was no stranger to the band. Stewart and Michael Tait also did a duet on ForeFront's *X: The Birthday Album*, and Pete went on to join Michael's solo band "Tait" for its first two years. Several years even later than that, their paths crossed again – the song "Guilty," performed by Michael Tait and the Newsboys for the *God's Not Dead* movie franchise, was written by Stewart and Juan Otero (a former backup dancer from the early dc Talk days who is now a major-league songwriter).

"Fearless" shows the three members of dc Talk getting equal shots at suitable vocal roles. The verses are quiet and thoughtful. A highlight is the introduction where Michael hums along to open guitar chords. The processing is appropriately dry for the intimate feel of the song. It's only during the rockabilly chorus that we hear layers. A surprising chord choice—a strummed A flat major—creates what essentially amounts to a key change between C Major verses and F Major choruses several times throughout the song.

Supernatural

It sounds like the musicians were left to their own devices during the outro to deliver what was probably a tightly-orchestrated jam session. Kevin Max ad-libs on top of it, improvising with an enthusiasm that hadn't been seen in an album cut since the end of *Free at Last's* "Socially Acceptable" or the "Lean on Me" cover.

"Fearless" was never released as a single. To this date, it has never been performed live.

Supernatural Album Track 07:
Godsend

"Godsend" is a light-hearted ballad... a "thank you" to the heavens for the band's spouses. It echoes the musical and lyrical vibes of "Between You and Me" in places. Which was fitting, as "Between You and Me" was *Jesus Freak's* exploration of love. Anyone who attended weddings where even the most casual dc Talk fan was getting married was sure to hear this song. It was the soundtrack to the start of many happy marriages.

"Godsend" was co-written with Michael Tait's friend Chad Chapin. Chad Chapin was also the drummer in a cover band that Tait had formed around the time that *Supernatural* was coming together. After the Supernatural Experience Tour was over, Chad and his brother Lonnie (a bass player) went on to help Michael form his solo band "Tait." Both brothers stayed with the Tait band for years as the group made two records and toured the world togther. After the Tait band folded, Chad stayed busy in the industry playing drums professionally and doing production work for several major acts. He also went on to found the Pro Music Academy, a music school that connects industry heavyweights with students of all skill levels.

Single:
"Godsend" was the last dc Talk single released in 1999 and the sixth from the album itself. It charted respectably, reaching number one on the major Christian music chart and breaking into the top ten on the Christian Adult Contemporary chart. It didn't

Supernatural

do quite as well as "Into Jesus" or "Consume Me," but by then, *Supernatural* had been out for a year already.

Alternate Versions:
One of the radio promo singles contained a version of the song called the "Godsend Loop Mix." It was essentially the album version of the song with a new drum pattern repeating throughout. The new loop was so unobtrusive, casual fans couldn't even tell that they were listening to a different mix.

Various karaoke versions of "Godsend" exist. Some have been produced by third parties without access to the original tracks, so consumers should read packaging carefully.

Live Versions:
"Godsend" was only performed during 1999's Supernatural Experience Tour. Every member of dc Talk got a spotlight number. This was Michael Tait's. Taking a few minutes to talk to the crowd before the song began, Tait would often crack jokes about his love life before urging the couples in the crowd to move closer together.

The song was performed with sparse instrumentation that allowed Tait's vocals to shine. He moved up and down the runway that connected the main stage to the acoustic stage while he delivered a knockout performance and reached out to meet outstretched hands as he went. Around the arena, dancing couples moved into the aisles. In a two hour show mostly made up of rock music, wailing guitars, and high-end special effects, this quiet moment was a breath of fresh air.

The musical and thematic elements of "Godsend" were so close to "Between You and Me," the songs were even placed next to each other on the setlist. Michael's "Godsend" performance literally ran straight into "Between You and Me" without missing a beat. After "Between You and Me" was over, the keyboard player continued the verse's chords with an airy pad sound while Toby shared scriptures focused on the importance of love. It slowed down the show enough for the band to begin the acoustic set.

Video:
The *Supernatural Experience* VHS/DVD included almost the entire performance of "Godsend" (and the after-credits bonus spot showed the live version of its companion, "Between You and Me"). It should be noted that the second verse was interrupted to show interview clips, though. Fortunately, dc Talk's management recently uploaded the uninterrupted version to internet video sites for fans who want to see an unabridged performance.

Supernatural Album Track 08:
Wanna Be Loved

"Wanna Be Loved" is a modern take on disco: a smokin' blend of Rhodes piano, guitar flange, and organ whirl that picks the album up and moves it to the dance floor. Michael does a standout job here, tapping into the "Soul" of "Rap, Rock, and Soul" more effectively than he'd done in years. If that's not enough, Toby narrates a fun bridge interlude that sounds like a vamp from *Nu Thang* but works well in this new, modern setting.

It's a great song, though something about the verse sounds unfinished. Perhaps it's the overdone doubling/chorus effect they put on Max's vocals, or perhaps the lower end of the verse arrangement lacks a bit of depth. It's certainly not Kevin's delivery. Perhaps it's that the album had so many grand moments and precise arrangements that it's just rare to find even a single bar that isn't perfection.

The song wasn't the most popular from the album, but it received a second life nearly ten years after its release when American Idol contestant Chris Sligh performed it live on national television.

Single:
"Wanna Be Loved" was released simultaneously with *Supernatural's* title track in the fourth wave of singles. It reached number one on the main Christian music chart.

Alternate Versions:
An instrumental version was released in the officially sanctioned karaoke line. Detail-oriented fans will notice that one syllable from Toby was mistakenly left in the bridge. Digital processing was used to offer the song in three different keys for those who sought a more comfortable vocal range.

Live Versions:
"Wanna Be Loved" kicked off the third act of 1999's Supernatural Experience show. After the mellow, worship-oriented acoustic set on the smaller stage, DJ Form entertained the crowd while dc Talk changed wardrobe and returned to the main platform.

The opening band, The W's, joined in as dc Talk played up the 1970s vibe of the song. Disco fever continued when "Wanna Be Loved" stopped at the bridge and went into an extended, twelve-minute-plus medley that included "That's The Way (I Like It)," "Le Freak," "Roller Coaster," and more. Each song transition was used as an opportunity to introduce a band member and give them room for a solo.

"Wanna Be Loved" has never been featured in any other tour or concert series.

Video:
A live performance is featured on the *Supernatural Experience* VHS/DVD. When comparing it against a raw feed of the show, numerous overdubs on Michael's vocal track are evident. Some of them are puzzling, as his original performance was superior to the edits that were made.

Unfortunately, the rest of the disco set couldn't be included on the VHS/DVD release. Modern audiences can finally see it almost in its entirety on dc Talk's social media channels.

Supernatural Album Track 09:
The Truth

As "Wanna Be Loved" fades out into the night, a dark, wispy tone enters behind it. Just as things start to get a bit spooky, a calming guitar riff arrives. The riff is catchy and could've held its own even on *Jesus Freak*, an album known more for its riffs than *Supernatural*.

"The Truth" is a song that understands drama and dynamics. Verses and choruses float into each other effortlessly. The vocalists buck some of their traditional roles and seem to take parts away from each other on a whim. The chorus is presented in several forms: a laid-back shrug (acknowledging that there's something strange going on), an insistent declaration that there's more to the world than meets the eye, and a wailing cry over an explosion of toms and overdriven guitars that blows the whistle on the whole conspiracy. It goes up and down, intensifies and retreats, and just when the listener gets lost in this mysterious world, that guitar riff is there to pull them back from the brink.

Rumor has it that "The Truth" was originally written for a soundtrack release based on the film *X Files: Fight the Future*. In a mystery fit for Mulder and Scully themselves, the song did not appear. The soundtrack album was released without dc Talk on June 2nd, 1998. Luckily, "The Truth" was filed away on *Supernatural*.

And here's more evidence of a conspiracy to keep "The Truth" away from us: the song was never released as a single, and it's never been performed live.

"I believe it's out there..."

Supernatural Album Track 10:
Since I Met You

Don't be fooled by the church organ. "Since I Met You" is a heart-pumping, fast-paced rocker with nods to the original masters of pop music. The brisk tempo and muted guitars make the perfect underscore for Toby's lead, while Kevin and Michael's vocal layers are thick, complex, and cover the entire sonic spectrum. The harmonies are as tight as anything The Four Seasons or The Beach Boys ever produced, and the backing track keeps pace with popular releases of the late 1990s.

The song sounds custom-made for a snowboard movie until the guitars grind to a halt at the bridge and Kevin Max brings the mellow vibe back. At the end, a jam session with an abrupt cutoff seems geared for a live performance.

The lyrics are tight, sunny, and fun. Despite sounding so much like other rock songs of the 90s, "Since I Met You" holds up well even today. As an album piece, it injects some much-needed adrenaline into a project that featured more mid-tempo songs than past dc Talk records. With rap no longer part of the dc Talk equation, it also gives Toby the mic longer and ends up recreating the old dc Talk formula of Toby-led verses with backup and bridges from Michael and Kevin.

Alternate Versions:
In what may have been a missed opportunity, "Since I Met You" was never released as a single. Official edits were created for rock

samplers with the shortest one nearly cutting the song in half. Radio stations with access to the promo could play the track if they wanted to, but nothing was ever captured in the charts.

An instrumental version was released through one of the officially sanctioned karaoke labels. The rock guitars, upper-range harmonies, and complex keyboard segments make for a terrific listen even without the vocals.

Live Versions:
In the weeks before *Supernatural's* release, "Since I Met You" was performed for confused audiences who, of course, had never heard the song before. Some of the concert-goers wondered which band dc Talk was covering.

During shows on the Supernatural Experience Tour, each member of dc Talk got a turn to speak directly to the audience. Kevin Max's slot was at the beginning of "Since I Met You." Usually the one to inject humor into the show, Kevin took the opportunity to be serious and express sincere gratitude for the decade of support that fans had given the group.

During the bridge of the song, Kevin would be back to hamming it up a little. He channeled Frank Sinatra in the same way that Michael Tait would sometimes channel Elvis Presley. The outro of the song was extended with audience participation and a microphone passed around during a call-and-response routine. "Since I Met You" was the third in an array of four songs from *Supernatural* that were performed back-to-back in the first segment of the show. It was the big rock piece before everything slowed down for "Godsend," "Between You and Me," and the acoustic set.

"Since I Met You" was cut from the setlist after 1999 and hasn't appeared, well... "since."

Supernatural

Video:
The full performance from the Detroit show, sans Kevin's message to the fans at the beginning, appeared on the *Supernatural Experience* VHS/DVD release. The version with Kevin's spoken introduction intact can be found on dc Talk's social media pages.

Supernatural Album Track 11:
Into Jesus

In almost every way, "Into Jesus" jumpstarted dc Talk's follow-up album to *Jesus Freak*. It was the first song written for the album, the first single released, and the first song performed live. "Hey you, the kid is back."

Michael Tait had taken up the guitar after *Free at Last*. When discussing "Into Jesus," he told interviewers at the time that he had been strumming in a ski lodge with Toby when the idea for the song came to him. A few minutes of guitar playing and a nice cup of hot chocolate were all it took for the core of the song to come together.

Like most songs based around the E Minor scale, "Into Jesus" has a haunting quality to it. The chorus is an anthem that can move a listener whether its hummed, sung, or belted. The arrangement is a step above the *Jesus Freak* album, the vocals are more seasoned and mature, and the group's knack for taking a simple phrase and turning it into something epic is on full display. The song is a classic dc Talk take-it-or-leave-it declaration of faith. No metaphors. No sugarcoating. "Into Jesus" made it clear that the success of the past few years hadn't done anything to change the band's message.

Single:
dc Talk had come out with "My Will" earlier in the year, but this was the first single released in support of *Supernatural*. It gained

major rotation before the album was released, reaching the top of the general Christian market charts and topping out at second place on the Christian Adult Contemporary charts. "My Will" had fared slightly better, but there was nothing to worry about – "Into Jesus" was a smash hit by any metric. And the next phase of dc Talk's career was only just getting started.

Alternate Versions:
The "Into Jesus" radio promo disc contained three different edits. Each one was the same basic mix of the song cut to different lengths. Also included was a teaser for the then-upcoming *Supernatural* album and a commercial announcing "Supernatural, available now." Rounding out the CD single were almost two dozen tracks of Michael Tait answering open-ended interview questions. Radio stations could splice them into their broadcasts however they saw fit to help promote the new album.

A completely instrumental version of the song was made available using the original mix. It's long been out of print, but sometimes it'll pop up for purchase online in cassette or CD form.

Live Versions:
"Into Jesus" was the first song performed from *Supernatural*. It appeared in a very raw state almost an entire year before the album was released. The live debut was at the October 25th, 1997 Billy Graham Crusade at the Oakland Coliseum. Several of the crusades were live-streamed, so a bootleg recording of this first performance of "Into Jesus" exists in many fans' collections. At this point, only the chorus had been worked on, and the song was called "Hey You, I'm A Believer." Despite the track being unfinished, this performance was one of the most passionate and powerful renditions of the song ever delivered.

dc Talk spent much of 1998 writing and recording the new album. Live appearances were sparse, but as the album neared completion, they hit the summer festivals hard. "Into Jesus" was left out of some of the fun, but toward the end, it was added back into the show. The first night it was performed again, Michael Tait couldn't get the lead-in right. Despite the band patiently giving him his cue over and over again, he kept singing the "see" in "I see the moon" on beat one instead of three. Toby stepped in to help him get back on track. By that point, Tait probably couldn't even hear the monitor mix over his own laughter.

Many fans prefer the earlier performances of "Into Jesus" over the later ones, though it was quite polished on the 1999 tour. It wasn't performed on the first leg of the Solo Tour, but since it was continually voted as one of the fans' favorite songs, it was wisely brought back for the second leg. "Into Jesus" wasn't performed on either of the cruises and mysteriously, it's been left off of some of the greatest hits collections.

Video:
Music videos were made for the album's second and third singles, but not for "Into Jesus." A powerful segment was included on the *Supernatural Experience* VHS/DVD, though. The video featured a live performance interspersed with interview clips of Michael Tait's father before he passed away. Tait and his dad take turns discussing their family, Michael's upbringing, lessons learned, and examples of how Mr. Tait had lived out the Christian message in his life.

Kevin Max's verse was cut from the video, but fans can finally see the full performance on dc Talk's social media channels.

Supernatural Album Track 12:
Supernatural (song)

Like "Into Jesus," "Supernatural" was originally devised by Michael Tait. On the *Supernatural Experience* video, he tells the story of how he was at home one night, couldn't sleep, and had begun strumming on his guitar. The chords and verse came to him quickly. So did that word... "Supernatural." The original demo he recorded featured only his voice over a single guitar track. A chorus was developed and he expanded on the song.

When the "Supernatural" demo was brought into the studio, the group helped Michael change the chorus, polish it up, and fine-tune the lyrics. The feel of the chorus changed from an upbeat pop melody to a mysterious, gritty rock affair. Innovative percussion effects drove the verses and bridge. While the title track to *Jesus Freak* was mostly an analog effort with nothing fancier than a distortion pedal and a rudimentary drum machine for the quieter segments, the title track to *Supernatural* was heavy on digital effects, reversed breakbeats, and the latest sampling techniques. The result was exactly the kind of digitally enhanced 24-bit rock that was starting to climb the charts in the late 90s.

Single:
The single was released simultaneously with "Wanna Be Loved." Even though the album bearing its name had been on the market for almost year, "Supernatural" shot up to second place on the Christian Rock charts. It was a respectable showing, though it would've been nice if it'd had the gas to climb up to number one.

Alternate Versions:
A few official karaoke releases have been put out there, but none of them are pure instrumentals.

A studio-mixed live version from the 1999 Detroit show was included on the limited-edition Australian gold disc release of *Jesus Freak*. Only 5,000 of these CDs were produced. They were individually numbered and featured signature prints of the band.

Michael Tait's original full demo version of the song, discussed in the opening summary, was available to listen to in the Black and White Lounge on the 2017 Jesus Freak Cruise. The original demo had more of a pop-oriented melody than the final *Supernatural* version. Michael's original take would've sounded right at home on his 2001 debut solo album, *Empty*.

Live Versions:
"Supernatural" has been a mainstay of dc Talk's live shows since the middle of 1998 – before the new album was even released. Early audiences didn't know what to make of it since the *Supernatural* album hadn't come out yet and they hadn't heard the song. It especially threw the crowds when it was the first song played in the set. "We tricked you a little bit!" Toby would tell them. "You don't know that one!"

On the 1999 Supernatural Experience Tour, the show opened with an esoteric DJ Form remix of the song as the fog machine pumped, the lights blinked "ready," and the band members took their places. Much later in the show, the group pushed through the exhaustion of a two-hour set to perform it in full. "Supernatural" was the concert's soft-close – the song they played to induce the crowd to demand an encore.

A notable performance took place at the 1999 Dove Awards. Michael was given the first few lines that were usually reserved for

Supernatural

Toby. Mark Townsend suffered a severe tumble at the end of the performance, but he came out okay.

"Supernatural" was featured on both legs of the 2001-2002 Solo Tour as a mainstay rock number from a decade's worth of hits. It also made a well-received return on the 2017 Jesus Freak Cruise, where something about the mix or the performance emphasized the vocal harmonies differently and gave the song a fresh feel. It was sung the same way on the 2019 cruise, too, but something about the cues used during the bridge threw the performers off. Bandleader and keyboardist Dave Wyatt was able to get them back on track.

Video:
No music video was produced, but a live performance was included on the *Supernatural Experience* VHS/DVD package.

Supernatural Album Track 13:
Red Letters

In many prints of the Holy Bible, the words spoken by Jesus are printed in red ink rather than black. "Red Letters," the longest song on *Supernatural*, is a powerful examination and exaltation of those words.

The song starts with an innovative piano passage that switches between C Major and C Minor. As the drama builds, so does the instrumentation and arrangement. The bridge is a thunderstorm of guitars, strings, percussion, and vocals. At its quietest, it's the softest part of the album. At its loudest, it's the most intense. "Red Letters" has the drama and dynamics with which records used to be made. It's so filled with showmanship that the track almost sounds like something from a Broadway musical.

Toby sounds fantastic over the piano-oriented opening section. Overall, McKeehan was underrated as a vocalist during the dc Talk years. His voice had an earnest, everyman quality to it with just a hint of Nashville. Side projects, like the 1997 song "Threads" he created with Geoff Moore & the Distance, showcase his 1990s vocal talents even better than his work with dc Talk. When it came to dc Talk, he just didn't have as many opportunities to shine next to Michael and Kevin.

Michael sings mostly at the top of his register on "Red Letters," a move that naturally adds more intensity to his voice. It couldn't have been the easiest thing to do during live shows, especially since "Red Letters" was at the tail-end of a long night, but he always handled it like a pro. Max's verse is somehow reminiscent of his work on "Colored People." He brings meaningful lyrics from a quiet ripple to a tidal wave in the span of just eight bars.

As with all songs on the album, Toby, Michael, Kevin, and Mark Heimermann are listed as co-writers. Also listed is Chris Harris, a long-time friend of the band and production partner of Mark Heimermann's who had pulled many different duties on dc Talk projects throughout the years.

"Red Letters" is a bittersweet end to the final studio album of Christian music's pioneering trio. The group ended as they began by singing about the virtues of "love," "truth," "hope," "peace," forgiveness," and "life." Their final plea: "Let Him in your heart."

Alternate Versions:
The fully-mastered live version from the 1999 Detroit show was included on the limited-edition Australian gold disc release of *Free at Last*. Only 5,000 of these discs were produced.

An instrumental featuring the original tracks was available on a karaoke cassette in 1999.

Live Versions:
The 1999 Supernatural Experience Tour was the only concert series to feature the song. It was part of the encore. As the trio took the stage again and spread out to their own spaces and spotlights, "Red Letters" was performed as a reverent number while the projection screen filled the backdrop with religious imagery. The live musicians stepped up their game to recreate the dense, complex arrangements of the album version and to help the vocalists deliver one of the standout moments of the show.

A Fan's Guide to dc Talk

Unfortunately, the song was not performed on either of the solo tours or the cruises.

Video:
The live version was included on the *Supernatural Experience* VHS/DVD in its entirety. When compared against the raw feed of the show, numerous edits and overdubs can be heard.

A few years ago, dc Talk's management uploaded the complete image projection screen loop that was used for "Red Letters" during the Supernatural Experience Tour shows. As of this writing, the video is still available. The images are a powerful complement to the message of the song.

Supernatural Album Track 14:
There is a Treason at Sea

Toby McKeehan has always said that he was a big fan of including spoken-word tracks by Kevin Max at the end of dc Talk albums. *Jesus Freak's* "Alas My Love" was a terrific surprise to anyone who left their CD player running. *Supernatural's* While "There Is a Treason at Sea" was a bit easier to find, it was no less remarkable.

The poem takes the imagery of the album's back cover and brings it to life: a lonely, tattered ship lost in an overcast sea sailing toward the break of dawn. Max is a superb poet, and this passage is him at his best. The backing track is an expansion of the intro to the album: a sonic sea of digital effects and synthesized loneliness that eventually finds its way back to the comfort of Toby's "supernatural... supernatural..."

Alternate Versions:
In an online chat, Kevin Max mentioned that a fully realized song was written based on "There Is a Treason at Sea." It was complete with a full instrumental backing track. If this version was finished, it has never been released.

Live Versions:
Though "Alas My Love" was performed on two different dc Talk tours, "There Is a Treason at Sea" didn't appear on a setlist until 2017. On the Jesus Freak Cruise, Kevin Max read the poem as his talented cruise band jammed behind him. In typical Kevin Max fashion, "There Is a Treason at Sea" ran seamlessly into a

rendition of "Riders on the Storm" by the Doors (where again, in typical Kevin Max fashion, he reoriented some of the lyrics to suit his audience).

Supernatural Era:
My Deliverer

Rich Mullins was a powerhouse in the Christian music industry. Among his many contributions, he was responsible for writing some of the most recognizable anthems of all time. "Awesome God" is his best-known piece.

In early 1997, Rich Mullins invited Kevin Max and Michael Tait to sing on a project based on the life of St. Francis of Assisi. The resulting album was titled *The Canticle of the Plains*. Both Tait and Max had two songs each: Tait sang "Cry for Freedom" and "Oh My Lord," and Max sang "If I Could Make It Work" and "Love's As Strong As Death."

The unthinkable happened later that year when Mullins and his close friend, singer/songwriter Mitch McVicker, were in a serious car accident. Tragically, Mullins died at the scene. McVicker survived, though he was hurt severely and still suffers effects from the crash.

A couple of weeks before his death, Mullins had spent the day in an abandoned church recording several demos for a new album. One of those songs, written by him and McVicker, was a hauntingly beautiful piece called "My Deliverer." After Mullins had passed, his musical group—the "Ragamuffin Band"—saw so much potential in the song (and the rest of the demos) that they vowed to finish the album he'd started. The Ragamuffin Band, with a founding member named Rick Elias at the helm, recorded

"My Deliverer" and released it with other re-recordings of the demos on July 21st, 1998. The Ragamuffin version of "My Deliverer" had the distinction of becoming the lead radio single. It quickly climbed to number one on the Christian charts.

dc Talk's *Supernatural* came out two months after the posthumous Mullins record. Two months after *that*, dc Talk released their *own* cover of "My Deliverer" on the *Prince of Egypt Inspirational Soundtrack*. The soundtrack project featured appearances by Boyz II Men, Jars of Clay, Take 6, and CeCe Winans. It was tied to 1998's *Prince of Egypt* animated musical by DreamWorks Animation, a studio later known more for computer-animated releases like Shrek. The album sold almost 250,000 copies.

dc Talk's version of "My Deliverer" is heavy, moving, and inspirational... one of the best songs in their catalog. Despite it being one of dc Talk's greatest releases, the dc Talk version of "My Deliverer" is relatively unknown to most fans due to it having never appeared on one of their main albums. Still, the track was released at a time when the country was still processing Mullins' death, so the musical gift felt even *more* special for those who did know about it.

Live Versions:
A brief portion of the song was performed during the 1999 Supernatural Experience Tour's acoustic set. It's never been included on any other tour. Another Rich Mullins tune, "Awesome God," *did* become a mainstay at dc Talk shows. They performed it consistently from 1997 to 2002.

Video:
dc Talk's live performance of "My Deliverer" was left off of the *Supernatural Experience* VHS/DVD, but an uncut version of the performance can finally be seen on their social media channels.

Supernatural Era:
Jaci Velasquez Tracks

In 1996, Mark Heimermann produced *Heavenly Place* – the first major Christian market album for a new artist named Jaci Velasquez. The project was released on Myrrh Records, the label that had brought the world Amy Grant in 1977 while she was just a teenager. *Heavenly Place* was wildly successful, so Heimermann was brought back to helm a follow-up album for Jaci Velasquez two years later.

Jaci's new project was a self-titled album released on June 2nd, 1998. As with most efforts led by Mark Heimermann in those days, the instrumentation was provided by the same studio ensemble that worked on dc Talk's albums. A closer look at the credits also reveals something else: two tracks on the album may have even originated as dc Talk songs.

The first is Track 3, a soulful, introspective song called "Little Voice Inside." It was written by Toby McKeehan and longtime dc Talk collaborators Joey Elwood (Toby's Gotee partner and co-writer for "My Will") and Chris Harris (long-time dc Talk collaborator and co-writer on *Supernatural's* "Red Letters"). The second is Track 7, a piano-based song written by Mark Heimermann and Toby McKeehan called "Speak For Me." This was the same songwriting duo behind "Jesus Freak," "Between You and Me," "Say the Words," "Socially Acceptable," and so many of dc Talk's hits.

A Fan's Guide to dc Talk

Based on the timing and album credits, many fans believe that "Little Voice Inside" and "Speak For Me" were, for all intents and purposes, dc Talk songs sung by a very talented outside vocalist. At the time that the *Jaci Velazquez* album was being recorded, dc Talk was busy formulating tracks for their *Supernatural* record. With both albums being worked on at the same time (though in different stages) and Mark Heimermann helming both, it would be natural for a few songs to pass back and forth between the projects.

Regardless if either song was ever considered for *Supernatural*, when dc Talk's two main producers put together music in any setting, it's music worth listening to. The market thought so, too. "Speak For Me" was released as the third single from the *Jaci Velasquez* album and went on to capture the number one spot in the Christian music charts. The *Jaci Velasquez* album itself went on to sell over 500,000 copies and helped solidify Velasquez' position as one of the industry's leading artists.

Supernatural Experience Tour (1999)

1997 had been a lighter year for the band, but things picked up as the 1998 summer festival season drew closer. dc Talk performed a number of shows with Gotee Records artists and headlined an E.R.A.C.E Festival on June 19th in Charlotte, North Carolina. It wasn't their first E.R.A.C.E show – they'd also performed at a Racial Reconciliation Rally in Little Rock, Arkansas on September 21st, 1997. During the summer of 1998, they played the Alive Festival, Creationfest, Sonshine, Spirit Song, Kingsfest, and several others. As *Supernatural* was readied for release, their thoughts turned toward the next major tour.

Just a week or two before *Supernatural's* release, they performed in Syracuse, New York with Jars of Clay and Jennifer Knapp. They also did a show at the Los Angeles County Fair and performed at a Billy Graham Crusade. Each of these outings gave them an opportunity to try out new songs from the upcoming album.

Supernatural was released on September 22nd, 1998. The next few weeks were consumed with album launch activities. After the rush died down, dc Talk played a Billy Graham Crusade in Tampa, Florida with Jars of Clay and took a few weeks off. As the year came to a close, they played a few shows in December. *Supernatural* had made its debut at number four on the mainstream Billboard chart, a feat that earned them enough recognition to appear at December's WPLT 93 FM Hootenanny with major artists like Semisonic (whose hit "Closing Time" was playing everywhere), the Goo Goo Dolls, Better Than Ezra, and Edwin McCain.

After these one-off appearances, the group got down to business. After a couple of weeks spent planning and rehearsing, the band played a practice show on January 15th, 1999 in Adrian, Michigan just twenty miles west of Lake Eerie. This was a dry run for the band's most dynamic and technologically complex concert series yet.

Over a week later, they performed for the Pope's visit to St. Louis. Three days after that, on January 29th, the Supernatural Experience Tour kicked off in Atlanta, Georgia at the Fox Theatre. Opening for the band was the Christian ska and swing act The W's and Gotee artist Jennifer Knapp. dc Talk's setlist contained over twenty-five songs, most of them performed on a futuristic stage setting with a spectacular lighting rig.

The Show
dc Talk's Supernatural Experience Tour showcased the group's unique talents better than any of the tours before it. Even the show's introduction combined the mystique of the Free at Last Tour and the energy of the Freak Show. After the lights dimmed and DJ Form treated the crowd to a brief remix of "Supernatural," the silhouettes of dc Talk appeared on a smaller stage near the center of the arena. Barely illuminated by white and blue floor-mounted lighting, the dark figures worked through the first verse and chorus of "Dive" before turning toward the main stage and making their way down.

"Follow me through the door to the great unknown," Kevin Max sang, motioning to his bandmates but speaking more to the audience. The trio hit the main stage just as the second chorus began and the arena was flooded with light. Bassist Otto Price (outfitted with a stylized gas mask) and Michael Tait (wearing wraparound sunglasses) tried not to run into each other as the sound of dc Talk's biggest tour ever shook the arena's walls.

"Dive" was followed by a newly stylized techno/rock version of "Jesus is Just Alright." Toby stopped during the bridge and declared "No matter what the say, Jesus is still alright for the new millennium!" A brief cover of the Beatles "Hello, Goodbye" led into the rocker "It's Killing Me" and the *Jesus Freak* track "Colored People" (which was capped off by a performance of "Give Peace a Chance"). A four-song *Supernatural* suite followed as "Consume Me," "My Friend (So Long)," "Since I Met You," and "Godsend" were performed. "Between You and Me" immediately followed. As the musicians set up in the middle of the arena for the acoustic set, Toby shared thoughts about the nature of love while keyboardist Jason Halbert continued to play chords from "Between You and Me."

The acoustic set opened up with an abbreviated, bass-heavy version of "What If I Stumble?" Then "Into Jesus" and "My Will" were performed next, followed by a very pensive cover of U2's "40" and the chorus of "How Great Thou Art." Short versions of the Rich Mullins classics "My Deliverer" and "Awesome God" finished out the acoustic set.

DJ Form was a new addition to the show, so he was given a spotlight segment while the band went through a wardrobe change and hit the main stage again to perform "Wanna Be Loved" and an extended disco set that served as an introduction to the musicians. It ended with Toby and his hype man, bassist Otto Price, performing an "Old School Medley" consisting of "Heavenbound," "Nu Thang," and the extra verse from the "Jesus Freak Gotee Remix." *Jesus Freak's* "Day By Day" brought the crowd back to its feet, but the show grew quiet again as Kevin Max performed a solo rendition of "Greensleeves" (for "all you cultural animals," as he put it). A stand-up version of "In the

Light" was performed, followed by the main set's closer, "Supernatural."

A dramatic version of "Red Letters" opened the encore, followed up by a no-holds-barred version of "Jesus Freak." At some shows, the crowd was so hyped that the band performed "Jesus Freak" twice.

After the last note had been struck, the stage lights had dimmed, and the artificial fog had begun to lift, Toby came back out onto the stage by himself to share with the crowd about how they could have a personal relationship with Jesus Christ.

Tour Dates and Major Stops
The tour schedule was packed with wall-to-wall shows, most of them on consecutive nights. The group made their usual stop at the Dove Awards – they sang "Supernatural" and won a Dove for their participation in the *Exodus* album.

They performed on April 10th at their alma mater. It was probably the biggest concert to ever pass through Liberty's hallowed halls. Their first Canadian *Supernatural* show was in May, followed the next day by the Auburn Hills / Detroit show that was filmed for a video project. A show on May 8th in St. Louis just about wrapped up the tour, but not before the band performed on the 9th in Little Rock, Arkansas to make up for a February 2nd concert that had been canceled.

The group began playing the festival circuit almost immediately. This was followed by several tour dates in Canada with Jars of Clay. They kept performing all the way through September, at which point Kevin Max splintered off to do a few solo shows of his own. dc Talk performed a Billy Graham Crusade as a band on October 16th, 1999 in St. Louis before Kevin Max resumed a short solo tour.

Supernatural Experience VHS/DVD

The May 7th, 1999 show was filmed for a live video project. The resulting VHS release, called *dc Talk: The Supernatural Experience*, included a relatively small percentage of live performances considering the number of songs that were filmed. Ten performances and two music videos were included, with the rest of the runtime filled with band interviews.

Released on November 2nd, 1999, the project won them a Dove Award in 2000 for Long Form Music Video of the Year. Fans held out hope that there would be a CD with a complete version of the concert like the group had done with *Welcome to the Freak Show*, but no release was forthcoming. A DVD version of the *Supernatural Experience* video was put out on October 21st, 2003, but the DVD contained the same material as the VHS version. In 2018, fans' wishes came true in a huge way when, in honor of *Supernatural's* twentieth anniversary, dc Talk's management made a full video version of the concert available on their social media accounts.

Like *Welcome to the Freak Show*, *The Supernatural Experience* video was directed by Eric Welch. Welch had also directed the videos used on the tour's live projection screen.

The video started with very brief interviews before launching into complete live versions of "Dive," "It's Killing Me," and the band's "My Friend (So Long)" music video. Semi-complete live versions of "Since I Met You," "Godsend," and "Into Jesus" came next, with interview segments featuring Michael Tait and his father during "Into Jesus." The clips of Michael's father had been filmed a couple of years prior for an E.R.A.C.E. project.

A live version of "My Will" and the music video for "Consume Me" were included next, followed by "Wanna Be Loved." The highlight of the VHS/DVD project, the live version of "Red Letters," followed. After that was the video's biggest rocker, "Supernatural."

The interviews featured on the project gave considerable insight into dc Talk's careers and personal lives. Kevin is shown at home with his first wife Alayna, and there's a segment featuring Toby's wife and their first son, Truett. Toby went the extra mile for the interviews by wearing one of the shirts that he'd worn almost every night on the Supernatural Experience Tour. Kevin's interview segment featured his "Greensleeves" performance, and Toby's interview segment included part of his "Heavenbound" throwback. Michael's interviews focused on his personal life, his father, his recent studio work, and the process he'd used to come up with *Supernatural's* title track.

After the credits is a dedication to the memory of Michael's father, Reverend Nathel Tait, Sr.

A live bonus version of "Between You and Me" was also featured.

Sales records for the *Supernatural Experience* VHS/DVD are hard to come by (and nothing is on file regarding Gold status at the RIAA), but fans enjoyed the release – even without an accompanying CD.

Spirit in the Sky (2000)

A television show called *Jesus: The Epic Mini-Series* starring Jeremy Sisto as Jesus was broadcast on CBS-owned channels in May 2000. The project, which also starred Debra Messing and Gary Oldman, cost about $20 million to make. Two months before it aired, a soundtrack featuring mainstream and contemporary Christian music artists was released.

Spotlighted on the soundtrack was a new dc Talk recording of Norman Greenbaum's "Spirit in the Sky." Greenbaum's original 1960's version of the song was one of the most popular tracks of its decade. Greenbaum's track sold over two million copies and reached number one on the Billboard charts when it was released. As a side note, Norman Greenbaum is Jewish – he'd seen a gospel singer on television and had simply decided to try his hand at the genre.

dc Talk's version wasn't released as a single by itself, but it was included as the B-side for a LeAnn Rimes single called "I Need You." Rimes' song was also featured on the *Jesus: The Epic Mini-Series* soundtrack.

dc Talk performed "Spirit in the Sky" as the opening number for the 2001 leg of the Solo Tour. A video of the group performing it can be found on a Luis Palau VHS tape from the era. Another performance of the song from a Billy Graham Crusade has been uploaded to official dc Talk social media channels.

Intermission (2000)

After ten years of bunking together, recording in close quarters, and near-constant touring, the members of dc Talk naturally wanted a break. Michael Tait and Kevin Max had been wanting to make solo records for quite some time, so they approached Toby and ForeFront Records with the idea. The label was on board to release whatever the two came up with.

Understandably, Toby wasn't quite as enthusiastic about the idea dc Talk splitting up in any capacity. And when it became clearer that Michael and Kevin's solo plans might be long-term, he had decisions of his own to make. Devote the rest of his energy to Gotee? Continue on as a solo act himself? By all accounts, this was a difficult time for him. In a conversation that he and Michael Tait recounted on the 2019 Jesus Freak Cruise, Toby revealed that after his bandmates went solo, he made it clear to them in no uncertain terms that he was *also* leaving dc Talk behind to focus on the future. As perhaps the most commercially successful Christian artist of all time, this move obviously worked out for him. Truthfully though, all *three* of them had made this decision. The demise of dc Talk was fairly obvious to anyone paying attention, but publicly, the trio continued to claim that dc Talk was *not* dissolving. The phrase they used was that they were on an "intermission." There were non-specific references to the "second half of the show," and most of those references implied that dc Talk would reunite and continue on. Most fans suspected that the breakup was much more final than the marketing lingo

Intermission

was letting on, and there were a *lot* of frustrated listeners left wondering what was going to happen. Regardless of what was said publicly, it seemed that the end of dc Talk was almost certain.

Thus, the word "intermission" is perhaps the most charged word in all of dc Talk fandom. One *positive* use of the word was that it became the title of a solid retrospective hits package: *Intermission: The Greatest Hits*. dc Talk had gone over ten years and five albums without putting out a greatest hits album, so there was a *lot* of ground to cover. Not only did ForeFront include some of the best songs from *Free at Last*, *Jesus Freak*, and *Supernatural*, but they included "I Wish We'd All Been Ready," "My Will," a new radio-friendly remix of "Say the Words," two brand new songs recorded specifically for the project, and two new interludes from dc Talk's famous next-door neighbors, the Morgans.

The album was jam-packed with content. It probably deserved a two-disc treatment, but in a world before streaming services and MP3 players, two-disc albums were unpopular. While paring it down to one CD, a few edits needed to be made to some of the classic tracks (most obviously to "Jesus is Just Alright," but some rare unreleased vocals were included to balance out the change). Nothing from the first two albums made the cut, but Toby was looking hard at releasing a remix album that would re-imagine *DC Talk* and *Nu Thang* tracks. It never came together, which was probably just as well.

Intermission: The Greatest Hits was released on November 9th, 2000. Included inside the packaging was a Willy Wonka-esque "Golden Ticket" that touted itself as the listener's pass to the "second half of the show." It had a website address that led to music videos and audio files from dc Talk's last three albums.

A Fan's Guide to dc Talk

Intermission reached number 81 on the Billboard charts, number 3 on the Christian charts, and was certified Gold in late 2003. Numerous greatest hits albums have been released since, but none as comprehensive as *Intermission*.

The next sections explore three of *Intermission's* new tracks.

Intermission Album Track 01:
Say the Words (Now)

Called "Say the Words (Today)" in some early pressings, the lead single from the *Intermission* project was a new take on an old *Free at Last* classic. The remix was created by Matt Bronleewe, an original member of the Christian band Jars of Clay who went on to become a celebrated songwriter and record producer.

The remix does the near-impossible task of improving on the original track in almost every way. The pulsing arpeggios, dirty basslines, and crisp drum beats take even the rhythm and feel of the song up several notches. And Bronlewee accomplished it all while still using the original 1992 vocals. Wouldn't it have been interesting to let him take a stab at the entire *Free at Last* record? At least in 2002, he got to reimagine "The Hardway" and even bring Toby, Michael, and Kevin in to record all-new vocal tracks.

One of Kevin's lines heard on both the original and the remix of "Say the Words" has caused some double-takes for some listeners over the years. The first line of his second verse is written "I think we all relate," but he's more clearly saying "I think we've all been late." Surprisingly (or not), most fans have assumed for decades that the line was "I think we've all been laid." Another *Free at Last* song, "I Don't Want It," would like to have a word with them!

Single:
"Say the Words (Now)" was one of dc Talk's most successful

singles in the late 1990s. It outperformed almost every track on *Supernatural*. A CD promo single that was released to radio contained several different edits of the song, allowing for quite a bit of versatility in how it could be included in rotations. Some of these different versions are discussed in the next section.

Alternate Versions:
There are almost too many edits of "Say the Words (Now)" to mention. Several appeared on the CD radio promo, and some appeared on a 2003 gold disc called *Free at Last: The Singles*. None of the edits change too much of the song's structure, though. The rap verse is missing from some of them, and the edits labeled "AC Mix" have removed some of the background instruments. An early, pre-release version of the song contains a voiceover announcing that *Intermission: The Greatest Hits* would be available in November.

Almost all of the edits begin with arpeggios that sound both retro and current at the same time. A staggering mess of bass makes the verses pop. No matter which edit is being played, the end result is a great new take on a classic.

Several official instrumental and karaoke versions of the song were also released.

Live Versions:
Several months after announcing their "intermission," dc Talk embarked on what they called the Solo Tour. During a series of concerts in 2001 and 2002, they each performed a solo set and came together for dc Talk sets. "Say the Words (Now)" was performed on both legs of the Solo Tour. After the song's three-part harmony ending, Kevin Max would often point at Michael and quip "I thought he was going to kiss me." "Never!" Michael would reply jokingly.

Intermission

The song was also performed on the 2017 and 2019 Jesus Freak Cruises. Proving the group's ageless versatility, the vocal harmonies were even tighter than they were in the early 2000s.

Video:
A video of dc Talk performing "Say the Words (Now)" can be found on an old commercial VHS tape of a Luis Palau Festival. A couple of years ago, dc Talk's management released an internet video of the group performing the remix at a 2001 Billy Graham Crusade.

Intermission Album Track 17:
Chance

"Chance" follows the "Colored People" formula of featuring Kevin Max on the verses highlighting TobyMac on the other passages. McKeehan and Max made great duet partners, but they weren't paired together nearly often enough. Toby's straightforward, almost folksy songwriting and delivery during the mid/late 1990s was the perfect contrast to Kevin's poetic, almost avant-garde approach. When the two of them met in the middle, the result was always amazing.

"Chance" delivers the strong but simple theme of viewing each day as an opportunity for giving and peace. It was co-written with Nathan December, a rock guitarist best known for his work as a touring musician for R.E.M. and a studio musician/tour guitarist for the Goo Goo Dolls. Shortly after his work with dc Talk, he left the music world behind to do lighting and electrical work on major Hollywood films.

Kevin Max has mentioned multiple times that "Chance" was special to him, particularly since it was the last song that the members of dc Talk wrote together as a group.

"Chance" was never released as a single and it's never been performed live. The only alternate version is a pre-release track of the song that had a brief voiceover announcing the release of *Intermission*.

Intermission Album Track 18:
Sugarcoat It

The song "Sugarcoat It" is a summary of the band's career... quite appropriate for a greatest hits album. It's a moment for the group to say "Hey, you thought that we'd have to sugarcoat our message to be successful. We didn't." They'd earned this bragging right. Critics had circled them for years, waiting for them to give in to mainstream pressure, but dc Talk had stayed the course. Nitpickers will find songs on their albums that aren't overtly Christian enough for their liking, of course, but hey – their most popular album of all time has "Jesus" in the title. Their final album was equally unambiguous with songs like "Into Jesus" and "Red Letters."

"Sugarcoat It" was one of the only songs from this era of dc Talk without any major input from Michael Tait. To make up for that (and for Kevin Max's spotlight on "Chance"), Tait was given the majority of the vocal lines.

In keeping with its theme of a career retrospective, "Sugarcoat It" even features a rap segment from TobyMac. This hadn't happened on a new dc Talk song since the *Jesus Freak* album.

Intermission's new songs, along with 2000's "Spirit in the Sky" and 2002's "Let's Roll," provides a small peek at what a sixth dc Talk album might've sounded like. The group was headed toward the electronic dance sounds that were taking over contemporary pop music. It even looked like some rap segments would've even started to sneak back into the fold. After one more song in 2002, the new recordings stopped there, though. We'll always be left to wonder what the next step would've been.

A pre-release version of "Sugarcoat It" had a brief voiceover announcing the release of *Intermission*. Like "Chance," the track was never released as a single or performed live.

Solo EP (2001)

By the time Intermission was released, Kevin and Michael's solo records were well underway. Toby was still wavering a bit. As he wrestled with the decision of whether to go out on his own or not, he was roped into writing the title track for an upcoming road trip movie called *Extreme Days*.

The soundtrack album came out on February 13th, 2001. Featured was an early version of Tait's solo track "Loss 4 Words" and a new song by Toby called "Extreme Days." Toby's said that writing and recording for the *Extreme Days* movie was such a rewarding experience that it finally cinched his desire to embark on a solo career.

The *Extreme Days* soundtrack was the world's first taste of how the individual members of dc Talk would sound on their own. A better sampling was offered on April 24th, 2001 when a dc Talk project called *Solo* found its way to store shelves. *Solo* contained a live dc Talk track recorded in 1999 and two new tracks from each member's upcoming solo records. It was the perfect metaphor for what was to come: fans could see "dc Talk" playing *old* material live, but everything else going forward would be solo.

The album packaging was clever. In the early 2000s, it was common for consumers to buy blank CDs and burn MP3 files onto them for each other... a slightly updated take on mixtape culture.

Solo ran with this concept and featured an album sleeve that looked like a blank recordable CD with a handwritten title font. Since the project technically included four different musical groups, this was a neat way to package it.

Track Listing:
1) dc Talk: "40 (live)"
2) Tait: "Alibi"
3) Tait: "All You Got" (co-written with Toby McKeehan)
4) Kevin Max: "Return of the Singer" (co-written with dc Talk guitarist Mark Townsend)
5) Kevin Max: "Be"
6) TobyMac: "Somebody's Watching"
7) TobyMac: "Extreme Days"

The tracks included on the disc are basically the final versions of the songs as they would later appear on their respective albums, though *Solo's* version of "Extreme Days" contained a different intro and a slightly different mix than the final *Momentum* version.

Even though the EP wasn't a cohesive album project, it was propelled all the way to the Grammy Awards because of the "dc Talk" name. It won a Grammy for Best Rock Gospel Album.

Solo EP Track 1:
40 (live)

Before *Solo* was released, it was advertised that the project would include an "unreleased dc Talk track." The name was kept secret, which prompted all kinds of fan speculation. "It's going to be a live track," one band member revealed. "It's kind of new, kind of old," another one teased. Most fans guessed correctly: it was dc Talk's cover of U2's "40."

U2's original version was released on their 1983 album *War*. The lyrics were based on Psalm 40 from the Bible. It was a popular track for them, and "40" was often used as U2's big closer even into the 2000s.

dc Talk used it as *their* closer in the early 2000s, too. dc Talk had first covered the song during the acoustic set on 1994's *Free at Last Tour*. It was dropped off of the setlist during the main *Jesus Freak* outings, but it was featured heavily again in *Supernatural*-era concerts. The recording used on *Solo* was from the Detroit show in May 1999 – the same show that the live clips for the *Supernatural Experience* VHS/DVD came from. Compared to a live feed from that concert, it's obvious that the version of "40" released on *Solo* had been edited heavily in post-production. The entire structure was changed (the chorus was duplicated between the verses), and a couple of problem notes from an overly ambitious and road-weary Kevin Max were overdubbed.

A ten-minute worship version of "40" was performed as the final song of the night during the first leg of the Solo Tour, but it was taken out completely on the second leg of the tour. Kevin Max sang it at solo shows on the Jesus Freak Cruise, and dc Talk even wandered into the chorus as a trio during 2017's third cruise ship performance.

Solo Tours (2001-2002)

dc Talk played very few shows together in 2000, though they did appear at Billy Graham Crusades and on a live PAX-TV special. As the Tait, Kevin Max, and TobyMac records were coming together, a tour was drawn up to feature all three solo acts. By going out as "dc Talk" and introducing their new solo material to the world, the band and ForeFront hoped to capitalize on the "dc Talk" name enough to launch the next chapters of their careers.

The first leg of the Solo Tour spanned from June 2001 to September 2001 in order to take advantage of the built-in audiences and venues offered by summer festivals and Billy Graham Crusades. For over twenty shows, each member of dc Talk was given a chance to perform a handful of songs from their upcoming records. At the end, they performed about a dozen dc Talk songs together as a band.

One of the highlights of early Solo Tour sets was the live version of "Spirit In the Sky." The song kicked off dc Talk's portion of the concert and was followed by a souped-up version of the Supernatural Experience Tour's take on "Jesus is Just Alright" and a rock version of "In the Light." Highlights from *Jesus Freak* like "Colored People" and "What If I Stumble?" came next, followed by "My Will," "Awesome God," "Say the Words (Now)," "Supernatural," and "Jesus Freak." An extended version of "40" and "How Great Thou Art" was used as an encore. "40" was probably highlighted because it was featured on the *Solo* EP.

A Fan's Guide to dc Talk

The Tait, Kevin Max, and TobyMac sets were intriguing because, at the start of the tour, none of the new records had come out yet. Fans were eager to hear what was coming. Tait's record came out in July, Kevin Max's came out in August at the end of the tour, and Toby's was still in production throughout.

The final date performed during the 2001 Solo Tour was on September 8th, 2001 – just a few days before the September 11th terrorist attacks. The shows had been scheduled to resume on October 4th, but the rest of the tour was suddenly dropped. Nine dates were moved to 2002 and eight were completely canceled. Rumors had already been swirling about dc Talk breaking up for good, so these cancellations threw the chatter into overdrive. Kevin Max publicly took the blame for the shows being moved, but it should be noted that most major tours for *all* artists were canceled in the aftermath of September 11th.

TobyMac's solo album came out on November 6th, so he *had* to start touring again. If he didn't, he risked botching his album's roll-out. Kevin was unable to join in, so Toby and Michael Tait's band went out to Florida to play a handful of dates in support of TobyMac's new album, *Momentum*. As this was happening, the 2002 leg of the Solo Tour was being finalized. The new shows were retitled "An Evening with dc Talk."

Starting in January, the "An Evening with dc Talk" rolled out with all three members of dc Talk in tow. In only a month's time, they were able to clock a whopping twenty-two shows.

On this leg, they tried something different. The dc Talk set was broken into pieces, and the solo sets took place at different points of the dc Talk show. After a Hendrix-style version of the National Anthem performed by one of dc Talk's guitarists, the group opened the show together, playing "Mind's Eye," "Colored People," a portion of "Luv is a Verb," "Jesus is Just

Solo Tours

Alright," and "Supernatural." Then after a brief set change, Tait's band played a set of five or so songs, followed by Toby's solo set. dc Talk then reconvened on stage. They started with "Alas My Love" / "The Hardway" and went through an acoustic set of "Into Jesus," "My Will," and a rendition of "Thy Word." Kevin Max performed *his* solo set, after which dc Talk took the stage again to perform "Say the Words (Now)," "In the Light," and "Day by Day." After being called back out for an encore, they performed "What If I Stumble?" and "Jesus Freak."

The tour ended in late February, though dc Talk went back out to play two make-up shows in April. After that, each member went his own way. They hit the summer festival circuit separately, coming together only for a June 29th Billy Graham Crusade in Cincinnati, Ohio – the same state where dc Talk had performed their first crusade together only eight short years before. Billy Graham got the group together one last time for an October 19th, 2002 crusade in Dallas, Texas.

Aside from the occasional Michael Tait cameo on TobyMac's live performances of "In the Light" or Toby delivering the rap on Tait's "Jesus Freak" if they happened to be at the same festival at the same time, dc Talk was essentially finished performing together. There was a brief reunion three years later on September 24th, 2005 when all three members of dc Talk happened to be at the Overlake Christian Church in Redmond, Washington at the same time. They performed "In the Light" and "Jesus Freak." Kevin Max made an appearance at a TobyMac concert in London later that same year. After Michael Tait joined the Newsboys in 2010 or so, he'd still occasionally cross paths with TobyMac on the road and invite him onto the stage for the "Jesus Freak" rap. One such rare occurrence was wasted when Toby's microphone had a technical issue and the crowd couldn't hear him.

Privately, they all remained friends and kept in fairly close contact that would ebb and flow the way most friendships do. They'd meet up or even exchange ideas for songs on occasion. dc Talk members would reunite briefly by guest-starring on each other's albums from time to time, too. But nothing remotely resembling a new era of "dc Talk" took place.

As the years went by, the window for a full-fledged reunion seemed to be closing. dc Talk's break-out record, *Jesus Freak*, had hit the stores in 1995. Twenty years went by in a flash with nothing promising on the horizon. Twenty years is a *long* time in the music world. In the back of their minds, the band must've wondered if dc Talk's old music would even be relevant or accepted in the current market. Nearly sixteen years after the sun had set on "An Evening with dc Talk," it would be natural to think that dc Talk's ship had sailed.

But a *new* ship sailed in 2017 – namely, the Jesus Freak Cruise. Not only had the dreams of long-time fans finally become a reality, but the response to dc Talk's back-catalog was so positive that it laid to rest *any* fears about the band losing relevancy. The cruises will be discussed in a bit, but first – there were a few times in the intervening years that dc Talk *did* reunite, though only briefly. Those tracks are explored next.

Let's Roll (2002)

One of the many tragic stories to emerge from the September 11th, 2001 terror attacks was the struggle of Flight 93's passenger's against the plane's hijackers. When the men and women aboard the hijacked plane found out through phone calls to loved ones about the crashes at the World Trade Center, they began formulating a plan to divert their plane away from whatever target the terrorists had chosen. A passenger named Todd Beamer, on the phone with a GTE Airphone supervisor named Lisa Jefferson, recited the Lord's Prayer with other passengers before announcing "Let's roll" and springing to action. Together, the passengers stormed the cockpit, overpowered the hijackers, and crashed the plane in an open field. Everyone on board lost their lives; a brave sacrifice made to protect countless other innocent people.

A 2002 album called *Let's Roll: Together in Unity, Faith, and Hope* was put together to pay tribute to these heroes. Even though dc Talk was in the process of going their separate ways, they came together to record a song for this important compilation.

Their song, "Let's Roll," is a powerhouse. It melds together a heavy beat, inspiring lyrics, rock guitars, rap segments, and a bridge where Toby recites the Lord's Prayer. Kevin Max's vocals let loose when the chorus comes back, and the three members trade vocal licks throughout an extended outro before the music fades. As the song ends, Toby shouts "Unite."

"Let's Roll" was released as a single. It didn't top the main Christian chart, but it rose all the way to number two on the Christian Rock chart.

Since it was released at the end of dc Talk's tenure together, "Let's Roll" has never been performed live. There were two alternate versions released on a CD promo: an "acoustic mix" and a "rock mix." Both of them contain significantly different instrumentation from the original version. The "acoustic mix" is stripped down to bare bones, offering the listener an unobstructed look into the group's recording session. The "rock mix" contains heavier guitars and thicker samples than the album version.

The Hardway (Revisited)

When *Free at Last* was reissued in 2002 for its 10th anniversary, the biggest boon for fans was the release of the long-shelved *Free at Last: The Movie*. Another, often-overlooked benefit of the reissue was a new version of the band's classic track "The Hardway."

Masterminded by Matt Bronleewe—the same producer who'd created the "Say the Words (Now)" remix for *Intermission*—the new version of "The Hardway" took the baleful sound of the original and transformed it into a modern dance number. Instead of having to re-use the vocals from the original sessions (as he'd done with "Say the Words"), the members of dc Talk actually came in and re-recorded their vocal lines to match the more aggressive, minor-key style of Bronleewe's new remix.

While "Say the Words (Now)" had been a smash hit, "The Hardway (Revisited)" was unfortunately overlooked. Several factors were working against it: the dc Talk brand was disappearing from the marketplace, the song was never released as a single, and the group never had an opportunity to perform it live. Additionally, it should be noted that "Say the Words" had never been a hit during the *Free at Last* years. Bronlewee's remix had turned it into one. "The Hardway" had already been a huge hit the 1990s, and when liberties are taken with a beloved classic, the new material isn't always appreciated by listeners. The remix has a lot to offer, though, and it was one of the only times in the 2000s that new vocal tracks by dc Talk could be heard together.

Alternate Versions:
In 2003, a gold disc of rare *Free at Last* tracks was produced in very limited quantities for select radio stations. On the disc were multiple versions of "The Hardway (Revisited)." The different edits eliminated some of the rap, extra vocals, and little touches that were found throughout the song. None of the changes were very radical, but they served to make the song a bit more radio-friendly.

"The Hardway" was performed on the Solo Tour in 2002, but since the "Revisited" version hadn't been created yet, the live version in 2002 was in the same style as the Freak Show Tour's version of the song. Kevin Max continued to perform "The Hardway" at select solo concerts throughout the 2000s, but his performances were usually acoustic and featured the chords from the original version. When dc Talk performed the song on the 2017 cruise, it was nearly a carbon copy of the Freak Show / Solo Tour version. Performances on the 2019 cruise were more like a mid-tempo acoustic rock ballad.

Atmosphere (2004)

TobyMac's first solo record, *Momentum*, was a major success in the marketplace. His follow-up, *Welcome to Diverse City*, went even further and improved on his debut project in almost every way. In fact, in the annals of Toby's solo career, *Welcome to Diverse City* is probably the most artistically significant record that he's yet to put out as a solo artist.

Significant for dc Talk fans was the inclusion of Michael Tait and Kevin Max on a remix of one of the album's main songs: a track called "Atmosphere." In an interview with the website jesusfreakhideout.com published on October 22nd, 2004, Toby mentioned that while he was writing the song, he felt from the start that Michael and Kevin would be perfect for the track. It sounded like a dc Talk song to him, so why not bring them in? He offered, and they accepted. Kevin also laid down vocal tracks for another song, but it wound up being cut from the album.

The "Atmosphere" remix was overseen by "Tedd T" (Ted Tjornhom), a producer known at the time for his work with Rebecca St. James, Code of Ethics, ZOEgirl, and various other groups in the Christian and secular markets. At the time of this writing, his career continues to flourish and he's just completed work on a For King & Country project.

A Fan's Guide to dc Talk

Some of the other musicians on dc Talk's version of "Atmosphere" included Damon Riley (who had done some technical work on the *Welcome to the Freak Show* project) and Brent Milligan (who had played bass on *Jesus Freak's* "Like It, Love It, Need It").

Kevin and Michael both enjoyed the experience, and they certainly appreciated that Toby had thought of them. Some folks have noted that it didn't feel like a "dc Talk" project, though. Part of that might have been because of a scheduling snafu that prevented Michael and Kevin from being in the studio together. As flawlessly as their voices came together, though, it would be almost impossible for a listener to know that. "I actually booked them to come into the studio at the same time," Toby told Christa Farris in an article for the September 2004 issue of *CCM Magazine*. "But one was late, and so I recorded one; and he had to go. But I did tell him the day before that they were both coming in for the same song. And they were both totally into it... It felt like old times and brand new times all at the same time."

TobyMac performed "Atmosphere" at several shows in the mid-2000s, but none of the dc Talk vocals were ever included in a live setting. Neither Michael or Kevin ever appeared with him live to perform the song.

The Cross (2007)

The "dc Talk" feeling was finally captured in the studio on a track for *The Blood*, a 2007 record by Kevin Max that served as a tribute to gospel standards from across different generations. Kevin went out of his way to feature interesting guest artists on the project. While stars like Joanne Cash, Amy Grant, Vince Gill, Erica Campbell of Mary Mary, and Chris Sligh gave incredible performances, none of the guests were quite so welcome to listeners as Michael Tait and TobyMac.

"The Cross" was a cover song from, of all people, the artist Prince. Appearing on his 1987 album *Sign o' the Times*, Prince's version of the track was a solid entry to one of his most critically acclaimed albums. Prince performed the song off and on throughout his storied career, most notably at a series of Las Vegas concerts in the 2000s.

Kevin Max's take on "The Cross" was quite a bit more rock 'n roll than Prince's. It would've fit well on any of dc Talk's past albums. The verse featuring TobyMac was especially solid; his vocal style had evolved to such a level that some listeners had a difficult time telling him apart from Michael Tait on this track. As a singer, being mistaken for Michael Tait is the ultimate compliment.

"The Cross" has never been performed live by dc Talk, but it would certainly make for a terrific surprise at a reunion show.

Love Feels Like (2015)

When Michael Tait took over as lead singer for the Newsboys, collaborations began flowing more freely. On the Newsboys album *God's Not Dead* (released November 11th, 2011), Kevin Max was a featured vocalist on the title track and on a song called "Second to None." Kevin appeared at a handful of Newsboys shows to perform the songs (and to perform an encore version of "Jesus Freak") with the band. On September 10th, 2013, the Newsboys released a record called *Restart*. Kevin Max was featured on a bonus track called "Man on Fire." It should be noted that on the same album, he was credited as laying down background vocals for another track, "The Living Years," but the liner notes were incorrect – Kevin doesn't actually appear on that one.

TobyMac, in the meantime, hadn't included his former bandmates on a song since 2004. When he wrote a meaningful new lyric called "Love Feels Like" for a new album called *This is Not a Test*, this was something he decided to rectify.

"Love Feels Like" was birthed from the struggle that the McKeehan family faced as they cared for Toby's father. Kenny. McKeehan had suffered from Alzheimer's disease for a number of years, and the condition had just claimed him as Toby was putting the song together. As Toby put his feelings into this new song, it resonated deeply with him on multiple levels. Before recording it, his thoughts turned to his former dc Talk bandmates. He invited them into the project, and they readily accepted.

"Love Feels Like" sounds more like dc Talk than anything they'd recorded since "Let's Roll." The verse melodies take the style of *Free at Last*, the lyrics take the style of *Jesus Freak*, and the musical complexity rivals the *Supernatural* album. These elements come together to form a new and most welcome addition to the dc Talk canon. "Love Feels Like" is Toby McKeehan and dc Talk at their finest.

To make "Love Feels Like" even more of a historic event, dc Talk reunited on-stage for the first time in over ten years to perform the song at the 47th Annual Dove Awards on October 11th, 2016. Aside from a spoken tribute appearance for their long-time road pastor, Michael Guido, and a celebration for Toby's 50th birthday party, the trio had rarely even been seen in the same room.

"Love Feels Like" was part of TobyMac's setlist on 2015's This Is Not A Test Tour and 2016's Hits Deep Tour. While Michael and Kevin didn't appear at any of those shows, a specially recorded video of them singing their parts to pre-recorded tracks was shown on the projection screens while Toby sang live. Movie clips from the *Free at Last* era were interspersed throughout. A video of one of these performances can be seen on TobyMac's 2016 *Hits Deep Live* DVD/digital project. The live dc Talk reunion for "Love Feels Like" at the Doves was broadcast on the Trinity Broadcasting Network on October 16th, 2016.

2017 Jesus Freak Cruise

After years of one-off recordings, sporadic appearances, and plenty of dashed hopes (like a much-talked-about "Jesus Freak 20th Anniversary Tour" that never happened), it finally seemed that dc Talk was finally getting back together for something substantial in 2016. There were cryptic changes at dc Talk's official website. Hints were dropped about a reunion for weeks. A marketing campaign began teasing some kind of grand reveal. The hype grew to a fevered pitch.

When the curtain was pulled and the reunion turned out to be a one-off dc Talk-themed cruise to the Bahamas, the reaction was somewhat mixed. There were more than a few disappointed fans, as they'd been expecting an album, a tour, or something else entirely. Others loved the idea and booked their staterooms at first opportunity. The majority were somewhere in the middle. They understood that the three members of dc Talk had gone their separate ways many years ago and realistically, they just couldn't abandon the lives they'd built up to roll the dice on reviving a band that hadn't put out an album since 1998.

Once the waters calmed on social media and people realized that *dc Talk was reuniting*, the venue mattered a little less. A reunion cruise was better than no reunion at all. And of course, there were still hopes that it would lead to something more.

On July 11th, 2017, a few thousand Jesus Freaks embarked from

2017 Jesus Freak Cruise

Miami aboard the MSC Divina – a spectacular ship with 18 decks and a 3,500 passenger capacity. The schedule was tailor-made for fans: a TobyMac show on Tuesday night, a Kevin Max set and a Newsboys show on Wednesday night, and the dc Talk shows on Thursday and Friday.

Armed with souvenir water bottles, fans participated in everything the Jesus Freak Cruise had to offer. There was a devotional with road pastor Michael Guido and another one with Diverse City member Nirva Ready and her husband. It was announced at the TobyMac show that Nirva, Toby's backup singer for many years, was leaving the band to pursue other projects. The cruise was her last performance. There was also a roundtable discussion with dc Talk's management, ForeFront Records' founders, bassist Otto Price, Denny Keitzman (dc Talk's road manager), and Juan Otero (former dc Talk dancer and now professional songwriter for the Newsboys and others). There was an auction and a memorabilia exhibit that displayed the original film stock for *Free at Last: The Movie*, one of Toby's old lyric notebooks, clothing worn by the band in old promo shoots, tons of old photos, tour schedules, unreleased songs, and more. While the parties and endless photo ops were grand, the best part, of course, was the dc Talk reunion concert.

dc Talk performed three times. Each passenger was assigned to one show, but shows that passengers weren't assigned to could be viewed via simulcast on large projectors at the rear of the ship on Deck 7 or at the Aqua Park on Deck 14.

At the start of the dc Talk set, a six-minute video explored the history of the band. After the lights went dark, the backing band entered the stage. Backlit against the crowd, the familiar "blues bridge" from "Jesus is Just Alright" played. Sixteen bars later, dc Talk entered and performed the reprise. The trio sounded like they'd come straight off the Free at Last Tour as they kicked it up into the full version of the song. "Luv is a Verb" came next, with a bassline that never sounded better. The "down with the dc Talk" part was emphasized, and the crowd was definitely down.

A mix of songs from their previous tours followed: "Mind's Eye," "Supernatural," "Between You and Me," "Colored People," "Say the Words (Now)," a DJ Maj interlude, "My Friend (So Long)," "In the Light," "The Hardway," and "What If I Stumble?" The nostalgia really hit during "I Wish We'd All Been Ready" and "My Will" (and at the final show, they played part of "40"). Earlier in the concert, during the introduction to "Between You and Me," Toby and the group gave a very heartfelt "thank you" to the fans who'd followed them throughout the years. They talked about how dc Talk originally started and gave background on how "Between You and Me" was written – during which Kevin gave a humorous apology for his "1990's self."

After performing "Jesus Freak," the concert's big encore was a recreation of the opening to the pinnacle of the band's career: the 1996 Freak Show Tour. "Help," followed by an extended version of "So Help Me God," reminded everyone on board why dc Talk was such a sensation in their day.

The only disappointing part about the cruise was that there didn't seem to be any plans to follow it up with anything else. At the end of the trip, it seemed a moment in space and time that would never be repeated. Fans were still holding out hope for a tour or new recordings, but given how long it took the group to get together for the reunion cruise, there was a lot of uncertainty. Luckily, the outing had been deemed so successful that the Jesus Freak Cruise would set sail again just two years later.

2019 Jesus Freak Cruise

The 2019 cruise was held on Royal Caribbean's Mariner of the Seas: a massive, 3,150 passenger cruise ship that had just undergone 120 million dollars in renovations.

On June 10th, 2019, the boat departed for the Bahamas from Port Canaveral near Orlando, Florida. Once again, the cruise featured parties, exhibits, speaker sessions, and activities. Of course, there were TobyMac shows, Kevin Max shows, Newsboys United shows (which also featured former frontman Peter Furler and bassist Phil Joel), and enough dc Talk shows to go around for everyone.

dc Talk's setlist was more or less the same, but the lighting rig was vastly improved over the 2017 concerts. The dc Talk set was a lot tighter and more energetic, probably owing to the fact that dc Talk's rehearsal time was scheduled for right before the cruise rather than several weeks in advance as they'd done in 2017. Rehearsal was only two days, but Kevin joked that it was plenty of time because Toby has such a detail-oriented personality that "two days can feel like two weeks."

The same video from the previous cruise was played before the dc Talk show, then the band was elevated from below deck onto the stage via a large "toaster" lift. They launched right into "Help" and "So Help Me God," just like on their historic Freak Show Tour. The middle of the show was the same as the 2017 cruise, but the band took more time to talk to the audience and explain what they'd been thinking when it came to some of their songs and even their "intermission." The band was surprisingly forthcoming about past fights, breaking up, and how these various triumphs and tribulations had shaped them.

The show's encore began with the "Jesus is Just Alright" reprise and a *Free at Last* version of the whole song in a similar setup to the 2017 cruise's. The only song on the 2019 set that didn't appear on the 2017 cruise was the closer: an energy-packed rendition of "Day by Day."

Some of the performances had *really* been polished since the previous outing. "The Hardway," in particular, was a far superior performance with new instrumentation and even an appearance by John Mark Painter, the original trumpet player on the *Free at Last* version. One of the most heartwarming moments of the week was learning that Michael Tait's brother Nate, who had been incarcerated for decades, had finally been released and was even able to join his brother on the cruise. Lynda Randle, Michael and Nate's sister and a powerhouse recording artist in her own right, was also on-board. She'd made a special appearance on the 2017 cruise, as well.

TobyMac's Solo Career

Momentum (2001)
When dc Talk announced that they'd be releasing solo records in 2001, TobyMac's album was probably the most talked-about. What direction would he take? Would he gravitate back toward hip-hop? Were Kevin and Michael the reason he'd stopped rapping? How much of dc Talk's success was Toby, and how much of it was Michael and Kevin?

Some of the questions were a tad on the ridiculous side, but people were actually having these conversations. And most of it wasn't gossip or disparagement. Fans really wanted to know what was happening with his new album. They already knew that Michael Tait was incorporating rock and pop on his record and would probably lean more toward one genre or the other depending on the song. They knew what to expect from Kevin Max, more or less, because he'd been so open with his recording process that he was even offering free downloads of demos and incomplete tracks. But with Toby, it was hard to say. It had been a long time since *Free at Last*, the final record in dc Talk's illustrious career where Toby had fronted most of the vocals. The majority of fans weren't aware of how instrumental Toby had been in leading dc Talk away from hip-hop and into rock and pop. At that point, many fans assumed that his solo record would sound like some of the latest Gotee tracks from GRITS or Out of Eden. They weren't wrong, but they weren't completely right, either.

A Fan's Guide to dc Talk

Toby has always loved experimenting with different genres of music. On his debut solo record, it seemed his desire to incorporate different styles of music went into overdrive. Hip-hop, rock, soul, and pop were only the tip of the iceberg. One of his songs was an expansion of "Do You Know," the theme from *Mahogany*. Another was a repurposing of Buffalo Springfield's "For What It's Worth" (the song "What's Going Down?"). Another was a takeoff on the Rockwell/Michael Jackson collaboration "Somebody's Watching Me" (and that song, incidentally, addressed many of the questions asked in this chapter's opening paragraph). It seemed he was keenly aware that all eyes were on him, that expectations needed to be managed, and that some people were even wondering if he'd even be able to sustain a solo career without dc Talk. There were moments when he was even wondering this himself.

The new record, *Momentum*, was released on November 6th, 2001. It was a triumph by any metric. And on the road, he handled himself just as well live as he did in the studio. The naysayers, and there were only a few, had to pack their bags and go home. *Momentum* was nominated for a Grammy, it reached 110 on the Billboard charts, it won a total of four Dove Awards (and was nominated for nine more), and it was certified Gold five years later.

To cross-promote *Momentum* with Tait's debut solo record *Empty*, ForeFront Records released radio singles with both Tait and TobyMac tracks on them. In addition to being promoted with his old bandmate and touring with dc Talk in 2001 and 2002, there were a few other ties to dc Talk on the record. Barry Graul, guitarist from the Supernatural Experience Tour, played some of the guitars on the album. Also, Tait's solo band (particularly Pete Stewart) contributed production and background vocals to the project.

TobyMac's Solo Career

There were a few more TobyMac releases during his first couple of years as a solo artist. One of them was a Christmas single featuring an original song ("This Christmas") and a TobyMac version of "Come All Ye Faithful." Both songs were re-recorded on later projects.

Another release was a 2003 album called *Re:Mix Momentum*. It took almost every song from *Momentum* and gave some of the hottest remixers and producers in the Christian music scene a chance to reinvent them.

Welcome to Diverse City (2004)

Momentum was the perfect title for Toby's first solo album: not only did it capitalize on the momentum of his previous group, but it added to the inertia and set his solo career on track for great things. TobyMac's sophomore album, *Welcome to Diverse City*, came out on October 5th, 2004. The album's title was meaningful here, too. It wasn't just a reflection of Toby's approach to life and music – "Diverse City" was also the name of his new backing band.

Welcome to Diverse City is perhaps Toby's best solo effort. Every track reached perfection. There's the sizzling "Catchafire" with Jamaican legend Papa San, the alternative rocker "Gone," the underrated "Stories (Down to the Bottom)," the unbelievably good "Burn for You," the quirky Soul-Junk cover "Ill-M-I," and especially, the reuniting of dc Talk for a second take on "Atmosphere." Speaking of dc Talk, their live guitarist Mark Townsend did guitar work on parts of the album (though not for the dc Talk track), and familiar faces from GRITS like Coffee and DJ Form appeared, as well.

The record, certified Gold within two years of its release, reached the 54th spot on the Billboard charts. In 2005, it won a Dove Award for Best Rap/Hip Hop Album of the Year. It was also nominated for a Grammy. The next year, TobyMac won a Dove Award for Rock Recorded Song of the Year ("The Slam" from *Welcome to Diverse City*) and Special Event Album of the Year for a soundtrack tie-in with the new *Chronicles of Narnia* movie, to which TobyMac had contributed a song called "New World."

On August 25th, 2005, he released a remix album called *Renovating Diverse City*. Rather than just giving remixers access to each track's prerecorded vocals and instruments, he was more involved and provided them with any new production that they needed. An all-new song called "West Coast Kid" (featuring Paul Wright, an artist on Gotee Records) was included, and Toby recorded some new vocal parts for a few of the songs. That approach had worked well on the previous remix album where the remixers were able to create almost an entirely new track with "Love is in the House." Some of the new remixes were so popular that they eclipsed the original album versions.

The only disappointing part of this era was that a new song featuring Kevin Max as a guest vocalist was not included on the album and still remains unreleased. A clip was featured on Toby's website at one point. The song itself is fantastic, but reportedly, some of the lyrics Toby had written didn't fit with the rest of the album.

Portable Sounds (2007)
TobyMac's next album softened its edges a bit and backed away from the hip-hop sound. *Portable Sounds*, released on February 20th, 2007, had much more of a pop and rock feel.

Highlights from the album include the smash hit single "Made to Love," an uplifting rocker called "I'm For You," party track "No Ordinary Love," and the earnest "Lose My Soul" featuring the legendary Kirk Franklin and American Idol sensation Mandisa. Mandisa went on to sign up with Toby's management team, True

Artist Management, and she also won a Grammy Award for her album *Overcomer*. She was featured as a guest on the 2019 Jesus Freak Cruise.

Toby was nominated for Artist of the Year at the 2007 Dove Awards. He *won* Artist of the Year in 2008. *Portable Sounds* won a Dove for Rock/Contemporary Album of the Year, and the music video for "Boomin'" won a Dove for Short Form Music Video of the Year.

Portable Sounds reached an incredible number ten on the Billboard chart. It also conquered the Christian music charts, taking the number one spot across the board. It was later certified Gold.

Alive and Transported (2008 live album)

It's rare that a live album/DVD/digital project outshines the original studio records, but by some metrics, that's exactly what *Alive and Transported* did. Released on May 27th, 2008, *Alive and Transported* was certified Platinum by the RIAA, having sold 100,000 units (note that Platinum certification for full-length studio albums requires one million units). This is TobyMac's only Platinum certification in his solo career so far (not counting "Ooh Aah," his collaboration with GRITS, which also went Platinum). He has thirteen Gold certifications, however, so he's certainly been no slouch in the sales department.

The setlist was pulled mostly from TobyMac's last two records, but there was a surprising amount of representation from his debut, *Momentum*. "J Train" and "Yours" were arranged particularly well. dc Talk fans don't want to miss Toby's solo versions of "In the Light" and "Jesus Freak." "Atmosphere" was performed, but it was without any of the Michael Tait or Kevin Max vocals.

Alive and Transported won a 2009 Grammy Award for Best Rock or Rap Gospel Album – the first Grammy of Toby's solo career. It also won a 2009 Dove Award for Long Form Music Video of the Year.

Tonight (2010)

TobyMac's already-impressive solo career was on a major upswing with the February 9th, 2010 release of his album *Tonight*, a project that continued *Portable Sound's* direction of moving away from hip-hop toward pop and rock.

Reaching number six on the Billboard charts and sweeping the Christian charts, *Tonight* and its hit single "City on Our Knees" took over the airwaves and earned Toby another Grammy nomination (unfortunately, this time he didn't win). "City on Our Knees" won a 2010 Dove for Pop/Contemporary Recorded Song of the Year, though. In 2011, Toby was nominated for another Grammy and *six* Dove Awards. That year, *Tonight* won a Dove for Rock/Contemporary Album of the Year.

On March 27th, 2012, TobyMac released a remix project called *Dubbed and Freq'd*. It contained remixes of tracks from both *Portable Sounds* and *Tonight*.

Christmas in Diverse City (2011)

Toby's first full-length Christmas album was released on October 4th, 2011. The first half of the record consists of TobyMac's takes on various Christmas songs (including an original and a re-recording of his song from the *Momentum* era, "This Christmas"). The second half of the album was given to his backing band, Diverse City, to make their own. Members were each given one track to showcase their talents. Some chose to write an original and some covered a traditional holiday tune. The album did well in the marketplace, reaching number 2 on Billboard's US Holiday charts and even getting to 84 on Billboard's main chart.

"Christmas This Year," an original TobyMac song featuring Leigh Nash from the band Sixpence None the Richer, was a hit single from this record.

Eye on It (2012)
The "TobyMac sound" had become a tad predictable on *Tonight*, but the next record shattered the mold. *Eye on It*, released on August 28th, 2012, made its debut at *number one* on the Billboard charts. With that distinction, TobyMac's solo career had officially eclipsed his work with dc Talk.

"Me Without You," the lead single, was an effective and efficient lyric in the spirit of "City on Our Knees." The song took the airwaves by storm. Other tracks on the album, particularly "Steal My Show," "Speak Life," "Family," and "Thankful for You" contained some of the best lyrics of Toby McKeehan's career... dc Talk or otherwise. "Made for Me," a love song to his wife, was also a high point.

The success of *Eye on It* translated to success at the awards shows. TobyMac won a Grammy, an American Music Award, and four Doves (including Artist of the Year and Pop/Contemporary Album of the Year).

The tour supporting the record harnessed the high energy of TobyMac's early shows and the polish of his later ones. It also contained one of the most impressive set pieces yet: a towering, high-rise platform for DJ Maj.

A remix album called *Eye'm All Mixed Up* came out on November 4th, 2014. It reached number 16 on the Billboard charts and number 4 on the US Dance charts.

This Is Not A Test (2015)
The idea that most careers travel on a Bell curve is not true in TobyMac's world. *This Is Not A Test*, released on August 7th,

2015, was the most solid entry of his career since *Welcome to Diverse City*. The track "'Til the Day I Die" (featuring a then up-and-coming rapper named NF) encapsulated TobyMac's mission statement better than anything he'd ever put out. Another solid entry, the single "Love Broke Thru," was a salad-days look back at when Toby first became a believer.

The album also featured the long-awaited studio reunion of dc Talk. The track "Love Feels Like," covered in-depth elsewhere in this book, gave a glimpse into an alternate universe where the group was still making hit albums. In another call-back to dc Talk days, "Joey E." from the *Free at Last* record even appeared on one of the album's interludes.

This Is Not A Test reached number four on the Billboard charts and number one on the Christian charts. It was certified Gold within two years of its release, won a 2015 Grammy Award for Best Contemporary Christian Music Album, and nabbed a 2016 Dove Award for Pop/Contemporary album of the year.

One of the best surprises on the *This Is Not a Test* album was that Toby's son, Truett, finally got to step up to the microphone in a serious capacity on the song "Backseat Driver." He'd been appearing in interludes on TobyMac albums for years. Behind the scenes, Truett had been writing his own music and crafting his own songs under the name "TRU." Later, he adopted the names "Truett Foster" and "Shiloh." In 2015, he even received credit for co-writing *This Is Not A Test's* "Lights Shine Bright" and Hollyn's "Alone" (a track he was also featured on).

Just as this book was going to press, news broke that Truett McKeehan had passed away unexpectedly at the age of twenty-one. Truett had immense musical talent and a future brimming with possibility. Not only was he a beloved son, brother, and friend to many, but he had just begun to share his artistry. Our hearts and prayers are with the McKeehan family and everyone who knew him. The world missed out on so much music and joy.

Hits Deep Live (2016 live album)
For several years, Toby had been following his major album tours with a "Hits Deep" concert series The idea was that an assortment of bands would go out together and play only their greatest hits. It was a takeoff on some of the more traditional label-based concert tours of the 1960s and 70s.

TobyMac had released three hit albums since his last live CD/DVD project, so the 2016 Hits Deep Tour was eyed as the perfect opportunity to record another one. The typical TobyMac show was a bit too long for the traditional CD format, but the Hits Deep show would be just about the right length.

Released on November 18th, 2016 to physical and digital media formats, *Hits Deep Live* was focused mostly on the *This Is Not A Test* album, but it also featured songs from almost every era of his solo career. Notable for dc Talk fans is the live audio/video of "Love Feels Like" featuring pre-recorded projections and vocals from Michael Tait and Kevin Max. The three got together and performed the song live as a trio at the Dove Awards that year, too.

Light of Christmas (2017)
On November 3rd, 2017, TobyMac released *Light of Christmas*, a project consisting of the Toby-led tracks from 2011's *Christmas in Diverse City* and a handful of new recordings. The new song "Bring on the Holidays" had been released in late 2016 with an animated music video put together by Allan and Nicole Rosenow, a team originally with Able Creative and now the proprietors of a family-owned animation company in Portland, Oregon. The album also contained the new track "Light of Christmas" (featuring award-winning mainstream artist Owl City) and "Can't Wait For Christmas" (featuring Reliant K).

The Elements (2018)

On October 12th, 2018, Toby's newest project, *The Elements*, was released.

While the entire album is solid, the first five tracks are an incredible suite of tunes that's become essential listening whether someone is a TobyMac fan or not. Track one, "The Elements," uses a thundering chorus and an innovative song structure to explore day-to-day human struggles. The second song, "I Just Need U," has a laid-back kind of magic. "Scars" is a universal pick-me-up. "Everything" is a retro-modern take on TobyMac's tried and true pop style. "Starts with Me," featuring new Gotee artist Aaron Cole, is a call to action and a thought-provoking exploration of race issues in the United States. Even though Toby has spent most of his career exploring the racial divide (from "Walls" to "Colored People" to the E.R.A.C.E. foundation and more), this song is the epitome of Toby McKeehan's approach of meeting diversity and inclusion issues with a message of acceptance, understanding, love, and initiative.

The Elements did well in the marketplace, reaching number 18 on the Billboard charts and number 1 on the Christian charts. At the time of this writing, the awards have yet to be given out for 2018 or 2019, but it's safe to assume that Toby will make another strong showing. The lead single, "I Just Need U," was by most accounts TobyMac's most successful single *ever*. The track was downloaded over half a million times in fifteen months.

Now in his fifties, Toby McKeehan shows no signs of slowing down. In addition to recording and touring as a solo artist, Toby stays busy as the president of Gotee Records. When he's not churning out Gold records or playing to crowds of thousands, he's mentoring new artists, collaborating with old friends, and keeping the same pace he's kept since the 1980s. He's asked more often than he'd probably like if he's ever going to retire. His plan is spelled out clearly in the 2015 *This Is Not A Test* album, though:

"Three, six, five, every minute, every day... 'Til the day I die."

This is good news for the millions of people who have been positively affected by his work over the past three decades. Even better for the ones who have yet to be blessed. One thing's for sure: Toby McKeehan will never be accused of resting on his laurels. Even if dc Talk never gets back together, fans still have a lot to look forward to.

Tait and the Newsboys

Tait: Empty (2001)
Collaborative by nature, Michael Tait's natural inclination as a solo artist was to form a band with close friends. His choice of drummer was an obvious one: Chad Chapin. Chad had not only been part of a small cover band called Curious George with Tait in the late 1990s, but the two had also roomed together for a time. Chad's brother Lonnie Chapin was an accomplished bass player, making him a natural choice, too. For guitars and additional production expertise, Tait turned to Pete Stewart.

Stewart, who had served as the frontman for a ForeFront group called Grammatrain, had collaborated with Tait on numerous songs in the past. He and Tait had even recorded a duet together called "Uphill Battle" for ForeFront's *X: The Birthday Album*. Grammatrain had put out hard-edged alternative rock, and Michael, who appreciated the sound of *Jesus Freak* and rock 'n roll in general, wanted to move a bit more in that direction.

Michael decided to name his new band "Tait." The name wasn't a tribute to himself; it was a tribute to his father, who had passed away in February 1998.

Personally and professionally, Michael Tait was one of the most respected names in the Christian music industry. When the schedule was set in 2001 for the release of dc Talk's solo records, fans and industry veterans alike were excited to see that Tait was up first. His band's debut album, *Empty*, was slated for release on July 3rd. "Loss 4 Words" came out ahead of the album on the soundtrack for *Extreme Days*. Featuring rock guitars and melodic pop vocals, "Loss 4 Words" was a good indication of what the rest of the album would sound like. It should be noted, however, that the version of "Loss 4 Words" on *Extreme Days* was much more raw than the one released on *Empty*. "Alibi" and "All You Got," released on the *Solo* EP, were well-received by fans and helped confirm Tait's overall rock/pop sound.

Toby McKeehan co-wrote two of the new songs on the album, plus a previously-unreleased dc Talk track that Tait recycled called "Carried Away." "All You Got," a song about being there for a friend during dark times, was one of the tracks McKeehan and Tait had written together. Fans couldn't help but wonder if the song was born out of the personal struggles that one or both of them were dealing with in the wake of dc Talk splitting up. The other song McKeehan contributed to, "American Tragedy," explored the country's history with racism. The album version of the song included historical narration clips that exemplified the racism found in America's past, including a clip that uses one of the most derogatory words in the English language. The pre-release version of the track lacked the narration clips, though. Michael Tait explained that he'd had to fight with the record company to include them.

Daniel Joseph, co-writer of "What If I Stumble" and "My Will" for dc Talk, co-wrote "Talk About Jesus" and "Unglued" on *Empty*. Mark Heimermann, dc Talk's producer, co-wrote "Tell Me Why."

Seeing as how the band was named for Michael's father, it was only fitting that the final album track be dedicated to him. "Unglued," one of the most touching songs in dc Talk's extended canon, explored the feelings that surround the loss of a loved one. The piano was played by none other than Tait's good friend

A Fan's Guide to dc Talk

Michael W. Smith.

A secret track with a jam session was included at the end of the album, and an *extra* secret track was included at the beginning. If the listener held the "rewind" button on a CD copy of the album before the first track began, they'd be treated to several minutes of Michael leaving humorous messages on his own answering machine.

Tait's *Empty* came out on July 3rd, 2001 as scheduled. Critics reacted positively to the album. Fans *loved* it. As Tait's band finished up on the dc Talk Solo Tour, ForeFront Records made plans for a follow-up.

Tait: Lose This Life (2003)

When Tait went back into the studio to record the band's second album, he brought a secret weapon with him: legendary dc Talk producer Mark Heimermann. Tait, describing Heimermann as a "musical genius," knew that the *Nu Thang*, *Free at Last*, *Jesus Freak*, and *Supernatural* producer was the perfect person to take his sophomore record to the next level.

The result of this collaboration was a strong rock/pop record that refuses to sound dated even fifteen years later. Missing from the Tait equation was guitarist Pete Stewart, though, who had left the band to pursue other projects. In his place was guitarist Justin York.

Lose This Life was released on November 4th, 2003. The record was even more successful than *Empty*, winning a 2004 Dove Award for Rock Album of the Year and having two songs show up on Billboard's Hot Christian Songs chart.

The record had several standout tracks. "Numb" was co-written with Toby McKeehan. Interestingly enough, the track had a rap segment, but the rap was *not* performed by Toby – Rob Beckley of Pillar delivered the verse. One of the big rockers on the album, "Wait," had been performed at shows earlier in 2003 with different lyrics. "God Can You Hear Me" was one of the best songs on the album and served as a highlight of their live show. A cover of "Electric Avenue" and a symphonic, classic rendition of "The Christmas Song" made for a solid and varied track list.

In 2004, Michael Tait performed the lead part in the rock opera *!Hero*, a modern take on Jesus' ministry set in Bethlehem, Pennsylvania. The project was written by long-time friend Eddie DeGarmo of DeGarmo and Key, one of the folks who had founded ForeFront Records and had launched dc Talk's (and thus Michael Tait's) careers. Tait's former bandmate, Pete Stewart, was the soundtrack's audio engineer and producer. In addition to plenty of critical acclaim, Michael Tait and his fellow performers won a Dove Award.

The Tait band was successful, but despite a killer record and dynamic live show, attempts at a third Tait album eventually lost steam. The album was planned and partially recorded, though. It was titled *Loveology*. The producer was Evanescence's Ben Moody. Only one song from the album ever surfaced: a track called "Glimmer." It was featured on Michael Tait's online social media profile for a time, but it's since been removed.

After numerous personnel shifts, Tait's last show as a band was performed in 2007.

Newsboys: Born Again (2010)
Back in the 1990s, as dc Talk was making hit records and headlining concerts, one of their old touring buddies was also enjoying *their* fair share of success. The Newsboys, dc Talk's partners on 1991's Nu Skool Jam Tour, had released over a dozen records since they were founded. With over twenty-five hit

singles, a handful of Dove Awards, Grammy nominations, and several critically acclaimed tours with over-the-top special effects, the Newsboys had been one of the most popular acts in Christian music for over two decades.

Shortly after their 2009 album *In the Hands of God*, the Newsboys made the surprising announcement that Peter Furler, the lead singer, would be departing the band to travel with his family and embark on a solo career. Filling in for him as the new lead singer of the Newsboys would be their old friend: Michael Tait.

Some fans found the change a bit jarring at first, though it wasn't the first time that the Newsboys had changed lead singers. For the first several years of their existence, the a singer named John James had been lead vocalist. But to add a little confusion to the mix, Tait, who had been living in Malibu and spending a little time away from the industry, wasn't even initially sure if he was a temporary fill-in or a permanent replacement.

Peter Furler continued to make special appearances with the Newsboys throughout the rest of 2009 as their live show was revamped to capitalize on Michael Tait's talents. dc Talk songs like "My Will," "Colored People," "In the Light," and "Jesus Freak" were brought in and out of the show. Behind the scenes, the group (sans Furler) began recording new material. Much of it was debuted on tour as it was finished. Tait became entrenched in the process, audiences responded positively to the new live shows, and the band released a five-song EP to test the market. It seemed that the change would work, so Tait became permanent.

The EP was released on January 5th, 2010. Former dc Talk dancer Juan Otero co-wrote all five of the songs featured. All of them except for "On Your Knees" became part of the new show. A few months later, "I'll Be" was released as a single. Response continued to be positive, so the group began a quick, intensive recording process. On July 13th, 2010, the aptly-titled *Born Again* album was released.

Born Again was a smash hit, debuting at number *four* on the mainstream Billboard charts and taking number one on the Christian charts. Though "I'll Be" had been a successful single, it was mysteriously absent from the album's final track listing. The record *did* feature a brand new recording of the song "Jesus Freak" though, with Tait doing both verses and the rap portion going to an artist named KJ-52. Reportedly, TobyMac had been approached about providing the rap verses for the new cover. He'd declined for undisclosed reasons, though it certainly wasn't because his relationship with Tait or the Newsboys had soured – they remained close friends and would cross paths often over the next several years.

The new singles "Born Again" and "Way Beyond Myself" were also released that year as the Newsboys embarked on the wildly popular Born Again Experience Tour to support their new material. Less than a year after *Born Again's* release, the band put out a deluxe version of the album. It contained the new singles "Save Your Life" and "We Remember" – the latter written by members of *another* former dc Talk touring partner: Audio Adrenaline. "I'll Be" and Tait's version of the 2009 Newsboys song "Glorious" was also featured on the album, along with a few other bonus tracks and remixes.

Newsboys: Christmas! A Newsboys Holiday (2010)

2010 was a busy year for the Newsboys. To ring in the holiday season, they recorded a Christmas EP with their new lead singer. It consisted of four newly-recorded tracks and "The Christmas Song" from Tait's *Lose This Life* album. It was released on October 12th, 2010. All four of the new songs on the project charted as singles on Billboard's Hot Christian Songs.

Newsboys: God's Not Dead (2011)

Tait and the Newsboys didn't know what a day off looked like in 2010 and 2011. Coming off the heels of a successful tour, they went back to the studio to record a new album.

God's Not Dead, released on November 15th, 2011, leaned more toward the worship genre and consisted mostly of cover songs. Major highlights for dc Talk fans were the two tracks that reunited Michael Tait with Kevin Max. The title track, which was also the album's lead single, featured background vocals and a bridge by Max. Kevin's other contribution, "I Am Second," sounded like a modern-day dc Talk song.

The album reached number 45 on the mainstream Billboard charts and took the number one spot on the Christian charts. It enjoyed a second wave of success when the title track was featured in a 2014 film also titled *God's Not Dead*. The Newsboys themselves had a small acting role in the movie.

Later that year, the album was certified Gold. In 2015, the single was certified Platinum – the only Newsboys release in over three decades to ever achieve that distinction.

Newsboys Live in Concert: God's Not Dead (2012)

On July 12th, 2012 and July 14th, 2012, the Newsboys shows at Lifest (in Oshkosh, Wisconsin) and Sonshine Festival (in Willmar, Minnesota) were professionally recorded. To bridge the gap between Newsboys albums, the shows were edited, mastered, and packaged for a live CD/digital release called *Newsboys Live in Concert: God's Not Dead*. Hitting the market on October 22nd, 2012, the album contained live versions of hits from *Born Again* and *God's Not Dead* as well as Tait's version of Newsboys classics like "Something Beautiful" and "He Reigns." A live version of "Jesus Freak" was included on the album with the rap portion performed by UN1ON's George Moss.

Tait and the Newsboys

Newsboys: Restart (2013)
Veteran Newsboys producer Seth Mosley was joined by Joshua Silverberg for the Newsboys' next album, *Restart*. Released on September 10th, 2013, *Restart* was the revamped Newsboys' most solid effort yet. It took the pop and rock elements from *Born Again*, added some of the worship-oriented focus of *God's Not Dead*, and sprinkled in modern electronic dance sensibilities for a monster sixteen-track (on the deluxe version) extravaganza. *Restart* conquered the Christian charts and made an impressive showing at number 38 on the mainstream Billboard chart.

In interviews leading up to the record's release, Tait told the media that he hadn't been this excited about an album since *Jesus Freak*. While some of that may have been marketing speak, the project did produce some of the best tracks of the Newsboys' storied career. "Live with Abandon" and "We Believe" were standouts, the latter being featured on a compilation honoring Billy Graham. "We Believe" went Gold in 2017, having been downloaded over half a million times. "That Home," a moving tribute to a dying mother co-written by Juan Otero, was a timely inclusion: Michael Tait's mom passed away two days after the album's release. Kevin Max appeared on the deluxe edition's "Man on Fire." The album's packaging lists him as a guest vocalist on "The Living Years," but he's nowhere to be found. One of the other bonus tracks sounds suspiciously like a TobyMac song and was even created by TobyMac producers Christopher Stevens and David Garcia, leading to speculation that an earlier version of the song had failed to make Toby's *Eye on It* record and had been rerouted to the Newsboys instead.

Newsboys: Hallelujah for the Cross (2014)
Somehow, the Newsboys found time in a wall-to-wall touring schedule to record *Hallelujah for the Cross* – an album consisting of modern but respectful takes on classic hymns. Produced by Seth Mosley, the album was released on November 4th, 2014. A

notable track was Michael Tait's version of the 1992 Newsboys classic "Where You Belong/Turn Your Eyes Upon Jesus" from their classic *Not Ashamed* album. The final track, "All Hail the Power of Jesus' Name," was an a cappella song with Michael Tait joined by Newsboys guitarist and backup singer Jody Davis.

Newsboys: Love Riot (2016)

Love Riot, the band's next album, was released on March 4th, 2016. Consisting of ten tracks (six of which were played on the Newsboys' next tour), *Love Riot* dropped most of the electronic dance production for a more streamlined rock, pop, and worship approach.

Thanks to new label Fair Trade Services and a partnership with Columbia Records, the album received wide distribution. In addition to coming in at an incredible number 14 on the mainstream Billboard chart, it swept the number one spot on the mainstream Rock Albums and Alternative Albums charts. It couldn't claim the top spot on the Christian charts, as that position was the sole domain of a project called *Hymns that Are Important to Us* – the final album recorded by husband-and-wife duo Joey + Rory as Joey was dying of cervical cancer.

The movie *God's Not Dead 2* was released within weeks of *Love Riot*. "Guilty," *Love Riot's* fourth track, was featured on the film's soundtrack. Other notable songs from *Love Riot* included "You Hold It All (Every Mountain)," "No Longer Slaves," "Crazy," and the title track. When the song "Hero" was performed during encores, it featured some of the most impressive vocal performances of Michael Tait's career.

Newsboys United (2019)

In 2017, former lead singer Peter Furler reunited with the current line-up of the Newsboys to record a single called "The Cross Has the Final Word." After joining them for a few concerts and seeing the fans' enthusiastic response, the band formulated a plan to bring Furler back into the fold.

"Newsboys United" kicked off their first tour in the spring of 2018. Consisting of the regular Newsboys line-up and joined by former members Peter Furler and Phil Joel, the supergroup toured more than forty cities. Most shows consisted of a short set with Michael Tait on lead vocals, a full retro Newsboys set with Furler and Joel on stage, and another set with Michael Tait leading the group. It ended with both Tait and Furler singing "The Cross Has the Final Word."

The outing was successful enough to book Furler and Joel for *another* United tour. As that geared up, Newsboys band members from the past and present began working on an album together. Released on May 10th, 2019, the new album *Newsboys United* featured both Michael Tait and Peter Furler on lead vocals. Shooting up to number 20 on the Billboard chart and number one on the Christian charts, the newest hit record from the Newsboys continued in the pop/rock/worship mold of past releases. The single "Greatness of Our God" was well-received. dc Talk fans found a gem in "Love One Another," a track that featured a brief guest appearance from Kevin Max.

What does the future hold for the Newsboys? The Newsboys brand is as strong as its ever been, so we'll likely be seeing a lot more from Michael and crew over the next several years. And it should be noted that at this point, Michael Tait has been with the Newsboys almost as long as he was with dc Talk!

Kevin Max's Solo Career

Stereotype Be (2001)
Kevin Max had been exploring the possibility of a solo record since before *Jesus Freak* was released. In the mid-1990s, he'd gone on a small tour with his group "The Strangers" to test the waters. At the time, dc Talk was booked for nearly a hundred shows a year, so long-term solo plans never came together. But at the conclusion of the Supernatural Experience Tour, both he and Michael Tait were finally ready to strike out on their own. Kevin began writing songs in earnest, finding new collaborators and recording dozens of demos. As the demos moved into the studio, Max assembled a team of all-stars including Adrian Belew as producer and guitarist (King Crimson, David Bowie, Frank Zappa), Tony Levin on bass (John Lennon, Stevie Nicks, Paul Simon, Tom Waits), and Matt Chamberlain on the drums (Pearl Jam, Tori Amos, Bruce Springsteen). One of his writing partners for the album was a familiar face: dc Talk guitarist Mark Townsend. The vast majority of the songs were co-written with an up-and-comer named Erick Cole. Max and Cole continue to collaborate and perform together even today.

The record that resulted from these efforts, *Stereotype Be*, was a magical trip through several genres. Songs ranged from electro-pop to alternative rock to Beatles-inspired numbers and even tracks with a Middle Eastern flair. Entries like "The Secret Circle" and "Existence" were masterpieces. "Blind" was a blend of progressive rock, show tune, and jazz. The legend himself, Larry

Norman, appeared in the background of a track called "On and On." Two spoken-word tracks rounded out the effort. The album was received well by critics, sales broke the 100,000 mark, and it charted on the Billboards Christian Music ranking for four weeks (peaking at number twelve).

Like Toby and Tait's records, *Stereotype Be* was released on ForeFront Records. For a variety of reasons, ForeFront and Max decided to part ways after this album. The decision was ultimately a good one. History has shown that the less interference Kevin Max has from record labels, the better his albums are.

Stereotype Be was an auspicious start to an incredible and varied solo career. Being a Kevin Max fan has always been a rewarding experience. Listeners who expect an artist to find a formula that works and stick to it may be turned off, but his catalog is so deep and wide that folks from almost any walk of life can find something amazing to explore.

For fans of the *Stereotype Be* record, Kevin Max has released two projects that expanded on it. The first was an album called *Stereotype Be-Sides* that contained several early, alternate, and cut tracks from the album. The second was an acoustic EP which contained four new unplugged recordings of *Stereotype Be* tracks.

Raven Songs 101 (2003)

On April 7th, 2003, Max released a spoken-word project called *Raven Songs 101*. The album contained poetry by Kevin and backing tracks by the incomparable Adrien Belew. Of note was the track "Black Leather and a Microphone" which served as the background music for kevinmax.com during this time period. The project contained eleven entries in total.

Between the Fence and the Universe (2004)

In the years that followed the release of *Stereotype Be*, Max continued to write songs at a feverish pace. At one point in 2004, he had a handful of solid tracks that worked well together, but not enough to form a cohesive album. Friends and fellow artists urged him to release them anyway, and so the EP project *Between the Fence and the Universe* was born.

The project included some of Max's best work yet. Songs like "Seek" and "Stranded 72.5" still get played at some of his shows, and "Irish Hymn" was one of the best mid-tempo rock ballads ever recorded by anyone. Also notable was a personal, intimate song about relationship struggles called "To the Dearly Departed."

The Imposter (2005)

Kevin Max's first project for Northern Records, *The Imposter*, can be considered his full-length sophomore album. Released on October 11th, 2005, *The Imposter* contained several standouts. Songs like "Confessional Booth," "Sanctuary," "Your Beautiful Mind," and "Fade to Red" worked well with any audience. One of Max's best vocal performances ever can be found on the song "When He Returns," a cover of the Bob Dylan classic. Like the *Between the Fence and the Universe* project, many of the lyrics were very personal and introspective. "Platform" was perhaps the best example of this, revealing some of Max's frustrations and questions about having been tasked with being a role model to such a large audience.

Holy Night (2005)

Released only a few months after *The Imposter*, Kevin Max's classic Christmas album *Holy Night* deserves shelf space next to any of the holiday offerings by Andy Williams or Elvis Presley. At times reverent, at times joyous, and always managing to capture both the sanctity and the mystery of the Christmas season, Max's *Holy Night* is undoubtedly an annual tradition for the holidays in many households.

The Blood (2007)
Even dc Talk fans who hadn't explored much of Kevin Max's solo work found much to love on *The Blood*. Released on December 18th, 2007 for a new record label, Kevin Max's *The Blood* was a gospel and blues record that paid homage to the roots of the genres. A must-listen was track two, a cover of Prince's "The Cross" featuring Michael Tait and Toby McKeehan. Collaborations abound on the record with Chris Sligh, Amy Grant, Vince Gill, Erica Campbell of Mary Mary, and Joanne Cash all making appearances.

Crashing Gates (2008)
A record that sounds like it picked up where 2005's *The Imposter* left off, *Crashing Gates* was the warm-up for a full-length album that Max was working on called *Cotes D' Armor*. His first release on dPulse records, *Crashing Gates* came out on December 9th, 2008. "Traveler" was one of his best recordings to date, and a new acoustic version of "Beautiful Mind" sounded just as good as the 2005 version. "The Saint of Lonely Hearts" was part of a remix contest: the individual track stems (including the vocal track) were given away for free, and listeners were challenged to make their own version of the song. Entries ranged from electro-pop to rock to jazz: perfect representations of Max's penchant for moving effortlessly through genres.

Cotes D' Armor (2010)
One of Kevin Max's most eclectic offerings was *Cotes D' Armor*, a dPulse Recordings label project released on August 24th, 2010. Along with a reimagining of songs from *Crashing Gates*, one of the highlights of the album was "On Yer Bike!," an innovative track where New Wave hitched a ride with 60's surf music and took off down uncharted roads. "Walking Through Walls (Just To Get To You)" and "Even When It Hurts" were the most radio-friendly offerings, though many fans preferred the demo of

"Walking Through Walls" to the album version. "Unholy Triad" was classic Kevin Max – heavy with the mysterious, poetic, pop feel that Max excels at. He wouldn't make another track quite like it until "That Was Then and This Is Now" on 2015's *Broken Temples* album. One more track should be noted: an instrumental found near the end of the album called "Death of CCM (Cybergenic Cyclic Machines)." The "CCM" term was taken as a humorous play on the "contemporary Christian music" industry label that Max was drifting in and out of during this period of his solo career.

Fiefdom of Angels: Side One (2012)
One of the most incredible projects from the mind of Kevin Max is definitely the *Fiefdom of Angels* concept: a novel/comic book/album/future film project that builds a world around the concept of Lucifer's fall. One of the *Fiefdom of Angels* products released in 2012 was the first half of the soundtrack: a collection of four covers and a re-recording of a *Stereotype Be* demo that dealt with the concept of angels. Synthetic strings and light orchestration surrounded Max's otherworldly voice, making for innovative re-imaginings of Real Life's "Send Me an Angel," Queen's "Dragon Attack," Joy Division's "Shadowplay," and Muse's "Take a Bow."

Demos and early versions of *Side Two* were put up on social media a few years ago, but a final product has yet to surface. The release was complicated by Kevin Max joining Audio Adrenaline as lead singer later that year. One of Side Two's highlights was an amazing cover of David Bowie's "Scary Monsters."

Audio Adrenaline: Kings & Queens (2013)
dc Talk's had spent years touring with their old label mates and opening band, Audio Adrenaline, throughout the mid-1990s. After gaining their own fanbase and finding their own footing, Audio Adrenaline had stepped out of dc Talk's shadow to

become headliners in their own right. Albums like *Some Kind of Zombie*, *Underdog*, and *Lift* had charted well, produced several hit singles for the group, and had led to other projects like live VHS/DVD releases. But when their lead singer, Mark Stuart, developed vocal problems in the 2000s, it looked like the band might be finished.

Taking an idea from the Newsboys (who had recently acquired Michael Tait as their new lead singer), the machine behind a new version of Audio Adrenaline reached out to Kevin Max and offered him the frontman position. Given dc Talk's longstanding history with the band and Kevin's friendship with original bassist Will McGinniss (who was part of the new effort) and former lead singer Mark Stuart (who was even married to Toby McKeehan's sister at one point), Kevin Max accepted the position and moved into the role as if moving in with extended family.

On March 12, 2013, the new Audio Adrenaline—fronted by Kevin—released an album called *Kings & Queens*. The album's title track and lead single (co-written with former dc Talk dancer Juan Otero) was geared toward a charity that Audio Adrenaline had helped found in Haiti called Hands and Feet.

The album rose to number 70 in the Billboard charts – an impressive showing for what essentially amounted to a debut album. It reached number four in the Christian charts. Though it wasn't one of the songs frequently highlighted, the best song on the album was "Seeker." It showcased Max's vocal ability better than even most of his own solo work.

After *Kings & Queens*, there was much internal discussion about what future Audio Adrenaline albums should sound like. Max and some of the other members continued working toward a pop/indie sound, while the group's management started steering them toward the praise and worship genre. In an open letter (currently still published on a website called *hallels.com*), Max explained that the praise and worship direction wouldn't be the right fit for the style of music he was best at creating. After two years with the group, he left his role as Audio Adrenaline's lead singer and returned to making solo projects.

Broken Temples (2015)
If Kevin Max's 2015 album *Broken Temples* sounds a lot like a follow-up to his Audio Adrenaline album, well... it *is*. Many of the songs (particularly those found on the deluxe version) were taken from early sessions for the follow-up to *Kings & Queens*. Highlights on this album include "Good Kings Highway," "Light Me Up," and "Infinite" (featuring Rachel Lampa). The song "That Was Then And This Is Now" was released online with a slideshow of photos from Kevin Max's life and career. Derek Webb, a musician known for his work with Caedmon's Call and his own extensive solo career, contributed two remixes to the project.

Starry Eyes Surprise (2015)
Kevin Max's next solo entry was a sophisticated mix of standards and classics called *Starry Eyes Surprise*. Released in October 2015, the project covered everything from "Moon River" to "Sunglasses At Night" to "When You Wish Upon A Star." dc Talk fans particularly enjoyed Michael Tait's guest spot on "Nature Boy," the first track of this calming, haunting album.

Playing Games with the Shadow (2016)
After a long and storied career with dc Talk and after multiple collaborations as a solo artist, Max wondered what a true *solo* album would be like. Free of label suggestions and outside input; something directly from his mind to the pen and keyboard. He set about writing songs for a new project by himself. He didn't bring in producers or studio musicians to record it until the material was nearly complete. *Playing Games with the Shadow*, released on April 2nd, 2016, was the result.

Kevin Max's Solo Career

Highlights include "Girl with the Tiger Eyes" (one of the best songs of Max's career, produced in part with dc Talk cohort John Mark Painter) and "Muzick is Magic!," a solid rock song that Max performed on both Jesus Freak Cruises. Like most Kevin Max albums, several tracks written for this album didn't make it onto the final track listing. It's unknown if they'll ever be released, but fans hope they will.

Serve Somebody (2017)

Kevin's next solo project was a cover album called *Serve Somebody* released on July 7th, 2017. Two different covers of the title track, originally written by Bob Dylan, were featured on the project. Other highlights included "Pride (In the Name Of Love)" (originally by U2) and a cover of dc Talk's "Red Letters." Max's solo version of "Red Letters" was carried by acoustic guitars at a faster tempo. Another dc Talk connection exists here: the vinyl record arm of TobyMac's Gotee Records helped launch and distribute the album. *Serve Somebody* also featured covers of Rich Mullins, Larry Norman, The Call, and more.

AWOL (2018)

The first of 2018's jaunts back to the 1980s with Kevin Max was his album *AWOL* released on June 8th, 2018. According to a statement by Max on his website, the album was about "paying homage to [his] heroes" and "creating songs that cannot be defined by a genre." Fans of groups like The Smiths, Duran Duran, and David Bowie found a lot to love about this album. As usual, Max didn't just imitate his influences – he channeled their essences and added his own style. Highlights of the album are many, but "Melissa," "Moonracer," and the title track are must-listens.

Romeo Drive (2018)

Fans could hardly keep up with Kevin Max's superhuman release schedule when his second album of the year, *Romeo Drive*, was released on October 31st, 2018. Fully dedicating himself to electronic music and synthesizers, *Romeo Drive* is Max's most immersive concept album ever. It was created with the synth-pop group Service Unicorn (members "Chrys Anthemum" and "Dan D. Lion"). Around the time of the album's release, Max performed a couple shows featuring several New Wave covers.

Black Sheep of the Fold (2019)
Max's latest release is a greatest hits project with a very specific theme: individuality. Titled *Black Sheep of the Fold*, the compilation was first available on the 2019 Jesus Freak Cruise. It contained songs from several of Max's past projects.

More Kevin Max material is on the way. At the time of this writing, Kevin is in the process of formulating a tribute album to his late friend, the Christian music pioneer Larry Norman. Given Kevin's vast and varied discography, there will certainly be more exciting and innovative projects to follow.

My Friend, So Long!

Whether you're a casual fan or you're what they used to call an "ardent enthusiast," I hope you've enjoyed this trip down memory lane. With over ten years as a group and nearly two decades of solo work, there was certainly a lot of ground to cover here! Hopefully, this book will be a worthy companion as you rediscover (or discover for the first time) dc Talk's industry-shattering discography, tours, work, and (hopefully) upcoming live appearances.

This is the end of the book, but it's certainly not the end of the dc Talk story. At the time of this writing, dc Talk has just pulled into port after their second reunion cruise together. As the twenty-fifth anniversary of *Jesus Freak* is approaching, the buzz for new material and a new tour has never been louder. Numerous discussions and meetings have already taken place to determine just what can be done to bring dc Talk back in some form or fashion. To start out, Kevin Max is going out on tour with the Newsboys in just a few weeks for their fall 2019 dates.

But, honestly – even if the three of them never step foot on the same stage together again, they've already given us so much to listen to and think about. And even if the three of them never again utter the words "dc Talk," their continued solo work will always have echoes of everything they've achieved together.

Don't lose hope for more dc Talk, though. The future is brighter than it's been in a while.

Here's hoping that the next edition of the book will have plenty of new songs and concerts to explore.

Until then – My Friend, So Long!

Bibliography

The majority of the information in this book was pulled from album liner notes, official credits, press releases, fan club materials (shout-out to the Vibe Tribe!), various anecdotes and conversations that band members have shared with the author and other fans over the years, interviews and official videos published by dc Talk's record label / managers / social media accounts, and other primary avenues. Threads were followed from there through various discographies, newspaper articles, websites, archival materials, and other resources.

Concert history information was put together with the assistance of Bert Gangl. As I provided him concert listings from press releases, merchandise, fan club materials, advertisements, and even the backs of t-shirts, he meticulously verified each one with newspaper or magazine reviews, credible recollections from concert-goers, and a variety of other methods. He found dozens of entries that I had overlooked. Bert's assistance in painting a fuller picture of dc Talk's history on the concert stage was invaluable to this project. Thank you, Bert!

Significant sources of information in this book are cited within the text wherever possible. Other resources that were particularly helpful in constructing this project are listed on the next several pages.

Articles:
Adolph, Bruce and Konstantopoulos, Stefan. "Diversity Among Brothers." *Christian Musician*, November/December 2004, pp 20-35.

Akins, Debra. "dc Talk Inks General Market Deal." *CCM Magazine*. January 1997, p 10.

Atwood, Brett. "Maxwell Brews Righteous 'Freak'." *Billboard Magazine*, 11 November 1995.

Brown, Bruce A. "DC Talk: Def, Not Dumb." *CCM Magazine*, December 1990, pp 24-26.

Bubel, Kathy. "DC Talks At Last." *Release*, May/June 1994, pp 16-18.

"'Buttefly Kisses' Nabs Grammy for Country Song of the Year; dc Talk Earns Second Consecutive NARAS Honor." *CCM Magazine*, April 1998, p 16.

Carlozo, Lou. "Rich Mullins' Last Musical Vision." *Chicago Tribune*, 28 June 1998. https://www.chicagotribune.com/news/ct-xpm-1998-06-28-9806280334-story.html

"Christian Singer Killed in Accident." *Spartanburg Herald-Journal*, 22 September 1997.

"Christian Singer Mullins Killed in Auto Accident." *Sarasota Herald-Tribune*, 23 September 1997.

"DC Talk: Sometimes You Just Gotta Break the Rules." *Inside Music*, June/July 1990, p. 25.

"DC Talk Wins Big at First Annual America's Christian Music

Bibliography

Awards." *CCM Magazine*, November 1994, pp 14-18.

Degen, Matt. "dc Talk Members Test Solo Waters." *The Orange County Register*, 24 June 2001.

Dougherty, Steve. "Rap Finds God." *People Magazine*, 24 January 1994. p 85.

Faris, T.L. "In Concert: Nu Skool Jam Tour." *CCM Magazine*, December 1991, p 64.

Farris, Christa. "The Life and Times of tobyMac." *CCM Magazine*, September 2004, pp 28-33.

Fernandez, Mike. "Breaking Fire: Tait Shatters Stereotypes and Reaches Out to Empty Souls." *Music News & Review*, July/August 2001, pp 18-20.

Fischer, John. "Consider This: 'Jesus Freak' Re-visited." *CCM Magazine*, December, 1997, p 68.

Friebel, Melanie. "The Year of DC Talk." *Calendar*, Spring/Summer 1994, pp 12-14.

Granger, Thom. "Super Freak." *CCM Magazine*, December 1995, p 61.

Granger, Thom. "What's New: Freed Up." *CCM Magazine*, December 1992, p 42.

Hefner, April. "At Last: Getting to Know DC Talk." *CCM Magazine*, October 1994, pp 34-43.

Hefner, April. Rumburg, Gregory. Riddle, Melissa. "O Brothers, Where Art Thou?" *CCM Magazine*, May 2001, pp 36-46.

Hefner, April. "Still Billy." *CCM Magazine*, May 1998, pp 40-42.

Hefner, April. "Supermen." *CCM Magazine*, October 1998, pp 30-40.

Lutes, Chris. "DC Talkin': Three Jesus Freaks Speak for Themselves." *Campus Life*, November 1995, pp 12-16.

Lutes, Chris. "Expressions: The Ego Thang." *Campus Life*, May/June 1994, pp 23-26.

Lutes, Chris. "Much More Than Talk." *Shout!*, December 1995, pp 38-44.

McKelvey, Douglas. "Jesus Freaks & Silver Screens." *Release*, December 1995, pp 22-28.

Michael, Robert and Hoagland, Colleen. "DC Talk: Tearin' Down the Walls." *Christian Activities Calendar*, Spring/Summer 1992, pp 10-12.

Moring, Mark. "Out of This World." *Campus Life*, November/December 1998, pp 22-25.

Newcomb, Brian Quincy. "The Fast and Furious World of toby Mac." *CCM Magazine*, June 2003, pp 22-26.

O'Conner, Joey. "It's a Rap with DC Talk." *Brio*, March 1994, pp 17-25.

Oldenburg, Ann. "DC Talk Bless with Success." *USA Today*, 4 December 1995.

Pierce, Ray. "Give Peace a Chance: Christian Artists Mark Arkansas Racial Reconciliation Week." *CCM Magazine*, November

Bibliography

1997, p 15.

Pryor, Rona. "dc Talk: A Chord of Three Strands." *Christian Musician*, May/June 2001, pp 14-43.

Pryor, Rona. "Denny Keitzman: King of the Road." *Christian Musician*, May/June 2001, pp 34-40.

Rake, Jamie Lee. "Putting (DC) Talk Into Action." *CCM Magazine*, November 1992, pp 30-33.

Ross, Michael. "Toby McKeehan: Walikin' His Talk." *Breakaway*, February 2001, pp 16-18.

Rumburg, Gregory. "The Rockford Files." *CCM Magazine*, December 1995, pp 32-39.

Stewart, Sheryl. "tobyMac Returns to His First Love." *Music News & Review*, July/August 2001, pp 28-31.

Walker, Abbie. "Just a Bunch of Freaks." *Youth 97*, June 1997, pp 20-21.

Books:
dc Talk. *Supernatural Tour 1999*. Print.

Key, Dana. *WWJD Interactive Devotional*. Zondervan Publishing House, 1997. Print.

Max, Kevin. *Unfinished Work*. Thomas Nelson Publishers, 2001. Print.

Videos:
"A Look at Gotee Artists & Repertoire." *Gotee Records*, 1994.

"ActionHouse TV: Inside Extreme Days." *Impact Entertainment*, 2001.

"Creation Festival: The Movie." *The Creation Festival, a div. of Come Alive Ministries, Inc.*, 2000.

"Creation Festival Live." *Creation Festival LLC.*, 2006.

"The dc Talk Video Singles." *ForeFront Records*, 1998.

"dc Talk: The Supernatural Experience with Jennifer Knapp and the W's Tour Preview VHS." *ForeFront Records*, 1998.

"dc Talk: The Supernatural Experience." *ForeFront Records*, 1999.

"dc Talk and Audio Adrenaline: Jesus Freak 1996 Tour Promo Video." *ForeFront Records*, 1996.

Fletcher, DeAnna. "Tobymac: New Record, That dc Talk Reunion Cruise, and More." *UCB (ucb.co.uk)*, 22 June 2016. https://www.youtube.com/watch?v=UiMvVmbKvdM

"Free at Last: The Movie." *ForeFront Records*, 2002.

"ForeFront Records: X: The Birthday Video." *ForeFront Records*, 1998.

"God's Late Night Show: The Works." *BGEA*, 1994.

"Keep the Faith." *TVFirst*, 1996.

"Narrow is the Road." *The ForeFront Communications Group*, 1994.

Bibliography

"On the ForeFront Volume 1." *The ForeFront Communications Group*, 1991.

"Rap, Rock and Soul." *The ForeFront Communications Group*, 1991.

"Sneak Peek of the Supernatural Experience." *ForeFront Records*, 1999.

"TobyMac and Michael W. Smith Guess 90's Christian Music." *WAY Nation*, 20 May 2019.
https://www.youtube.com/watch?v=L8NG-c0t62I

"Welcome to the Freak Show." *The ForeFront Communications Group*, 1997.

Websites:
Artist Pages at grammy.com. *Recording Academy*.
https://www.grammy.com

Blackwood, Danl. "RichMailList 204: The Jesus Record FAQ." 5 May 1998 (Updated 4 July 1999).
https://www.kidbrothers.net/rmml/rmml204.html

"CCM Magazine Chat with TobyMac." *CCM Magazine*. 28 September 2004. http://www.ccmcom.com/features/2828.aspx.

Chart Histories at Billboard.com. *Billboard*.
https://www.billboard.com/music/dc-talk/chart-history/

"Chillin' with TobyMac." *jesusfreakhideout.com*. 22 October 2004.
https://www.jesusfreakhideout.com/interviews/TobyMac.asp

"Dealing with Diverse City: A ccmbuzz Exclusive Interview with

tobyMac." *CCMBuzz*. 14 September 2004.
http://ccmbuzz.com/modules.php?name=News&file=article&sid=851

Entries at Recording Industry Association of America. *RIAA*. https://www.riaa.com/

Hartse, Joel Heng. "Jesus Freak." *Chrindie '95 essay collection at medium.com*. 17 November 2015. https://medium.com/chrindie-95/dc-talk-s-jesus-freak-7273f0a39059

Moring, Mark. "My Dad, My Hero." *Christianity Today*. https://www.christianitytoday.com/iyf/truelifestories/interestingpeople/9c6025.html?start=1

Official dc Talk Website. *True Artist Management*. dctalk.com

Official Kevin Max Website. *Max, Kevin*. kevinmax.com

"Past Winners." *Gospel Music Association*. https://doveawards.com/awards/past-winners/

Sarachik, Justin. "'Jesus Freak' at 20." *CCM Magazine*. 15 January 2016. https://www.ccmmagazine.com/features/jesus-freak-at-20/

Sarachik, Justin. "TobyMac Says 'DC Talk' Was Originally His Rapper Name." *rapzilla.com*. 28 January 2019. https://rapzilla.com/2019-01-tobymac-dc-talk-original-name

"Toby Mac: Musician/Record Executive." *CQBibleStudy.org*. https://www.cqbiblestudy.org/page-896

"Who Sampled: Exploring the DNA of Music." *whosampled.com Limited*. whosampled.com

www.ingramcontent.com/pod-product-compliance
Lightning Source LLC
Chambersburg PA
CBHW022057090426
42743CB00008B/638